This is a book about railways such as has never been told before. Wonders and blunders, supernatural experiences, ritual customs, and a wealth of weird tales that sound as if they might be true. But surely they aren't? Or are they?

A lifelong interest in both trains and folklore, a willingness to sit sharing a pint or three with fellow enthusiasts, plus the practised ear of a professional journalist. All these have given Paul Screeton the unique ability to collect and write about this wonderful web of weirdness and ever-evolving lore.

Crossing the Line provides a wealth of tales to make even the delays on a train journey enjoyable. Then take an active role in keeping these tales alive by recounting the more perturbing ones to fellow passengers or unsuspecting 'gricers'…

Paul Screeton is a prolific writer and editor. He re-founded *The Ley Hunter* magazine in 1969 and in 1974 wrote *Quicksilver Heritage*, a pioneering overview of 'earth mysteries'. He currently edits *Folklore Frontiers* which he founded in 1985. For many years Paul combined working for the *Hartlepool Mail* with his interest in railways, contemporary folklore and local pubs.

By the same author:

Quicksilver Heritage: The mystic leys – their legacy of ancient wisdom

Seekers of the Linear Vision

The Lambton Worm and Other Northumbrian Dragon Legends

The Man Who Ate a Domino

Whisht Lads and Haad Yor Gobs

Who Hung the Monkey? (A Hartlepool Legend)

Crossing the Line

Trespassing on railway weirdness

Paul Screeton

Heart of Albion

Crossing the Line

Trespassing on railway weirdness

Paul Screeton

ISBN 1 872883 96 6
EAN 978 1872 883 960

Published by

Heart of Albion Press
2 Cross Hill Close, Wymeswold
Loughborough, LE12 6UJ

albion@indigogroup.co.uk

Visit our Web site: www.hoap.co.uk

Printed in England by Booksprint

Contents

Several abbreviations are used throughout:

BR	British Railways
ECML	East Coast Main Line
EWSR	English, Welsh and Scottish Railway
GWR	Great Western Railway
LMS	London, Midland & Scottish Railway
LNER	London & North Eastern Railway
LNWR	London & North Western Railway
SR	Southern Railway
WCML	West Coast Main Line

Introduction

When railway pioneer George Stephenson attempted to cut through a reputed fairy hill in County Durham his efforts were hampered by sides of the cutting supposedly pushed down by indignant faery folk. Whether simply a technical problem or one concerning little Luddites' supernatural intervention, Stephenson was forced to seek extra funding from his line's backers.

There is a cherished belief among diehard fans of the former Great Western Railway that not all their beloved 'Grange', 'County' and '47XX' class steam locomotives perished at the breakers' yards. Some fanatics are convinced that as a contingency measure a cache of redundant engines is secreted away deep beneath the rolling Wiltshire hills to be rolled out again in the nation's darkest hour.

My mate's uncle's pal was going for an interview and found himself with two hours to kill while changing trains at York. His efforts at summoning Dutch courage in the station buffet had unfortunate consequences when he failed to reach the toilet in time. Luckily there was a clothing shop on the forecourt and he ran in demanding 'Levis, size 36.' In the train toilet he took off his trousers and pants, pushed them out of the window, cleaned himself, opened the bag… to find a size 36 denim jacket.

Survivors of one of the worst massacres of the February 2002 sectarian riots in Gujarat filed a compensation claim against the western Indian state's ruling Hindu nationalist Bharatiya Janata Party. Hindu mobs killed more than 120 people from the minority Muslim community in riots triggered by claims that a Muslim mob had torched a train carrying Hindus, killing 59 people. A subsequent official report stated the train fire was an accident.

For all their differences, each of the above brief chronicles are examples of folklore. The study of folklore has advanced from the era of my first tale with its subject matter of a supernatural agency undermining the great civil engineer, but just as ancient dragon stories are found dotted around Britain. So my second example is what folklorists call an 'urban legend' – this example has been found from Lancashire to Hampshire and Yorkshire to Wales. An indication that folklore need not be po-faced is revealed by the fellow in the third story whose compounded embarrassment was relayed at several removes: by a friend of a friend who heard it, what is known as a FOAF-tale. Whereas the fourth account of mayhem in India presents rumour – another aspect of folklore – at its ugliest.

As a typical railway enthusiast myself, were it not for my interest in the broad spectrum of folklore I would not readily or necessarily consider much of the content of this book folklore. For instance, what have those ubiquitous 'leaves on the line' got to do with folklore? Well, I term this 'medialore' as it and 'wrong type of snow' when transmitted by the media bond commuters together into a jointly-suffering affiliation. It is through such fraternal experiences that folklore and other common

1

interest information is disseminated, be it the gricers' grapevine on the Internet, the industry's shared TOPS computer (which once mysteriously 'lost' loco No. 60097 and put out an alert for anyone seeing all 100 tons of the mislaid asset) or shelves of W.H. Smith emporia.

Not all the material is – or was ever intended to be – folkloric. Many items are included for their humour or strangeness. The wholly folkloric parts are the chapters dealing with the supernatural, the rites of passage from birth to death, and many contemporary legends, including an in-depth inquiry into the strategic steam reserve. Other less obviously folkloric sections assess the world of rail enthusiasm; real people associated with railways such as the clergy, royalty and politicians; criminal activity; and commuters' trials.

Some notes on terminology

Although the terms 'myth' and 'legend' are often used interchangeably (most of my sources misunderstand the difference so I have not adopted a strict division), for the deadly serious folklorist they have separate and specific meanings. Each are stories with plots and cast of characters, but myths have godlike or supernatural beings/animals and take place in the far past, while legends are accounts of purported incidents involving ordinary people in more recent times. Although both are told as true, they are not necessarily believed to be the literal truth, either by the tellers or their audiences.

There is also a wider milieu where in our postmodern world larger themes and archetypes form what a cultural mythologist would see as providing coherence in the face of change and carry forward patterns of life. Here myth can engage the larger events within literate culture such as Hiroshima or the Holocaust and, most typically, national identities. Railway-related examples include the GWR with its 'Bulldog' class locomotives and, when the first 'Class 20' was shipped to France to work on the Channel Tunnel project, it was specially named *Marianne* in deference to the French icon of nationhood and freedom.

As for 'contemporary legend', I prefer this term, but 'urban legend', 'urban myth', 'urban belief tale' and 'FOAFtale' are also used. They are all cautionary tales which voice our fears and concerns in the form of stories which supposedly tell of what happens to transgressors of ideal behaviour or confirm our belief that the world is dangerous and the government is engaged in secret machinations. These tales are commonly equated with falsity and the majority are sheer invention, although a handful turn out to be based on real events. An original account can be confabulated to cover more people and places than could be reasonably believed.

Rumour can in its milder form be no more than wishful thinking where a subject is weighted with emotional ballast, as when John F. Clay in his book *Jubilees of the LMS* (Ian Allan 1971) said that 'Platform end rumour before and after the building of the first "Jubilee" suggested that a four-cylinder version was under construction.' At its strongest, information generated by hysteria is considerably distorted until it reaches a lynch-mob stage. In *Rumour, Fear and the Madness of Crowds* (Ballantine,

New York, 1959) J.P. Chaplin posited that rumours appeal to five types of basic requirements:

- **animal needs** when deprivations are blamed on others, from mute acceptance rising to psychotic behaviour (see for example the berserk railfan with girlfriend trouble in Chapter Ten);

- **the need for safety and security** – Chaplin devoted a whole chapter to the Mattoon 'gasser' (for wider discussion see Chapter Five);

- **the need to belong** – racial, political, partisanship (for fundamentalist-strength preferences see Chapter Three);

- **the need for power and prestige** – amateur detectives out to beat experts at their own game (Kennedy assassination sleuths replaced in railway context by strategic steam reserve investigators, see Chapter Eight);

- **the need for self-expression** – where an outside stimulus brings individuals to life for the first time (typified by trainspotting giving the disenfranchised a meaningful role in life; see Chapter Ten).

Rumour is closely linked to conspiracy theories – Was Diana murdered? Is there a secret world government? Were moon landings filmed in a Nevada desert? And so on. These lead to the realm of 'forteana'. Named after the collector of anomalous phenomena Charles Hoy Fort (1874–1932), 'forteana' suggests that our apparent reality is partially false, untrustworthy or mischievous. In Fort's philosophy all theories propounded should be tentative and temporary. He posited a continuous universe and adopted the policy of inclusionism and fought against categorisation. The data he spent a lifetime collecting he termed 'The Damned'; that is events and phenomena which conflicted embarrassingly with orthodoxies. Such topics as covered here being wildmen, alien big cats and entombed toads (see Chapter Seven).

I have already touched upon my term 'medialore'. By this I mean any event which by repetition has entered public consciousness. A good example is the way 'leaves on the line' and 'the wrong sort of snow' has expanded to make any excuse for a train delay newsworthy because the interrupted journey is a strong folk motif and we enjoy repetition (see Chapter Four). The success of the comedy sketch show *Little Britain* works on the premise that a play of variation within a given structure is a winning formula. Unlike previous humour, *Little Britain* makes a virtue of the predictable. Items on rail delays also win sympathy as they are a shared human experience. And does the sheer volume of myth and legend surrounding Isambard Kingdom Brunel scattered throughout these pages make the engineer a sort of Colossus of Railroads? Yeah but no, but yes, but no, but...

I need also mention 'ostension', a nebulous term at the best of times but used here only to refer to a real event patterned on a contemporary legend; when fact mirrors fiction. This is best exemplified by the series of almost certainly apocryphal tales of injury resulting from urinating on a live rail, but eventually leading to a real death and a coroner's court (see Chapter One).

There is also the term *blason populaire*, best described by Robert Chambers more than 100 years ago and I cannot better it. He wrote:

> There is a nationality in districts as well as in countries; nay, the people living on different sides of the same stream, or of the same hill, sometimes entertain prejudices against each other, not less virulent than those of the inhabitants of the different sides of the English Channel or the Pyrenees. This has given rise to an infinite number of phrases, expressive of vituperation, obloquy, or contempt, which are applied to the inhabitants of various places by those whose lot it is to reside in the immediate vicinity. Some of these are versified, and have the appearance of remnants of old songs; others are merely couplets or single lines, generally referring to some circumstances in the history of the subject, which originally called for the ridicule of the neighbours and continues to do so traditionally.

In this book *blason populaires* are scattered throughout the pages, emanating from Hartlepool, Gotham, Marlow, Saltley and Drumuillie.

This book is very much the product of two extraordinary happenings in my life, both of which occurred during railway journeys. The earliest may be perceived as some kind of shamanistic experience which led me to quitting my job in the hopes of writing full-time (see Appendix); the second was a UFO sighting which rekindled an urge to complete this book (see Chapter Two).

That benevolent biographer of George Stephenson, Samuel Smiles, so understood the achievements, uniqueness and numinous quality of the railway system that he described it as 'a magician's road.' Railways are bewitching and the tales, rumours and folklore collected here will, I hope, deliver something of the fun, spirit and enchantment of the magical railroad.

Chapter One

Stations of the sun

The fitting title for this chapter is taken from Ronald Hutton's book of the same name; a glorious compendium of folk rituals specifically linked to the passage of the year. I, too, examine festivals associated with the turning year, but deal more generally with customs relevant to stages in human lifetimes. This chapter formed itself into a two-tier structure: firstly, birth, childhood, marriage, retirement and death; and, secondly, the classic folkloric 'book of days' approach, working its way around the timetabled circle of the year.

The history of railways has been one of constant change, and the folkloric dimension is no different. The birth of the 'baby train' legend (of which more shortly) can be traced back more than a century, while the licensing for civil weddings of railway premises is very recent. The tradition of naming locomotives goes back to the railways' antiquity, whereas Thomas the Tank Engine events so derided by purists and lucrative Santa specials embrace modern financial acumen.

Birth

Britain is the birthplace of railways. That can be said without contradiction. Yet in almost every sphere of the growth of railways there is contention and 'folk history' can be used as an appropriate yardstick in measuring who or what was significant or deserves attention, prestige, praise or notoriety, rather than who or what was first past the post.

That railways were important is indisputable, but historians seem to see the development as arbitrary at best. R.A.S. Hennessey observed: 'Although born rather casually, and by chance, nevertheless the railway was a massive agent of change – perhaps the greatest ever.'[1] And: 'If one meaning of industrialisation is the replacement of human or animal power by mechanical forces, then the significance of railways is unmistakeable,' wrote Harold Pollins, adding the rider, 'None of this means that the development of railways was in some sense inevitable.'[2] My mentor Charles Fort certainly did not think railways were a matter of serendipity. He wrote: 'I think of our existence as an organism... it's logic is only the adjusting constructiveness of all other growing things. A tree cannot find out, as it were, how to blossom, until comes blossom time. A social growth cannot find out the use of steam engines, until comes steam engine time.'[3] Or steam locomotive time.

The Stephensons rocket ahead

The invention of the railway is commonly ascribed to George Stephenson, born fortuitously in a cottage alongside the Wylam wagonway on 9 June 1781 and, though this honour is not entirely accurate, it can be argued as such with some justification. Despite the fact he neither invented tramway, steam engine nor locomotive, it is 'folk-history' which has justifiably made him the inventor of the railway. The reasons for this are fourfold. Firstly, Stephenson had the vision to see the mechanically-worked tramway, or railway, not merely for parochial colliery tracks, but as general traffic arteries for a broader area, purpose and time-scale. Secondly, his self-taught engineering skills displayed him as a mechanic of genius proportions. Thirdly, he was shrewd. Fourthly, lucky. Even as early as 1836 he was called the 'father of the railway.'

By vision and discipline, Stephenson had shaped the steam locomotive to contain virtually all the basic elements such a machine required. However, his son Robert refined some aspects, having replaced the cumbersome arrangement of beams atop the boiler, which gave *Locomotion No. 1* a spider-like appearance, in preference to inclined cylinders and connecting rods to drive direct to the wheels.

This development had been successfully applied to Robert's *Lancashire Witch* in 1828 for the Bolton and Leigh Railway. When the directors of the Liverpool and Manchester Railway issued a public challenge, with a £500 prize, to any engineer who could create a locomotive able to pull three times its own weight at a minimum 10 mph along 1¼ miles of track 20 times (just over the railway company's line's length) and repeat the procedure after refuelling, Robert rose to the occasion. On 7 October 1829, he arrived at Rainhill, near St Helens, with his brand new 0-2-2 design, the boastfully-named *Rocket*. The specially-designed contender – the others being *Sans Pareil*, *Novelty* and *Perseverance* – followed his *Lancashire Witch* layout, except for an increased heating surface created by fitting a series of small copper boiler tubes rather than a single large one. This revolutionary aspect enabled the locomotive to exceed 30 mph and won him the prize purse. George Stephenson, contrary to general public and sometimes scholarly belief, is thought to have played no significant part in *Rocket*'s design.

Later engineers brought the steam locomotive's design, size and performance to higher standards, but the basic Stephenson model has never been replaced. That is until midway last century when diesel and electric traction took ascendancy.

The baby train

There are many versions of the baby train legend; in fact, doyen of contemporary lore Jan Harold Brunvand used it as a title for one of his amusing and scholarly books. However, international though the tale is, I prefer a jokey, rustic English version with tortured vernacular which harks back to the pre-Beeching days of the branch-line pick-up freight.

Here a student engaged in a thesis on birth statistics was advised to visit a small village which would likely provide him with valuable information. Let not the village's name of Waggling Hampton be a drawback to the essential fundamentals of the much-travelled tale. Whereas the population was static throughout the surrounding area, Waggling Hampton had a phenomenal birth-rate. Upon arriving to make his investigation, the student made his way to the village pub. He quickly discovered that a few jars of scrumpy cider loosened the locals' tongues.

'Aah!' intoned an old farmer. 'Oi can tell 'ee, young feller, why we 'ave more beebies yere, an Oi've got four'een to prove it. 'Tis cos ye railway.'

'The railway?' queried the student.

'Aye,' reaffirmed the farmer, 'that ol' milk train what comes along, ten past foive, each mornin'. Allus blows 'er whistle as she comes roun' the bend, then she pulls up with them brakes a screechin' an' they get busy an' rattle all they churns 'cross the platform, then 'er blows 'er whistle again an' shunts up an' down a time or two to get the empty milk van into the sidin' for the full churns, then 'er whistles again an' rattles off. Wakes everyone she does.'

'Go on,' urged the student.

'I can tell ye've never lived in the country, lad,' observed the farmer, ''cos if you 'ad, you'd know as ten past foive be an akward hour of the mornin'. Bit too early to go to work, bit too late to get off to sleep again.'[4]

Brunvand heard the story in the early 1950s while a student at Michigan State University, where it was believed the married student housing units had the highest birth-rate on campus because of a scheduled early morning freight train awakening the residents. He had heard the offspring of such dawn lovemaking called 'whistle babies', though wondered why the couples' young children did not awaken too and disrupt any intimacy.

The professor's book gives two more versions from Utah, where he teaches, and also Australia, South Africa and a small village in Shropshire as long ago as 1900.[5]

Another version I found to reveal its ubiquity was supposedly sent from a news agency in Moscow. Here an express train which thunders through the town of Malakhitovo at 5 a.m. each day was blamed for a baby boom. It would wake everyone up for early-morning sex sessions and a hospital spokesman commented: 'People can't get back to sleep so they kill time making babies.'[6]

Premature birth

I have come across a couple of versions of this next tale from China. The most complete features young farmer Wu Ming and his unnamed wife, who was seven months pregnant. While they were travelling on a train it stopped at Wuxiang, in Shaanxi province, and she went to the lavatory with stomach pains. After the train pulled out twenty minutes later her husband found her unconscious and covered in blood. She had given birth and the baby had fallen down the toilet chute on to the tracks. Luckily it was rescued unhurt despite the freezing weather.[7] Yet somewhere I saw the tale challenged as the umbilical cord and afterbirth would have been pulled out by the baby's fall. However, that did not deter the Zimbabwe Broadcasting Corporation including an item, suspiciously on Christmas Eve, in its foreign news of a baby falling through a train toilet on to the track. Two TV newscasters, Tsitsi Vera and Noreen Welch, burst out laughing and for this loss of composure were suspended from duty for three months.[8]

Tunnel vision

That engineer of genius, Isambard Kingdom Brunel, had energy, insight and originality, but it was style which led him to align Box tunnel so the rising sun shines through it each year on 9 April, his birthday. Legend had it that only on that particular day would the sun's rays strike directly through the tunnel near Chippenham, Wiltshire. Although admitting that gangers on the line have reported the occurrence as late as 17 April, Philip Atkins, archivist at the National Railway Museum at York, suggested that the eerie shaft of sunlight was more likely to appear three or four days before Brunel's birthday.[9] In response to Atkins, John Powell, librarian of Ironbridge Gorge Museum Trust, added that the story was first reported in *The Daily Telegraph* in April, 1859, the last year of Brunel's life. It later became the subject of correspondence in *The Railway Magazine* in the mid-1960s, when the conclusion was reached that though the great engineer and his surveyors attempted to achieve this natal exploit, insufficient information concerning atmospheric refraction resulted in the dawn sun piercing the tunnel on dates ranging from 6 April to 8 April, but not on 9 April.[10]

Childhood

When I was a youngster 50 years ago any large station had as many young train-spotters as adult passengers. Today it is a very different story. Almost all trainspotters are middle-aged men, 'Children today have a phobia about being trainspotters,' commented Colin Garratt, international photographer of trains. 'They don't want to be seen as spotty-faced nerds who are open to national ridicule.'

Terrifying Thomas

According to a learned shrink, stories featuring Thomas the Tank Engine make children afraid to travel by train. The bizarre claim was made by Dr Brian Young, a psychology lecturer at Exeter University, who believes the great number of crashes on the televised series 'terrifies' youngsters. Seems no one previously noted that the Rev Wilbert Awdry's entertaining books created fear during their half a century of publication or twenty years of broadcasting. Dr Young says the pre-school kiddies who watch Thomas and his friends as they potter around the island of Sodor, with avuncular narration by Ringo Starr, have not learnt to differentiate what they see on television and what they see in real life. Hence they assume most trains crash. Responding to criticism that the safety aspect of trains should be stressed, an ITV spokesman said witheringly: 'We are confident that the latest Thomas series is suitable for children.'[11]

Marriage

Asked to define a railway in the simplest term it is essentially a marriage: the union of two previously separate fruits of technology. A railway is the merger of an artificial track and mechanical traction. Visually it is that 'road' of parallel iron or steel rails upon which runs a wheeled engine hauling its 'train' of carriages or wagons.

Bridal trains

Stations, museums and other railway facilities are becoming popular venues for marriage ceremonies. So, in autumn 2004, guests crowded on to the tiny station on multi-millionaire enthusiast Sir William McAlpine's private standard gauge railway at Fawley, Oxfordshire, to witness the marriage between Carole Cuneo, a widow and daughter of the late railway artist Terence Cuneo, and retired engineer David Moss. After the formalities, the newly-weds left the station between two raised paintbrushes (like her trademark mouse-in-the-picture father, Carole had been staging an art exhibition at Yeovil Steam Centre) and signed the register in a GWR coal truck. Several trains were then run for guests before a wedding supper of typical station fare, which included pies, mash and mushy peas. Sir William gave away the bride and guests included fellow artists David Shepherd and Barry Freeman, and former *Flying Scotsman* owner Alan Pegler.[12]

After the wedding of Rachel Fortnam, granddaughter of Thomas the Tank Engine creator the Rev Wilbert Awdry, and teacher Nik Barton, at Highworth in Wiltshire, the reception was held in the new running shed on the Swindon and Cricklade Railway. They and guests were taken there in a train hauled by 'Thomas', on loan from the Mid-Hants Railway.[13]

Following its acquisition of a licence to hold civil weddings, Chesterfield couple Christopher Boyden and Katherine Bates became the first couple to marry in a signal box when they tied the knot at Swanwick Junction at the Midland Railway Centre.[14]

David Lowery and Railtrack secretary Sam Heffer wed on the Royal Platform at York's National Railway Museum[15], while Dee Yoto-Mee and Lee Oker, plus one hundred guests, piled into a carriage to take their vows on an underground train in Tokyo during the rush hour.[16] Dee and Lee had first met on a train during the morning rush hour, while Peter and Shirley Dobbin, who work at London's St Pancras station, had their marriage blessed on the train where they fell in love. Midland Mainline employees, the train operating company has no fewer than eighty of its nine hundred staff married to each other or in long-term relationships together.[17] Also, love blossomed on the footplate for driver Dave Jones and fireman Kirsty Skinner who, after marrying at Whitby register office, held their reception in the North Yorkshire Moors Railway's 1947-built GWR inspection saloon, attached to that day's 1.40 p.m. working from Grosmont.[18]

Another coupling was planned in New York where Paul Batterman and Carolyn Frome had applied to wed on the subway's tracks. They told officials their relationship was 'electric', although the authorities planned to turn off the power during the ceremony, at which priest and guests would stand on the platform.[19] Another novel venue now licensed for wedding ceremonies is the Great Engine Shed at Beamish, based on Timothy Hackworth's Shildon building, with a package offered including an early 1800s-style ride hauled by one of the museum's replica locomotives, *Locomotion No. 1* or *Steam Elephant*.[20]

Model behaviour

Lastly, superstar Rod Stewart's marriage to supermodel Rachel Hunter. Are tales of his preferring to enjoy his model train sets more than sex true? Maybe his lust, drinking and leisure pursuits should be seen in mythological terms as an amalgam of Priapus, Bacchus and Frank Hornby meets the Sirens, Amazons, the ex-wives' sisterly fraternisation akin to the witches in *Macbeth*, and being currently caught between Scylla and Charybdis. More model trains than supermodel; more Hornby than horny.[21]

Death

Queen Victoria, George V, George VI and most recently Sir Winston Churchill made their final earthly journey by rail. Those were state funerals, marked by pomp, circumstance and solemnity. Today the ordinary working man or the lifelong trainspotter can be afforded a similar but less grandiose send-off to that great motive power depot or busy terminus in the sky.

Modern mortality

Preserved lines are nowadays in the business of replacing the funeral procession of glossy black Daimlers with a steam locomotive hauling mourners in ex-BR Mark I carriages with the wake being held sedately in the dining car. The body would 'lie in state' in the guard's van, doubtless in a biodegradable coffin of cardboard or willow basketwork, or cremated remains of the enthusiast would be fed into the steam engine's firebox. The grave could be a woodland spot at the side of the track. A time not for sadness but celebration.[22]

Peace Burials, a Lancashire company which specialises in themed funerals, arranges packages which range in price from just £25 for the coffin's carriage in a hearse van to several thousand pounds for full catering and haulage by favourite chosen locomotive. Director John Mallatrat said: 'When the men in black suits come and take away the body of a loved one, it's a bit impersonal and the family aren't involved. On a steam-hauled funeral train, we are involving the family in the celebration of a life in a way that we think the deceased would have appreciated. But it doesn't have to be a burial. We can arrange a cremation, with the ashes being put into the firebox or a wake on the train, or whatever. We will try to be as flexible as possible to people's needs.'[23]

Peace Burials had problems at Carrog, beside the Llangollen Railway, where the Corwen Community Council clerk summed up objections as it being 'a bit undignified. It's against our way of life. We like quiet burials here.' Commenting on the Carrog cemetery division into three for various religious groups, Tristan Davies sniped: 'Nothing... for anoraks or duffel bags.' [24] Even less complimentary on the debate was James Bedding, who reflected that earlier the 'residents of the quiet, leafy Dee valley had kicked up such a fuss at the thought of their gardens being coated in anorak ash that the plans had been shelved.' [25] No such trackside cemetery hitting the proverbial buffers hiccup occurred at the Midland Railway – Butterley, where a 1½ acre graveyard has been accommodating the deceased at Golden Valley Halt Woodland Burial Ground at Swanwick Junction after being given the green light by Amber Valley Borough Council. [26]

The Japanese have also seen idle railway land as an attractive commercial opportunity. *The Nikkei Weekly* announced annual deaths in Japan are forecast to double by 2036 and already several of the railway companies in the Land of the Rising Sun have diversified into the funeral business, providing work for surplus employees arranging graves on vacant land. [27]

Following the many occasions now on private railways where the deceased's ashes have been added to coal in the firebox, the A1 Steam Locomotive Trust has offered a fast-track trip to the hereafter. The multi-million pound project by the charity to construct a new 'A1' class Pacific loco, to be named *Tornado*, has offered to shovel the ashes into the smokebox for anyone pledging £1,000 towards the cost of the first main-line steam engine to be built in Britain for almost forty years. Trust chairman David Champion said: 'I'm sure there will be people who want to do it. It's not so different from mariners who have their ashes scattered at sea.' [28]

Rather than the ashes be fed from firebox to chimney, others have had their remains scattered on the tracks. Station supervisor Willie Dickson had his dying wish granted when his ashes were dispersed at his beloved station at Perth in Scotland. [29] Similarly former Main Line Steam Trust member Derek Freshney, who left the Great Central Railway £124,000 was to have his ashes scattered beneath the platforms at Leicester North station, where his bequest will help fund new station buildings. [30]

There has even been an 'instant' railway funeral for a dog! Arriving at Wansford on the Nene Valley Railway, Cambridgeshire, the driver in charge of a preserved Swedish steam loco was made aware that he had struck the animal near Orton Mere. The distraught owners of the Labrador were left with a sizeable body to dispose, so it was arranged that the next train would stop so that their late pet's remains could be cremated in the firebox. Railway staff assisted the unnamed dog owners in manhandling the animal's remains into the fiery furnace. Perhaps as an act of revenge from beyond the grave, the Labrador's body became firmly wedged in the fire-hole. Brute force and several size nine boots finally achieved their objective, but that was not to be the end of their troubles. The carcass hardly burned merrily and the crew were in fear of the loco running out of steam on the following trip. After stopping for a blow-up, they managed the final journey to Wansford. [31]

But what of a dog committing suicide? After his owner, Giovanni Cera, 59, was killed when his car was hit by a train in Rome, the next day his faithful mutt lay on the line and was killed.

11

Hughie Gallacher in his prime. The Scots striker scored 387 goals in 541 games, but his life ended in suicide on the railway at Gateshead.

Suicides

Hughie Gallacher was hailed the 'King of Tyneside.' The Scotsman, who trounced England in the Twenties, was a deadly centre-forward and one of the most prolific goal-scorers of the last century. In a lengthy and detailed portrait of the Wembley wizard and his life and mystery death, James Dalrymple wrote: 'To me, and to every Scottish schoolboy saturated in football folklore, Hughie Gallacher was, quite simply, the greatest of them all.' [32] His career took him to clubs all over the country, but he eventually returned to north-east England and Gateshead Football Club. 'It's grand to be back on Tyneside,' observed Gallacher as he alighted from his train. 'I intend to spend the rest of my life with my adopted folk in Gateshead.' Yet in 1957 two young trainspotters saw a small man, agitated, weeping, talking to himself. At 12.08 he heard the whistle of a northbound express, moving swiftly, only pausing briefly to mutter 'Sorry' to the boys, he walked into the path of the train. His decapitated body was found one hundred yards down the line. The spot was known locally as Dead Man's Crossing.

The whole of Tyneside went into mourning. Crowds packed Newcastle for his funeral. Young and old, men and women, wept as if saying farewell to a personal friend. His exploits were remembered. His self-destruction saddened. He was 54 when he died. He enjoyed his legend status, revelled in being feted in pubs and dressed like a dandy. So why commit suicide? He had been accused of mistreating one of his three sons, who was taken into care. By all accounts, in exasperation Gallacher had thrown a small plastic ashtray which hit Matti on the temple. It did not even break the skin, but somehow a zealous NSPCC officer learned of the incident and police and social workers removed the boy. Unable to see his son and with a court case looming, the distraught Gallacher took his leave of Tyneside, sublimely by train.

As a footnote, perhaps Dalrymple and his purple prose got one of the pertinent points wrong. Instead of passing Dead Man's Crossing on an Anglo-Scottish express, it has always been my recollection that 'V2' No. 60934 arrived at Newcastle Central light engine from Gateshead motive power depot across the Tyne to relieve an incoming passenger train. In fact, I was there that day and saw 60934. However, what I do not recall was Gallacher's head on the buffer beam. That was what truly happened, at least so I recall being told.

In another suicide, there is an element of 'if only... ' Born Clive Horrocks, the 30-year-old who changed his name to John Yoko Ono Lennon horrified waiting travellers as he lay down in front of a train at Fratton station, Portsmouth, and was killed. His body was so mangled it could only be identified from fingerprints.[33] Just weeks later the Fab Four released their first single for 25 years. If only ...

A verdict of suicide was recorded upon eccentric Wilfred Crone, 87, a health freak who lived on a diet modelled on that of cavemen. He refused to kill plants for food and ate only fruit, nuts and seeds. He knelt in front of a train and was decapitated. A note was found at his home near Southampton which read: 'Sorry folks – don't want to become a burden to anyone.' [34]

An example of sympathy bypass came at the end of a public notice issued by Taiwan's Taipei Mass Rapid Transport Company threatening a fine not exceeding 50,000 Taiwanese dollars (nearly £900) for unsuccessful suicides. It concluded: 'In recent months there have been up to four cases each day of people jumping in front of speeding trains on the mass rapid transit lines and these incidents are leading to unacceptable delays. Furthermore many of our track workers have acquired stains on expensive shoes that simply won't come out.' [35]

Misadventure

Superstition led to six people sleeping on a railway line dying after being struck by a freight train. Police at the scene of the tragedy in southern Texas, near the Mexican border, believed the victims were all illegal immigrants. Mark Davis, a spokesman for Union Pacific, said the rail company had worked with the American border patrol and Mexican authorities to discourage people from sleeping on the tracks. He added: 'There is a great misbelief that if you sleep between the railroad tracks, snakes won't get you. Unfortunately, trains will.' [36]

Another death in the United States which could have been averted happened to Charles McFerron, 82, a veteran of more than a dozen marathons. He was killed instantly while he was out on his daily training run in Castle Rock, Colorado. Running along a railway track, he was struck and killed by a train because he was deaf.[37]

Yet another person tempting fate was an unnamed 22-year-old convinced he was a wizard, who was killed when he tried to stop a train with his mystic powers. He lay down in front of a 28-wagon freight train in Shanghai to demonstrate his abilities to his mother.[38]

More supernatural tales are given in Chapter Two, but a death which has the spectre of the Chinese art of *feng shui* about it is another case of superstitious action. The first working railway in China, the seven-mile Tangshan-Xukozhuang Railway, opened in 1880. However, an earlier line was constructed from Shanghai to Woosung, but never opened to traffic after a workman was killed shortly before its projected opening. The Chinese authorities purchased the line compulsorily from its British constructors and immediately tore it up.[39]

Staying abroad, the 150-mile line from Ambla to Delhi carried what has been described as the world's most dangerous train, where one day during October, 1977, it killed nine people all in separate incidents and did not stop once. So much for the value of life in India.[40]

Also so much for sympathetic headline writing. A romantic wedding proposal on the platform at Leissling, East Germany, ended in tragedy. Silvia Cahle, 32, broke free from an embrace to ask Uwe Harken, 36, to marry her. But when he declined she threatened to kill herself and ran towards the platform edge as a train sped towards the station. Devoted Uwe blocked her path but fell to his death. Heartbroken Silvia, under sedation in hospital, told police: 'He fell backwards and seemed to be hanging in space forever and clung on to my left index finger. Then he lost his grip and was gone.' No prizes for guessing which paper's sub-editor wrote 'Dying to marry ya.'[41]

An item about two youths who lost limbs while 'train surfing' brought to mind a reader's recollection of a tombstone situated to the right of the main door to St Mary's Church, Harrow-on-the-Hill. It read: 'Here lies the body of Richard Port of Burton-upon-Trent who used to ride on the axles of wagons on the London and Birmingham Railway near this spot. In 1876 he lost both his legs after losing his hold.' There follows the inscription:

> Bright rose the morn
> And vig'rous rose poor Port
> Gay on the train
> He used his wonted sport
> Ere noon arrived
> His mangled form they bore
> With pain distorted
> And overwhelmed with gore
> When evening came
> To close the fateful day
> A mutilated corpse the sufferer lay.[42]

While on the subject of tombstones, these form part of the line-side fencing west of Goonbarrow on Cornwall's Newquay branch. A correspondent, suspecting the legend that generations ago a local farmer needing to repair a fence could only afford to buy old gravestones was apocryphal, noted that responsibility for fencing presumably lay with the railway authorities rather than the landowner.[43]

Similarly I suspect a journey to the family graveyard in the heart of Romania as told is a legend. Unable to afford a hearse to take a dead uncle three hundred miles, three family members sat their relation's corpse upright in a seat on the night train from Bucharest and doused him in alcohol to conceal the smell of mortality. The carriage being unheated and unlit, no one on the train noticed anything amiss.[44]

One newspaper account blamed a track death on the Royal Train's movements being kept secret, so the man, who was a railway employee, trainspotter and expert on timetables, would not be aware of its impending presence. Roger Breeze, 50, a fitter at Crewe Works of Burland, Cheshire, was struck as he stood with his back to the train at a remote spot around eight miles north-west of Crewe. The accident happened at 10.50 p.m. as the Duke of Edinburgh was travelling back from Chester to London after an official engagement. Prince Philip was unaware of the tragedy, which was the first fatality involving the Royal Train. The verdict: Accident.[45]

Evidence of the Grim Reaper's persistence could apply to an unfortunate crane driver who had helped remove the form-work at Stanway viaduct, Gloucestershire, and was standing below Number Ten arch when it collapsed and he had to be rescued. He then sheltered under Number Nine arch before it too fell down, leading once more to his rescue from the rubble. However, forty minutes later he was struck once again by brickwork when arch Number Eight collapsed. This time he was fatally injured, as were three other people during the whole incident.[46]

Seemingly irony is part of the Grim Reaper's stock in trade. That the first casualty of the Railway Age was one of the foremost proponents of the Liverpool and Manchester Railway might be apt. Having travelled against the advice of his doctor, the accident-prone Member of Parliament William Huskisson was chatting to the Duke of Wellington when Stephenson's *Rocket* despatched him to that chamber in the sky.

At least the facts surrounding Huskisson's death are incontrovertible (unless someone knows otherwise). Not so the demise of Dugald Drummond. Railway historians are split more or less 50:50 as to whether the engineer died after a domestic accident or on the footplate. Drummond was chief mechanical engineer of the London and South Western Railway when the redoubtable O.S. Nock claims he received a severe scald to the leg while riding on a locomotive, and the resulting amputation led to shock from which he died. More prosaically, the august C. Hamilton Ellis says Drummond was scalded at home in Surbiton having a hot mustard foot-bath after getting his feet wet and cold while at work, and neglected the blistering, gangrene set in, and after refusing anaesthetic for amputation, the shock of the operation killed him the following day. He was 72. Even the various learned tomes by so-called experts cannot agree upon the date of death; 7 or 8 November. It is also reported that some of his footplate men were so afraid of his wrath, that after his funeral they piled half-a-ton of used brake-blocks on top of his coffin to make sure he could not return to haunt them.[47]

A more bizarre blurring of fact and fiction followed the televised death of the character Victor Meldrew, played by Richard Wilson in the BBC's *One Foot in the Grave*. Viewers of the last episode saw the grumpy pensioner mown down by a car outside the railway station at Shawford, near Winchester, Hants. Within hours bouquets with messages such as 'Goodbye Victor – we can't believe it' and 'Victor, keep moaning' began arriving as mourning fans laid flowers and wreaths in tribute at the spot where he died.[48]

Finally one of those silly fillers which has virtually no veracity but deserves an airing for its outrageous unlikelihood: 'Lucky Juan Veras cheated death by surviving four train crashes in two months – then got a fatal electric shock in Mexico City, Mexico... as he played with his son's train set.' [49]

Down the Tube

London's Underground is replete with tales, such as 'The Maniac on the Platform' (see Chapter Five) and the death of musician Graham Bond (see Chapter Nine). As for death, there are frequent tales of kinks in the layout being linked to avoiding plague pits, but this urban legend can be dismissed on the grounds of engineering necessity and the great depth of the tunnelling.

On more solid ground are stories such as this true one with a twist of irony. When the body of a man found decapitated by a train in a Tube tunnel near Leytonstone station was examined, the only distinguishing mark was a vertical scar on his abdomen. There were no other clues to his identity, although he was wearing a black T-shirt with white lettering predicting 'Have A Very Bad Day.' [50]

Urinary authority

It may seem to most people apocryphal as they read of yet another unfortunate soul innocently caught short and urinating unknowingly on to a live rail. However, it seems that at least in the cast of Afghan asylum-seeker Saliamin Akrami, 32, death was truly caused in this manner. An inquest heard the man was found by workmen repairing the tracks at deserted Kensal Green station, London. It was presumed Akrami relieved himself and six hundred volts flashed up the stream of urine to his penis, and as he convulsed in agony he fell on to the live conductor rail. The victim's alcohol level was more than twice the drink-drive limit and it is probable Akrami, of Willesden, was drunk. Pathologist Dr Rufus Crompton said the only injuries to the body were burns, including a tiny mark on the end of his penis. He added that a stream of urine hitting electricity was the only way this injury could have been caused. Verdict: Misadventure.[51] When urinating onto an electrified line claimed the life of Ho Lee, compensation culture awarded his widow Sang Yeul Lee one million pounds from the Chicago Transit Authority.[52] Two similar tales, both featuring hoboes standing up on the roofs of freight trains to urinate and being zapped by 25,000 volts from above, end with the victims – Ray Charman, 47 [53] and John Moore, 33 [54] – being so seriously burned their penises and testicles had to be amputated. Same story repeated three times, each featuring a train in China, had the urine not hitting electricity but chemicals in a truck which reacted to give off a lethal gas. The *Xinmin Evening News* reported the chemical reaction produced toxic hydrogen phosphide gas and when the train pulled into the northern city of Tianjin the guard was found unconscious.[55] In the other version it was a soldier guarding a bridge in Peking or Wunchung who peed over the bridge into a stationary wagon.[56]

You know that old chestnut of the man getting comfy to do a number two, lighting a cigarette and, because of a build-up of gas, blowing himself off the toilet seat? When the first thirty British Rail 'Class 56' diesel-electric locomotives were being built at Craiova, in Romania, such a death allegedly occurred. Perhaps the health and safety regime was sufficiently lax to allow this to happen – or else give substance to an apocryphal version. Apparently the workshop lavatories were situated below the erecting shop floor. Acetylene welding trolleys were parked directly above and one night the stopcock on an acetylene canister leaked the heavier than air gas into the toilets. Along came the worker, he lit a cigarette and there was one fewer 'Grid' builder.[57]

Conspiracy

A train explosion in North Korea on 22 April 2004, thought to be caused by a power cable touching rail wagons loaded with ammonium nitrate fertiliser, killed around 160 people and injured 1,300. The blast at Ryongchon wiped out many buildings and damage extended for four kilometres. The official news agency later claimed many of the victims died going into their burning homes to rescue portraits of their leader, Kim Jong-il.[58] It happened just hours after Kim passed through on his way home from a trip to China and by the June officials investigating the devastating explosion believed the blast had been an assassination attempt. They reckoned a mobile telephone was used to detonate the train's cargo of chemical and fuel. The remains of a mobile handset, with adhesive tape attached, was found at the scene of the blast. Kim's itinerary was frequently changed for security reasons and this probably saved his life.[59]

Freak weather

Abnormal weather conditions have claimed lives in bizarre circumstances. Firstly, journeyman carpenter Henry West, 24, was working on the roof at the GWR station at Reading, Berkshire, when a particularly strong gust of wind lifted him and a four-ton glazed section of roof, carried it some two hundred feet before crashing to the ground, killing him instantly. His body was taken to the Boar's Head Inn, in Friar Street, to await the inquest, and he was buried in St Laurence's churchyard the following Sunday. A memorial board is still in situ recording that 'he lost his life in a whirlwind' and a plaque on Platform Four is inscribed: 'In memory of Henry West who lost his life in a whirlwind at the Great Western Reading Station 24 March 1840.' The accident had occurred around 3.30 p.m., only six days before the station opened to the public.[60]

Secondly, in an another more recent freak accident, a 57-year-old grandmother was killed when a mini-tornado struck the village of Corfe Castle, Dorset. Part of a pine tree collapsed on the Swanage Railway station and although firefighters managed to free her grandson, the unnamed woman was pronounced dead at the scene.

Necropolis Railway

The notion to use railways to ferry London's dead to new rural cemeteries had been mooted some years before Sir Richard Brown proposed buying a huge tract of land, around 2,000 acres, at what is now the Surrey village of Brookwood, near Woking. By 1852 Brown's scheme had come to fruition with an Act of Parliament creating what became The London Necropolis Company, with its ground consecrated and the dead and mourners being carried in rolling stock loaned by the London and South Western Railway to two stations on a branch line off the Waterloo to Southampton main line. There were first, second and third-class carriages, each offering a few more home comforts than the one below it and charged accordingly, and the dead were given an equally wide choice to their living companions. Two stations were built at the cemetery; one serving the Church of England area on the sunny south side, the other the non-conformist plots on its chillier north side. Mourners were issued with return tickets while 'coffin tickets' were, of course, singles! [61]

As wariness passed to acceptance, the public began to refer to the service by tasteless nicknames such as 'the stiffs' express' or 'the dead meat train.' [62] Trains had their own timetable and London terminus separate from Waterloo; first on York Street and in 1902 from Westminster Bridge Road. Operations ceased after an air-raid on the night of 16 April 1941 severely damaged the Necropolis sidings and station at Waterloo.

Calendar rites

Preserved railways have developed both special events for differing times of the day and the seasons of the year. During lax periods in the daily timetable special charter freights can be slotted in and, also for photographers' benefit, staged atmospheric night locations of simmering engines, plus the now traditional and lucrative dining trains. During the year private railways hold Thomas the Tank Engine events to attract youngsters, though the die-hard volunteers and serious enthusiasts often deplore the smiling wooden faces disfiguring smokeboxes and cardboard names applied for the day. To get around strict copyright licensing some niftily call the occasion 'Friends of Thomas'. Santa Claus faces adorning locos can elicit the 'bah humbug' reaction.

January to December

In imitation of the internationally-renowned Pirelli calendar, British Rail Engineering Limited produced six black-and-white photographs by Garie Hind of model Wendy Bracken posing against a background of BREL products in heavy engineering settings. A limited edition of 2,000 calendars were printed in 1986 and sent to BREL customers and railway administrations throughout the world. Depending upon your viewpoint, thankfully or unfortunately it predated Rylstone and District Women's Institute's entry into the softest of porn market and so Wendy's nipples stayed unrivettingly ungreased and covered. [63] Nine Derby-based women working for Midland Mainline and female members of staff working for Virgin Trains and other rail businesses produced two saucy charity calendars for 2005. [64]

A mischievous computer hacker attempted to convince rail travellers that there would be no trains over a New Year weekend. The hoaxer entered Railtrack's website – used by 1.2 million people each week – and wrote that all services were cancelled. Railtrack said it was impossible to estimate how many people might have been misled before the damage was rectified.[65]

While Santa specials provide a financial lifeline for some struggling railways, the phenomenon is not as recent as most supporters or detractors imagine. The fifteen-inch gauge Fairbourne Railway ran 'Father Christmas Trains' as long ago as 1949 for pupils from the village school in Beach Road. New owner John Wilkins erected a large illuminated Christmas tree at Fairbourne while a locomotive's casing was removed and the engine transformed into a reindeer. A moth-eaten stag's head appropriated from the Fairbourne Hotel was attached to the front of the grille and a bearskin rug draped over the engine cover. Santa Claus rode in a suitably-decorated flat truck. Altogether not a bad inspiration for a beach-based tourist railway intended only for operation during the summer months. This commercial principle was reborn on the Bluebell Railway at a time when steam-hauled trains were still a daily sight on the national network. It was not long before Santa mania gripped other heritage railways, much to the chagrin of the hardcore enthusiasts who comprised their membership and volunteer workforce. Yet that additional income had to be acknowledged as funding those selfsame enthusiasts' projects all the year around. Such a marketing masterstroke and family attraction has proved irresistible to all but a few preserved lines.[66]

April Fool spoofs

When *Rail Enthusiast* magazine announced that a Brush 'Class 31' loco had been named *Railtour Enterprise*, the 1 April joke caused the reprint of at least one motive power book and embarrassed a Sunday newspaper. The wooden plate with name on red background was attached to loco No. 31200 for only half-an-hour, just long enough for the fake photograph to be taken. However, it was not long before the names of various heritage railways were applied to British Rail engines, culminating in a 'Class 73' electro-diesel being named *Hertfordshire Rail Tours* (the nameplates currently adorning 'Class 90' electric loco No. 90028). The spoof extended to a planned allocation of names to more 'Class 31s', those recently fitted with train-heating equipment, Nos. 31457–31468. Names selected included *My Little Pony*, *Power of Grayskull*, and *Frankie Goes to Hollywood*. Yet members of the reading public still did not cotton on to the fact the offending article was in the April issue and the editor's postbag doubled with irate letters.[67] It also led to a Sunday 'red top' belatedly shooting itself in the foot by not following journalism's first rule of checking your facts: 'Britain's most famous rodent is getting the ultimate accolade – his own train. British Rail are naming a new engine *Roland Rat Megastar* in a ceremony at London's Marylebone station in July. *Boy George, Arthur Scargill* and *Adrian Mole* will also have locos named after them in the ceremony. BR say the figures "reflect contemporary British society".' [68]

A far more subtle spoof was created by humorists at *Rail Express*, whose explanation for renumbering EWS 'Class 66' No. 66074 to 66474 was cunningly logical. The argument for creating a thirty-strong electric heat variant of the Canadian-built freight locomotives was persuasive and renumbering strategy sound. A colour photograph of the hybrid pioneer on a Middlesbrough to Boulby empty potash train was digitally manipulated to back up the writer's claim. The spoof took in a number of notable figures in the railway business: a senior EWS manager was surprised his superiors had not notified him of this important development, a railway magazine editor rang his EWS contact to demand why he had been beaten by a rival to such a scoop and a rail tour operator was eager to ascertain the story's veracity so he could be first to hire such a usefully-modified loco for a charter special.[69]

The magazine *Rail* had its readers bemused and angry when it claimed British Rail was to dispense with easily-observed numbers on the sides of locos and rolling stock in favour of large barcodes.

On the steam front, Severn Valley Railway members were informed of planned fitting of tachographs to the steam loco fleet, because of concerns over the hours being worked by footplate crews. It is to be wondered how many of its 16,000 members were fooled when the spring issue of *Severn Valley News* noted that 'as several engines have already been fitted with speedos, the rest of the new installation should not be too much of a problem. Not only will the tachograph show the hours the crew work, it will also be linked to a valve which will apply the brakes if the speed exceeds 25 mph.'[70] The same issue of *Severn Valley News* misreported more convincingly that Collett 2-8-0 No. 2857 was to receive a Giesel ejector. When that more famous GWR 4-4-0 No. 3440 *City of Truro* was shown in photographs to have been painted black in an enthusiasts' magazine there was widespread apoplexy. Enraged purists were not amused by the japester's argument that had *City of Truro* continued in general stock, BR would have deemed its wheel arrangement and duties insufficient to warrant a lined green livery and demoted it to plain all-over black.

Customs and traditions

Bringing luck and counteracting evil. Stag night stripped and paint stripper. West Highland to West Country. Here are a few rail-related customs, from the whim of an eccentric enthusiast collecting platform lavatory visits to pilgrims following in the footsteps of cinematic consciousness-expanding explorers of Britain's most remote halt.

Topping-out

It was fitting that when the National Railway Museum at York completed its new workshop, celebrity steeplejack and steam fanatic Fred Dibnah should perform the topping-out ceremony. He even did it in the time-honoured traditional manner, with a yew branch to ward off evil spirits. The £4 million conversion of the former diesel depot created a new exhibition area and workshop, allowing visitors to witness the restoration of locos and stock, while also housing thousands of small relics from the reserve collection, many having never been displayed to the public previously.[71]

Another topping-out was held at Bodiam, the new southern terminus of the Kent and East Sussex Railway, and carried out by the then Minister for Tourism, Film and Broadcasting, Janet Anderson, MP. More than 45 years after passenger services last ran to Bodiam, it was Miss Anderson's task to put the finishing touches to the restored station platform. She cemented the final edging bricks with a ceremonial silver builder's trowel, being presented with a coal model of a KESR loco mounted on a brick of the type she had laid. Miss Anderson, wearing a red hard hat, was a fine choice for the role as she is a vice-president of the East Lancashire Railway.

Pilgrimage

Sally Bliault and Keryna Booth, in their early thirties and living in Jersey, had spent more than £40,000 since their teens on their obsession with the Andrew Lloyd Webber musical *Starlight Express.* They had seen the dancers zooming around on roller skates pretending to be trains more than eight hundred times when they were invited to the show's fifteenth anniversary celebrations in London. On being introduced to his two greatest fans, Lloyd Webber looked puzzled and said: 'You must be mad.' I would think not. There can be nothing insane about getting hooked on the show's central theme that you can do anything if you really set your mind to it.

The antithesis of such a positive attitude is the sheer negativity of life revolving around scoring hard drugs. Author Irvine Welsh pathetically used rail enthusiasm as a metaphor for the tenuously-structured action within what is essentially a pointless existence lived by his anti-heroes in the novel *Trainspotting.* Since this cesspit reached the cinema, many film buffs have been making a pilgrimage to Corrour, following in the footsteps of its star Ewan McGregor and his pathetic friends on their awayday to the highest station on the British Rail network. Corrour, on the West Highland line to Fort William and Mallaig, has no village and no shop, though there is a fourteen-bed bunkhouse inside the former stationmaster's office run by two inhabitants. It is seventeen miles to the nearest road. At least if it gets film fans of Renton, Spud and Sickboy out of the house and breathing fresh Highland air, Welsh has achieved something. Heroin chic may be cool in the city, but at Corrour there are forests, deer, Beinn Na Lap for Munro spotters and more chance of copping an electric-heat 'Class 37/4' than scoring a Class A fix.[72]

Bachelor night

Naked, apart from a tie and Liverpool Football Club baseball cap, a would-be rail traveller presented himself to Bernard Rigby, manning the ticket office at Prescot station, near Liverpool. Appearing at the window with a beer mat covering his manhood to preserve his modesty, the unfortunate customer explained rather unnecessarily that he was on his stag night and his supposed friends had dumped him at the station with no clothes and no money. Taking pity on the bridegroom-to-be, the kindly railwayman made him a makeshift suit out of a grey bin bag, by cutting out holes for the suitor's head and arms, and waved him on his way with wishes for a long and happy marriage.[73]

Personal ritual

In *Steam Railway's* 'The Glorious Years' nostalgia series, contributor Peter Cotton discussed such familiar aspects of rail enthusiasm as shed bashing and performance

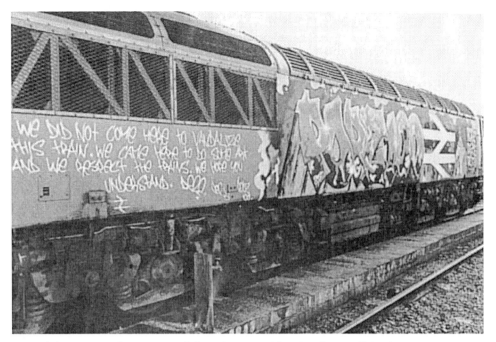

'We did not come here to vandalise this train,' begins the graffitists' message. 'We came here to do some art and we respect the trains. We hope you understand.' Understandably a complete repaint for 'Class 56' No. 56083 and loss of revenue-earning service was not appreciated.

logging, the guest photographer adding that he had come across an eccentric rail fan who 'griced lavatories (both up and down platforms if possible). Well, whatever turns you on! History does not record whether a quick sortie through the door counted or if you actually had to use the facilities!' [74]

Art attacks

It was in a lavatory (the up platform) at Newton Abbot, South Devon, that I spotted my favourite piece of railway graffiti. Like the sound of one hand clapping, it asked cosmically: 'Whither atrophy?' To which someone, perhaps an off-duty schoolteacher, had added: '10/10 very good.'

The modest scrawlings of toilet visitors pales in comparison with the lurid spectacle of urban rail-side art. Those who see this as a messy scourge, costing railway companies millions of pounds each year to erase and putting its perpetrators' lives at risk, would probably prefer to see the word 'art' in inverted commas. Yet others would view graffiti art as a distorted desire to be creative rather than destructive; a motivation which leads to the creation of murals which are often quite sophisticated.

Painted graffiti began to be seen as art some time last century. Some would single out the railroad depots of 1940s Los Angeles as the location where the spray can became an artist's tool, while others dated the cultural transformation to the 1950s

Philadelphia highways and the marking appearing there. Whichever, it was the railway subway cars of New York in the 1970s which seemingly changed artistic perception and transformed what had been viewed as crude vandalism into 'street art'. Since then it has stretched around the world. As a vibrant urban subculture, it has its own styles and techniques, separate vocabulary and specific conventions. The best of it creates a cosmopolitan calligraphy. Disney characters and blue Smurfs were common where I live and a passable portrait of The Cure's Robert Smith, was until recently a landmark on a railway bridge near my home for passengers to admire or deplore for the past 20 years.[75]

The excitement and aura of graffiti's iconography is captured in words and illustrations by Henry Chalfant and James Prigoff. 'In New York, writers have an almost mystical attachment to the trains, the giant worms, arteries in the belly of the beast,' they write in their most-shoplifted tribute. 'The drama unfolded on the trains, in the dark tunnels where writers encountered dragons, high voltage, cold crushing steel wheels, giant hurtling monsters. The trains were the arena where the writer could prove himself, and it is the adventure that caught everyone's attention.'[76]

When *Graphotism* published a special issue devoted to vandalised trains and railway property, editor Mark Sinckler dismissed illegality and trespass issues by saying the magazine was non-judgemental. The law, however, is. British Transport Police confirmed that under the Criminal Damage Act 1971 anyone found guilty of criminal damage can face six months and/or a £5,000 fine when tried in a magistrates' court – or ten years' imprisonment from a crown court. The traditional reluctance of courts to take graffiti seriously was turned on its head when graffitist Daniel Koroma, 28, was successfully sued for damage he caused to London Underground and he was ordered at Northampton crown court to pay £3,000 over a five-year period.[77]

However, despite having a sneaking admiration for some of this 'art' (does having an 'A' level in art from 1963 make me a suitable critic?) and wondering if those adopting a zero tolerance approach might be better employed protecting the public, I cannot but wonder if the use of colourful advertising displays on train exteriors is not capitalism imitating art.[78]

Chapter Two

Supernatural realm

I prefer to use the term 'supernatural,' but this chapter could just as easily have been named 'paranormal', 'fortean' or 'mysteries' – but not 'occult.' All these terms define phenomena that orthodox science cannot or will not examine. The 'paranormal' happens without our conscious intervention; the 'occult' is where we 'dabble' and can supposedly cause changes by our will. Anyway, 'supernatural' sounds more folkloric!

Being devoted centrally to railways rather than being a book on parapsychology, any labelling of phenomena is loose and the sub-divisions used are for convenience only. Fear not, dear reader, this is not the place nor the time to beat you over the head with yet another doomed-to-failure unified field theory of the paranormal.

Spectral sphere

Frankly, the basic insubstantiality of ghosts themselves and general paucity of detail in tellings has – doubtless to many readers' surprise, in the context of this book's subject – left me underwhelmed and the subject under-represented. What I have selected is a single old-fashioned station-setting ghost story, a fitter's modern reminiscences of a spooky diesel loco and an author's fabrication of fiction into fact.

Phantom rail clerk's attack

As a youngster in the mid-Fifties, I would join the throng at that redoubtable haunt of trainspotters, Bank Top station, Darlington. In unison the cry 'Streak' would echo as an 'A4' would thunder past on *The Elizabethan* or *The Flying Scotsman*, its chime whistle shrieking like a banshee. Earlier in the day we would probably have tried to 'bunk' the engine depot. The afternoon 'dead hour' was set aside to view the North Road works yard from a handy footbridge. We could either walk there or catch a train to North Road station, first stop out of Bank Top on the branch to Bishop Auckland. Before heading to see what was being repaired or built at the workshops, we would pay our last respects in the scrap yard outside the neglected and already spooky-looking, dark, dirty and depressing halt. This sad pilgrimage would witness aged steam engines whose long, illustrious and loyal service was being rewarded by withdrawal, ignominious haulage by diesel shunters into the sidings, and finally destruction at the hands of oxy-acetylene torch-wielding assassins. Here proud 'B16', 'Hunt' and 'Shire' class locos were being insensitively dismembered to become slabs of steelworks furnace fodder; rust was eating into the 'G5' and 'A8' tanks ousted by multiple units; the oldest tender engines born of the North Eastern

Railway were falling as the shadows lengthened towards the 'J27' and 'Q6' next-in-liners. Memories of those adolescent times live on. Paradoxically the station (which also once acted as a temporary refuge for condemned engines when withdrawals outstripped the scrapmen's abilities to keep up with the pace) now houses steam stock exhibits as a museum devoted to the historic Stockton and Darlington Railway and its development.

This restoration may have met with approval from the station's little-known spectre, but it was in no friendly mood 150 years ago when it and a dog attacked a man. The victim was teetotal nightwatchman James Durham, who had worked at North Road for fifteen years and would be on duty between 8 p.m. and 6 a.m.. The traumatic events were recorded in a deposition he made:

> At about 12 o'clock or 12.30 I was feeling rather cold with standing here and there, so I said to myself: "I will away down and get something to eat." There was a porter's cellar where a fire was kept on and a coalhouse was connected with it. So I went down the steps, took off my overcoat and had just sat down on the bench opposite the fire and turned up the gas when a strange man came out of the coalhouse followed by a big black retriever. As soon as he entered, my eye was upon him, and his eye upon me, and we were intently watching each other as he moved to the front of the fire. There he stood, looking at me, and a curious smile came over his countenance. He had a stand-up collar and a cutaway coat with gilt buttons and a Scotch cap.

Then came the attack.

> All at once he struck at me and I had the impression that he hit me. I up with my fist and struck back at him. My fist seemed to go through him and struck against the stone above the fireplace and knocked the skin off my knuckles. The man seemed to be struck back into the fire and uttered a strange, unearthly squeak. Immediately the dog gripped me by the calf of my leg and seemed to cause me pain. The man recovered his position, called off the dog with a sort of click of the tongue and then went back into the coalhouse, followed by the dog. I lighted my dark lantern and looked into the coalhouse, but there was neither dog nor man, and no outlet for them except the one by which they had entered.

Mr Durham was sufficiently intelligent and curious as to make inquiries and ascertained that some years previously a railway clerk named Winter had committed suicide by shooting himself on the station platform. A fierce black retriever was his constant companion. So as not to alarm passengers, the body was moved to the coal cellar until police inquiries were completed. Winter's description was exactly what Mr Durham had witnessed.

The ghost story was a 'scoop' for W.T. Stead, the crusading Darlington journalist – and spiritualist – who went down with the *Titanic* in 1912. His source was an old friend, the Rev Harry Kendall, minister of Union Street Congregational Church, which James Durham had attended for twenty-five years.[1] Mr Kendall was quoted as regarding what the witness had encountered as 'genuinely apparitional.' Yet the Society for Psychical Research was unconvinced that the nightwatchman had not had a nightmare, and Mr Kendall made a further attempt to assure the society by citing Mr Durham's integrity of character.

The fireplace where the assault victim grazed his knuckles was bricked up many years ago, but in the mid-Eighties a boy performing a security night shift during an Easter exhibition heard footsteps. Nicholas Blackett, 15, said: 'There was no one there and no one could have got in because it was all locked up. I was terrified and I just can't explain it.'[2]

Olive Howe, a member of the Friends of Darlington Railway Museum, and her friend, Irene McCloud, trawled archives and discovered that a clerk named Thomas Munroe Winter, aged 29, had committed suicide in 1845. 'When we bought a copy of his death certificate we were elated to find that his cause of death was "shot himself with a pistol, being in a state of unsound mind" and his occupation was "ticket clerk." We had found the ghost,' commented the sleuths.[3]

Never alone with '69'

It could be said that for Thornaby depot fitter Hugh Watson every day's a busman's holiday. When centenary celebrations were held at Darlington's Bank Top station, Hugh was there helping look after preserved 'Deltic' class loco No. 55009 *Royal Highland Fusilier*. On the adjacent track was one of his Teesside depot charges, pristine 'Class 37' No. 37069 *Thornaby TMD*, close to its 1962 birthplace at Robert Stephenson and Hawthorn's works in the famous railway town.

Hugh recalled:

> One night I was in the 'Deltic's' cab, and glanced across at 69, and was convinced someone was in her cab. I knew at the time no one should have been in there so I went to investigate. When I reached the loco I looked in both cabs and engine-room windows. There was no one there, but there was a definite feeling that someone was around. After a while I returned to *Royal Highland Fusilier* and occasionally looked across at 69. Suddenly a diesel horn sounded. It was definitely not the 'Deltic', and no other working loco was in the station. It must have been 69, but no person was near her. All I could say looking at her was a very strange aura around.

A couple of days later, it was a really hot summer Saturday afternoon, and Bank Top station was very busy. All of a sudden my son Craig burst into the 'Deltic' shouting, "Dad, *Thornaby TMD*'s on fire." Immediately a friend and I charged over to 69 and noticed what looked like smoke coming through the engine-room louvres. My friend opened the engine-room door and became engulfed by the contents of the fire bottles, causing slight injury to his arms. After making sure he was OK, I returned into

Parked alone. Haunted 'Class 37' No. 37069 at Thornaby depot on May 14, 1989. (Paul Screeton)

the cab alone to make certain nothing was wrong. I was alone, yet I knew I wasn't, although there was no one there. Yet the hairs on the back of my neck stood up, and there was a definite presence. I turned and went into the engine-room. No one was there. I ran through into the other cab. No one was there either: it was very eerie. Once recomposed and realising that previously that day the loco's cabs had been open to the public, I checked to see if the fire bottle levers had been pulled, but they hadn't. Nor had there been a fire in the engine-room. It appeared the fire bottles had gone off on their own accord. I looked around and thought 'This isn't real.' But it was.

Celebrations over, *Thornaby TMD* was supposed to tow the 'Deltic' and the supporting 'Peak' class diesel back to Thornaby depot, but 69 refused to start. Eventually all the locos arrived back at Tees Yard, and 37069 was back home. [4]

Hugh mentioned the experiences at Darlington to colleagues and a strange picture began to emerge. It was said at Thornaby depot that night or day, if a horn should sound or fire bottles went off without explanation or no one present, 'It's only 69 at it again.' Also Hugh learned that while hauling a southbound freight along the ECML between Northallerton and York, pre-TOPs numbered D6769 approached a Deltic-hauled northbound express, when suddenly an object was thrown up, smashing through D6769's windscreen, hitting the driver on the head, killing him, but luckily not disabling the secondman.

Hugh reported: 'Persons approaching the loco are said to have seen the apparition of a man sat in the driver's seat, believed to be the fatefully-killed driver. One driver explained he never felt alone on 69, and many times had occasion to look in the engine-room or back along the loco to see if anyone was there – but there never was. Once I learned of 69's reputation, I could hardly believe it. Strangely enough, while talking to Paul Screeton he commented on the loco always appearing to be either parked alone or on the end of a line of locos. I, too, have noticed this. She's like some guardian angel looking over the flock, but to me Old 69 is never alone.' [5]

Today 'The Ghost', as it was also known, is employed mostly on hauling nuclear flasks for its new owner, Direct Rail Services, a wholly-owned subsidiary of British Nuclear Fuels. Hugh Watson, author of *The Deltic Years* (Patrick Stephens, 1989), is employed by EWS at Thornaby depot.

Clouded vision

How a fictional story of a spectral loco could have seeped into factual life among the fanatic fraternity makes interesting reading. I came by an insight into author William Barry Herbert's methods when a review I wrote and published [6] was read by a former railway preservation society publication editor. Herbert had a chapter wherein a diesel loco, No. 55020 *Nimbus*, seemingly reappeared in ghostly fashion charging through a Home Counties station seven months after it had been well authenticated as cut up in a Doncaster scrap yard.

Mark Valentine wrote:

> I must lay the ghost of 55020 *Nimbus*, before it passes altogether from fiction to folklore. The source for the story of this spectral 'Deltic' diesel locomotive, supposedly 'spotted' at Hadley Wood station months after it was scrapped by BR, is an article 'A Trick of Light?' published in *Deltic Deadline*, journal of the Deltic Preservation Society. W.B. Herbert, in *Railway Ghosts*,[7] repeats the story and acknowledges this source, and you mention the sighting briefly in your review of his book. As editor of the *Deadline* at the time the story appeared, I can categorically state that it was a spoof, contributed by a member under a pseudonym in order to jog memories of the departed loco, and underline the fate in store for other locos in the same class. W.B. Herbert wrote to me seeking permission to use the piece while he was compiling material for his book. While I had no objection on behalf of the society, the copyright obviously belonged to the member who wrote the story, and the matter was referred to him. Herbert wrote again, very close to the book's publication deadline, telling me that he would be using the story with the usual acknowledge-ments. It was only at this stage that I realised that his work concerned supposedly authentic railway ghosts. I replied to Herbert telling him that the piece was a hoax. In response, he said he was surprised to hear this as several other people had reported curious incidents in the general area of Hadley Wood station.

I have never received a copy of Herbert's book, but I know now that he appears to have presented this story as a possibly authentic case despite being clearly told that it was a work of fiction -- a 'Winter's Tale', if I remember, for our Christmas issue. And although it is no great matter, I am also aware that he did not receive permission to use the story from the original writer, the copyright-holder. If Herbert has indeed been told by other witnesses about strange happenings at Hadley Wood, I have no doubt they must also stem from the *Deltic Deadline* story. The magazine had an average circulation of about 1,000 and rail enthusiasts are apt to exchange gossip and tales of this kind at the slightest prompting, so that the piece could quickly have become a friend-of-a-friend phenomenon.[8]

So Herbert ignored copyright and published as fact what was fiction. Discovering my interest in the supposed strategic steam reserve, he sought permission to reproduce an article on the subject I had published in a magazine of 'studies at the fringe of human experience.'[9] This I granted and he promised me a copy of the book in which it would be republished 'as a token of my appreciation.' Herbert reproduced a shortened version – though the longest piece in his book – without crediting me directly (although my name appeared in the general acknowledgements) and failed to send a courtesy copy of the book (a review copy being supplied by the publisher). When reviewing Herbert's second collection,[10] I took the opportunity also to clarify the 55020 tale.[10] His publisher then chose to combine both his books in a single volume, still with no indication that the 'Deltic' story was anything but fictional.[12]

Prophecy

Just as psychic research has become an 'ology' – parapsychology – so science has nowadays rationalised prophecy and other clairvoyant matters under the respectable term extra-sensory perception. Here are some persons who saw the future with a railway theme.

Life and death of 47216/47299

Numerous articles and television programme snippets have featured a particular 'jinxed' locomotive. In one of the best-authenticated cases of prophecy, a humble, workaday diesel-electric engine was propelled to infamy after its renumbering failed to avert the crash a psychic had foreseen.

The culprit heading for a day with destiny was 'Brush Type 4' No. 47216. Old in tooth and with the track record of a showbooth pugilist, this celebrity of dubious provenance was finally cut up as surplus to requirements. 'This machine which has defied all predictions of its doom, even now, must surely be offered to preservationists,' wrote a rail enthusiast magazine staffer.[13] This was when against all the odds the loco had been reinstated although boatloads of General Motors 'Class 66s' were on their way as replacements for aged British workhorses.

As D1866, the 'Class 47/0' diesel-electric left the Brush company's Loughborough works in May 1965. In February 1974, it was renumbered to 47216 on the TOPS computer database. In 1981 it became 47299, the remaining unallocated number before the 47/3 slow-speed control variants began (though a few other numbers before it remained vacant). The reason for this new renumbering has about it something of the magical ritual – a banishing one – for normally new numbers are only allocated when a machine has a major modification necessitating the TOPS computer to identify its new sub-classification for assigning it duties commensurate with its re-equipped capabilities. In the case of 47216 there were no mechanical changes; only a psychic component. As a keen rail fan, I had never understood the reason for the renumbering. The first inkling came when the loco was involved in a crash, where one magazine reported: 'After predictions of impending doom, BR even renumbered 47216 to 47299... but it obviously made little difference.' This brief news item also claimed that 'the jinx that has haunted an Immingham-based Class 47 for over two years followed it to a remarkable crash.' [14]

This occurred at Wrawby junction, a convergence of lines just west of Barnetby, North Lincolnshire. At about 18.18 on 9 December 1983, 47299 was hauling the 15.02 Drax-Lindsey 900-ton empty oil tanks when a set of points, which had been hand cranked but not clipped, reset themselves in front of the freight train. A collision then occurred with the 17.32 Cleethorpes-Sheffield two-car diesel-multiple unit ('Class 114s' 53049 and 54049). Student Rachel Taylor was killed and a dozen passengers injured.[15] Both cabs of 47299 were stove in and the DMU severely damaged. The official report stated 'the weather was fine and visibility good,' yet another account claimed 'emergency services were stretched to the limit in appalling weather conditions,' while adding the renumbering came 'after a soothsayer predicted a crash involving its earlier guise, 47216.' [16]

So, who was the psychic with a line to mediumistic ferroequinology? Perhaps we'll never know. The report with greatest detail did not say and even the 1 April dateline should not concern the reader unnecessarily. Graham Bell's by-lined article in the *Sunday Express* was as accurate a railway news story in a national newspaper as I have ever come across; particularly as in this case an offbeat, human interest story. A clairvoyant had a recurring vision of a train crash involving a big blue engine hauling oil tankers, nothing could stop it and someone would die. She could even decipher the number 47216. She called British Rail and insisted her name be kept secret before revealing the accident in minute detail. Apparently those in authority found her predictions had previously been taken seriously in police investigations. After the crash an enthusiast contact of Bell's recalled phoning Immingham depot to ask why 47216 had been renumbered and was told staff had been warned of a clairvoyant's predictions and made a special application to BR headquarters in London to change the number. According to Bell, who checked his story out with BR and confirmed 47299's history, the prediction was not mentioned at the collision inspectorate hearing, and the spokesman said: 'We regard the whole thing as an amazing coincidence.' [17]

Does all this give the story credence? The Press loves supernatural stories and with police, BR spokesman and depot officials, you either accept the reporter was

Jinxed 'Class 47' No. 47299 at Carlisle in 1996. Its earlier crash at Wrawby junction had been predicted. (Alan C. Hopkins)

thorough or you mutter about 'authority figures' and 'urban belief tales'. I wrote about 47216/47299 in 1984 [18] and in slightly larger context in 1985.[19] Meanwhile, 47299 was back in traffic, recognisable because its new cabs were two inches higher than the rest of the bodyside lower profile, and the buffer beam lacked the usual raised edge.[20] Author Jenny Randles used the fulfilled prophecy in a number of books; her reports being generally sound, though the renumbering explanation being in error. Don't worry Jenny, seasoned spotters and rail employees can be equally baffled by what appears to be an arcane numerology system.[21]

But there was to be a note of scepticism abroad. Dave Rapson profiled the loco and focused upon it as the 'Demon' as the spotting fraternity termed it, and stated that 'its sudden change of identity had never been revealed, although it is generally believed a visionary foretold of impending doom... even the depot staff at Immingham having been sworn to secrecy, though the general belief was that, as 47216, the locomotive had been involved in a number of incidents.' [22] But many locos have had chequered careers without such publicity (Great Train Robbery 'Class 40' No. D326 being an exception) or renumbering (an exception being Hatfield and Great Heck accidents victim renumbered from 91023 to 91132).

As Rapson pointed out, 47299 was condemned on 5 September 1989, only to be reinstated three days later when a replacement wheel set was found. He concluded: 'Whether or not this stay of execution is merely temporary, time will tell, and we may never know just how sinister the tale behind 47299 is!' In another magazine, a detailed caption of the loco as D1866 disputed two points: stating 'BR officials at

York' – not London – permitted renumbering and its worn tyres reprieve came after seven – not three – days. Trivialities, perhaps.[23]

Eventually, after twenty years on Humberside, the loco moved to Tinsley, near Sheffield, and on 28 June 1991, was applied the painted unofficial name *Ariadne*. It then suffered fire damage, but was sanctioned repair and intermediate overhaul,[24] emerging in Railfreight Distribution livery in January 1992. It was at this time I decided to dig deeper into the loco's past. I got in touch with 47299's former home, Immingham depot, and have a letter dated 13 February 1992 from S.D. Boner, Area Fleet Manager. I specifically asked about the psychic, renumbering and any earlier accidents to the loco. The brief reply states: 'I refer to your letter dated 5 February and the "folklore" surrounding locomotive 47216/47299 and the Barnetby crash. This is not a matter about which I have any knowledge. I personally have been here since April, 1989, and this is the first time it has ever been raised. Renumbering of locomotives occur quite frequently for many varied reasons, all of which are decided at Headquarters level. I am sorry that I cannot be more helpful. Hopefully the foregoing is of some assistance.'

No really, actually. In fact, very disappointing. So what conclusions can be drawn? There are several possibilities: that he was too busy/bored to inquire further; that there was no mystery psychic; or the conspiracy theory that the depot staff had been sworn to secrecy.

However, the matter does not quite end there. Researchers for TV programmes on the paranormal twice contacted me regarding 47299; on the second occasion I was told authoritatively that an exorcism was carried out upon 47299 at Tinsley, though I could not get details. I wrote a couple more lengthy articles on 47299 [25], ghost-hunter Barry Herbert resurrected it [26] and a Sunday tabloid's three-page special lumped it with cellar spirits, cursed highway and alien kidnapping.[27] A massively-detailed life history appeared on what the obituarist called the 'Devil's Chariot' [28] for after a multitude of defects led to its owner losing patience, 47299 was hauled off to Wigan Springs Branch, where component recovery took place with inordinate haste and it was completely disposed of on 7 January 2000. R.I.P.

The Brahan Seer

On the face of it, whoever foresaw the Barnetby crash did so with astonishing clarity. Not so in olden days when predictions were given in verse with the prophetic vision so alien to the time when received that it was too technologically advanced to fit into the age's cultural matrix, resulting in the revelation being couched within the seer's limited vocabulary, literary ability and descriptive scientific capability. It would be opaque. The soothsayer of 47216 fame remains anonymous, but not so a man who had a vision of the coming of railways.

When it comes to considering predictive hits, the man who became known as the 'Brahan Seer' stands head and shoulders above the others. Coinneach Odhar Fiossaiche, or Kenneth Mackenzie in English, was an uneducated labourer working on the Brahan estate in east Ross-shire, who around 1675 became famous for his visions throughout the Gaelic Highlands, where the sixth sense was not uncommon, but was so uncannily pinpoint accurate that he became regarded as a prophet's prophet. The year of his birth is unknown and there are more than one versions of how he came supernaturally by the white, or blue, holed stone he used for scrying by holding it up to his blind eye. The farmworker psychic was consulted for domestic affairs, but his inner eye focussed not only on the mundane in time and space, but ranged over two hundred or more years and, in fact, beyond today.

A long and detailed analysis of Mackenzie's claims appears on the Internet,[29] anonymous but I believe it was written by two Newcastle University dons. The analysis is broken down under:

- intuitive prophecies;

- doubtful prophecies;

- prophecies, all or partly fulfilled; prophecies unfulfilled.

'Intuitive' simply means making a claim which could be easily construed from extrapolating known facts, so it might be guessed from the geography of the country, with its chain of great lakes, that the Caledonian canal could be predicted; similarly 'that the day will come when there will be a road through the hills of Ross-shire from sea to sea, and bridge upon every stream.' This area of ascribing natural shrewdness leaves the unbeliever only a fraction of the Seer's output, and doubtful prophecies number only one, being possibly relocated from another parish.

The fulfilled prophecies, fully or partially, are many and varied, several pertaining to the downfalls of distinguished Highland families, particularly the intricate Doom of the Seaforths, the savage battle at Culloden, piped water and gas, and one pertinent to this book, predicting the formation of a railway through the Muir of Ord, appearing in the stanza stating in literal translation:

> When there shall be two churches in the Parish of Ferrintosh,
> And a hand with two thumbs in *I-Stiana* [the Black Isle],
> Two bridges at *Squideal* [Conan] of the gormandisers,
> Soldiers will come from *Carr a Chlarsair* [Tarradale],
> On a chariot without horse or bridle,
> Which will leave the *Blar-dubh* [Muir of Ord] a wilderness,
> Spilling blood with many knives,
> And the raven shall drink he three fulls
> Of the blood of the Gael from the Stone of Fionn

The writers had been told by an eyewitness of a man with two thumbs (and another with two navels as also predicted!) and translated the 'chariot without horse or bridle' as the 'iron horse.' As for the remainder of the prophecy, they suggest that having been so accurate previously, the Seer had seen scarily for us 'something serious is looming not very remotely in the future.' A simpleton called Farquhar of the Gun 'entered into the spirit of the prophecy' recorded the writers when he compared the first train to pass through the district, to the funeral of 'Old Nick.' Another version attributed to the Seer was 'that after four successive dry summers, a fiery chariot shall pass through the "Blar Dubh".' The authors added that it had also been reported that a man with second sight living in the Beauly neighbourhood had a vision of a train moving at great speed while he was heading home one autumn night, this being several years before the notion of a railway in those whereabouts was mooted.

Back on track with the Seer, the adjudicators take 'The day will come when long strings of carriages without horses shall run between Dingwall and Inverness, and more wonderful still, between Dingwall and the Isle of Skye' as hardly necessary to require comment as this so obviously refers to the railway carriages running two hundred years afterwards to the places mentioned.

Before reaching the unfulfilled prophecies, I found another railway-connected reference, for the Seer made remarkable predictions about the Mackenzies and Fairburn Tower. 'The day will come when the Mackenzies of Fairburn shall lose their entire possessions; their castle will become uninhabited and a cow shall give birth to a calf in the uppermost chamber of the tower.' In the Seer's day the tower was an important stronghold. It eventually became a ruin and in 1851 it was being used by a farmer to store hay. One day a cow, following a trail of hay, had a good feed and became stuck. She gave birth to a healthy calf in the uppermost chamber. 'A special train trip was organised from Inverness for visitors to witness the cow and calf' [30] or 'the prophecy was so well known that the people came via the railway to Strathpeffer or Muir of Ord and then by coach to see the cow.' [31] Having given the incredulous sufficient time to see the prophecy fulfilled for themselves, after five days both cow and calf were manoeuvred down to a more convivial pasture. Those sceptics who said Kenneth could have second-guessed the Caledonian canal found this bovine event more difficult to dismiss.

The sympathetic sceptics finally ran through the unfulfilled prophecies, one of which featured Gairloch House. This is one made before he was burned to death in a barrel of tar by the angry Countess of Seaforth. The Warlock of the Glens predicted what Justine Glass suggested could be the detonation of a nuclear submarine, 'a dun hornless cow will appear in the Minch,' whose 'horrid black rain' will depopulate Scotland and whose blast 'will knock the six chimneys off Gairloch House.' In the Seer's time the construction was a mere thatched wattled-turf-and-hurdles dwelling without chimneys. The present, rebuilt Gairloch House has six chimneys. Terrorism ahead? Scotland beware! [32]

Mother Shipton

Mother Shipton, a witch and seer with an acute mind, was born Ursula Sonthiel in the North Riding town of Knaresborough in July 1488. Her mother, an unmarried orphan and beggar aged 17, had fallen in love with a handsome gentleman on a black horse. He is supposed to have been the Devil. Strange phenomena surrounded her childhood, she moved from school to school and eventually married Tobias Shipton and the couple moved to Skipton, West Yorkshire, where she lived out the rest of her life, dying peacefully in her bed at home in 1561, just as she had prophesied.[33] She turned her powers to the art of prophecy and healing. Sceptics might say that those prophecies which were about events that took place in her own lifetime or shortly afterwards were explainable as the astute predictions of a capable commentator on current politics, i.e. intuitive. Also that visions of events and inventions not to happen until centuries later were more wishes than visions of the future. But among these prophecies recorded in clever rhymes are references to aircraft, divers' suits, worldwide communications and pertinently for the purpose of this book, 'horseless carriages'.

Her words included 'around the world thoughts shall fly, In the twinkling of an eye, Through hills men shall ride, And no horse or ass at their side, Under water men shall walk... in the air shall men be seen, Carriages without horse shall go, And accidents fill the world with woe... fire and water shall more wonders do... '[34] In the Brahan Seer's prediction the 'horseless carriage' was decoded as a train, though here it could be judged to be the motor car and the 'fire and water' perhaps refer to steam, i.e. a steam locomotive. There are even two more optional couplets: 'When carriages without horses run, Old England will be quite undone' and also 'A carriage without horse shall go, Disaster fill the world with woe.' However, that great arbiter 'folk history' is on the side of railway rather than automobile development, and anyway these and other famous Shipton lines have been claimed to have been forged in 1862 by Charles D. Hindley, a seller of almanacks.[35] In an introductory note distinguishing early records of Mother Shipton's prophecies from those later attributed to her in a reprint of a 1916 account of the sybil's life, John Michell comments on the 1862 supposedly confessed couplets that they 'became generally known only after the introduction of railways, though before the motor car' and that such 'rediscovered' prophecy expressed popular feelings of the time and traditional orthodoxy.[36]

The Witch of Tebay

The horseless carriages prophecy attributed to the Brahan Seer and Mother Shipton also attaches to another elderly woman with second sight, but whose party trick was to turn herself into a hare and dash around annoying a neighbouring squire's hunting dogs. Even at the best of times hares have been mysterious, indeed rather sinister, animals associated with witchcraft and given fine names by country folk such as the 'long lugs', 'the race-the-wind', 'the sitter-still', 'the ring-the-hill' and the (honestly, and I don't know why) 'gobshite'.

Folklore is replete with geriatric crones whose shape-shifting ability made them sprightly beasts on occasion,[37] but as far as I know Mary Baynes is the only one to exercise a sixth sense in addition to lithe limbs. This sporty dame predicted that 'carriages without horses will run over Loups Fell.' Her vision took physical form when the Lancaster and Carlisle Railway Company began services and opened a station at this very spot, calling it Tebay after a tiny nearby hamlet.[38] Mary Baynes, sometimes known as the Witch of Tebay, died in 1811, aged 90. She became the subject of a fascinating Web discussion forum on ghost trains when a contributor pointed out that a favourite book[39] mentions that *The Westmoreland Gazette* in 1983 reported that rail enthusiast David Johnson photographed a 'Britannia' steam loco on a desolate stretch of line near Tebay. Presumably this would be in the dying days of steam in the late Sixties. When Johnson developed the film he could see a cloaked figure of an old woman standing on the embankment. He was certain she was not visible when he took the photograph. Knowledgeable in local lore, Johnson became convinced he had accidentally photographed Mary Baynes and believes that perhaps she was proudly checking out her prophecy. Authors John and Anne Spencer considered another possibility. What if Baynes had somehow projected herself into the future and saw trains at the site? Then perhaps it was her projection that Johnson photographed; not checking up on her prophecy, but actually discovering the 'carriages without horses' which she was to prophesise. Or as the Internet commentator 'Thistle' adds: 'or did he just notice an old woman standing at the side of the embankment at the time????' After some cyber correspondence with 'Cufflink' tangentially touching upon unclean underwear, the lewd Scotswoman replies that she cannot locate a copy of Johnson's photograph (apparently it did not accompany the Press report), but had learned that Mary Baynes supposedly haunts the Cross Keys Inn at Tebay.

Bullet trains and disasters

There were railways in every corner of the earth in 1892 when Jack McCullogh wrote *Golf in the Year 2000 or What We Are Coming To*. In 2005, an Edinburgh auctioneers sold a rare copy to an American collector for £1,200. McCullogh had predicted the invention of television, digital watches and what we now know as 'bullet trains.' [40]

An impressive precognitive dream comes from no lesser person than the engineer J.W. Dunne, who went on to write the classic book *An Experiment in Time*, published in 1927. In 1913 he dreamed of a high railway embankment, knowing with full certainty that it was a place just north of the Forth bridge in Scotland. He 'saw' a train going north fall over the embankment, with several carriages crashing to the bottom of the slope, followed by boulders. He tried to receive the date of the disaster, but succeeded only in having the vague feeling that it was March or April. On 14 April 1914, *The Flying Scotsman* fell on to the golf links from the parapet 25 kilometres north of the Forth bridge.[41] The contributor who wrote this tosh remains mercifully anonymous for his reputation. Like the ghostly 'Deltic' resurrected earlier, there is something seriously wrong here. Is the Flying Scotsman here the train of that name – if so it runs from London, terminates at Edinburgh Waverley station and does not go across the Forth bridge. Or is the Flying Scotsman here the locomotive of that name – if so it did not exist in 1913 or 1914, in fact not being constructed until 1923.

It is also claimed many people foresaw the Tay Bridge catastrophe, but the authorities discounted the dreams as too slight a reason to investigate the soundness of the structure. [42]

Another premonition of a railway disaster struck as a woman was crossing a railway bridge. It was 1952 and Betty Gayler was returning home from a day out with two friends. It was midnight and they were crossing the bridge at Harrow and

Wealdstone station. Miss Gayler wrote in a letter responding to an earlier tale of a prophetic dream: 'There were very few people about at that time of night and the station seemed very ghostly. As we crossed I suddenly felt a terrible panic and grabbed hold of my two friends and ran. When they asked me what was wrong, I replied, "I smell death".' Two days later, on 8 October 1952, one of the worst railway disasters in history happened at that bridge. Two trains crashed in fog and a third ploughed into the wreckage. There were 112 killed and 157 injured.[43]

Bird of ill omen and nodding donkey

The splendid magazine *Fortean Times* ran a couple of interesting letters; the second correcting the first on no fewer than five errors of fact in two paragraphs. So, piecing together the bones of the matter, it seems there may have been a legendary big black bird with leathery wings and red burning eyes known as the Skree which, having hovered over Culloden battlefield in 1745 and seen the Jacobites massacred, it next appeared over the men and officers of the 1st/7th Battalion of the Royal Scots embarking for overseas. The superstitious Highlanders spotted the bird of ill omen and refused to join the troop train at Larbert until forced on at gunpoint by the unsuperstitious officers. Railway archivist Mark Andrew Pardoe knew of no reference to the Skree bird or mutiny attempt, but referred to an unconfirmed report that after the train with the troops had crashed at Quintinshill, an officer was seen emptying his revolver into the wreckage, presumably to save trapped soldiers from the horror of being burned alive. The military special had collided with a local train ten miles north of Carlisle on 22 May 1915. Before protective action could be taken, a double-headed down express ploughed into the wreckage. The signalmen's error caused the greatest number of fatalities of any railway accident in Great Britain. At least 277 were killed and 246 injured, though the exact numbers were never known as the regimental records were consumed in the fire which burned for almost 24 hours. In fact, there was a second troop train and those on it reached the Dardanelles, only to be slaughtered there.[44]

Just to add a note of levity to proceedings, when journalist Chris Milner was sampling a cab ride in the Midlands, Traction Inspector Bill Soden asked if he had heard the tale of the Sharnbrook donkey. It had been said during the steam era that a donkey in a field on the southern approach to the summit would signal to footplate crews of northbound trains whether they would make it over the top. If he nodded, they would manage, but if he shook his head then they could expect the worst.[45]

Earth mysteries

The art of interpreting the landscape has several names: the dullest but correct 'geomancy'; the sinister-sounding 'psychogeography'; 'hermetic topography', the mystical but faintly pompous creation of Bill Porter; John Nicholson's workaday 'ancient skills and wisdom'; Julian Cope's romantic 'new antiquarianism'; and the memorial to the unknown sub-editor's apposite and winner by popular 'folk history' choice 'earth mysteries'. Whatever name is preferred, the interdisciplinary research engages archaeology, folklore, mythology, cosmology, symbolism, geometry, geology, dowsing, magic, divination and revelation, dragonlore, ufology, ecology, the paranormal and metaphysics. It is a study which has established itself as a discipline in its own right over the past forty years.

My role as editor of the seminally-significant magazine *The Ley Hunter* between 1969 and 1976, publication in hardback of earth mysteries overview *Quicksilver Heritage* and countless articles need not detain us. Back then the only living embodiment of a once universal planetary-wide appreciation of the topographical engineering was the Oriental practice of *feng shui*. Railway development by Westerners could not comprehend the warnings of Chinese geomants with their dragon lines followed by mysterious forms in the skies, even after the misfortunes befallen by George Stephenson as he railroaded the elven race.

Skull and cross fairies

It was appropriate that British Rail named 'Class 91' locomotive No. 91018 after novelist Robert Louis Stevenson (though with less romanticism Great North Eastern Railway renamed it *Bradford Film Festival*). Stevenson was also an accomplished poet and it was equally fitting that revolutionary railway photographer Colin T. Gifford named the two volumes of his best steam era portfolios after phrases in the last line of his poem *From A Railway Carriage*. I'll give four lines of his verse as a taster, particularly as I will be considering the machinations of faeryfolk and wizardry.

> Faster than fairies, faster than witches,
> Bridges and houses, hedges and ditches...
> And here is a mill, and there a river:
> Each a glimpse and gone forever!

Traditional Australian aborigines still believe each stone and tree has its own spirit and they journey along invisible 'song lines'. We modern Britons have all but lost contact with a landscape which was once enchanted. Occasionally tales surface of deeds which remind us that presences still guard the sacredness of the countryside scene.

One who chose to alter the landscape was visionary George Stephenson, a hard-headed railway pioneer whose surveying led him to drive his line through a reputed fairy hill in County Durham, at Middridge, but he found himself facing an engineering problem blamed upon supernatural intervention. The sides of the cutting through the hill were supposedly being pushed down by the indignant elementals and he faced a plea for extra money from the contractors to complete this section. Whether he believed the problem to be supernatural or technical, Stephenson was left no option but to approach the Quaker backers and put the case for additional finance.[46] Another railway line to Darlington was constructed shortly afterwards to transport ore from Merrybent mine on Gatherley Moor, apparently rich in copper deposits. Unfortunately the venture proved commercially nonviable and certain persons held the fairies which were said to inhabit Diddersley Hill responsible.[47]

Another example of mysterious forces hindering a railway scheme focuses upon a guardian or heirloom skull known as Dicky O'Tunstead. A long catalogue of

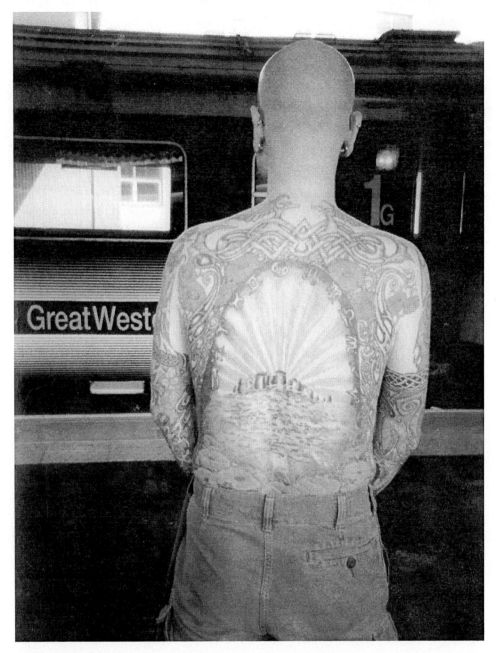

This splendid tattoo of Stonehenge adorns the back of a Geordie stranger I photographed at Bristol Temple Meads station. He was in a hurry to catch a connection so all I know is that it was copied from a magazine illustration and otherwise he had no interest in prehistory. Consequently he would not have known that the huge sarsen stones at Stonehenge came from Fyfield Downs some 30 miles to the north, where the remaining ones lie in such a way that archaeologists call them 'sarsen trains'. Incidentally, 'sarsen' is Celtic for 'stranger'. (Paul Screeton)

misfortune associated with the skull included farm beasts sickening, crops failing and strange sounds, yet when well-treated it was believed to bring good fortune. However, the skull was blamed for railway bridges built across the Peak District farmland collapsing in 1862 and causing the line to be re-routed. The bridge that eventually became permanent came to be known as Dicky's bridge. As for the skull – actually female and possibly prehistoric – in 1985 it was buried by the wife of the farm's present owner in the garden.[48]

When the Victorians forged northwards with what we now know as the West Coast Main Line (WCML), near Shap quarry they cut through the Neolithic stone circle now known as Kemp Howe. There are many accounts of woe befalling those who desecrate ancient monuments and I was not surprised to learn of problems at this Cumbrian location, even so long after engineers chose to bury half the terminating site of an avenue of sacred megaliths.[49] Discussing Virgin's present loco fleet and future plans, journalist David Brown asked if there were any upgraded current problems. As Jackie Townsend, Virgin Trains' Operations Manager West Coast, confided, 'current' was the operative word: 'We do have a mystery problem – our very own "X file" if you like! There is a disconfiguration problem on the WCML near Harrison's Sidings, Shap, which means we suffer loss of power in the afternoon. The locos have been tested and the overhead wires have been tested and so far we have not found the source of the power loss. So we'll keep on looking!'[50] Kemp Howe was not the only sacred site desecrated by railway construction, as is witnessed in a tale of geomantic prophecy. During the nineteenth century a line was being built between Neubrandenburg and Rostock, and when the workmen arrived in the manor of Gevezin, farmers implored the landlord not to allow the impending destruction of a small prehistoric burial mound. A 'tradition had been preserved by the local people for about 4,000 years' that in the distant past a king had ridden into the mound seated in a golden chariot. Undaunted, the line builders cut into the barrow and encountered a tomb containing a bronze wagon.[51]

As for prehistoric stone circles, one theory among many to explain their origin and specific siting is Terence Meaden's novel notion that Stone Age engineers built them where they saw a wind vortex in motion. This is not the place to argue the pros and cons of corn circles, but two railway associations with cereology are worth a mention. Noel Ingram was trainspotting at the bridge over the ECML at Swayfield, Lincolnshire, on 7 June 1962, when 'I was enjoying the countryside between trains when there was a sudden roaring in a crop field to the left of the [railway line]. A sudden whirlwind whipped up the crop skyward and then stopped as suddenly as it had begun – leaving a ring of flattened crop! I was too startled to use the camera hanging around my neck.' This bizarre event appears to be given in an extended caption recording the passing at 6.40 p.m. that day of 'Class A4' No. 60015 *Quicksilver* on the Tees-Tyne Pullman (which by my memory and reckoning should have been in London by 2.30 p.m.).[52] Quicksilver is another name for mercury and Patrick Harpur has suggested corn circles are created by the god Mercury.[53] Also among the rich lore which has attached to crop circles is the occasional manifestation of a low-frequency sound which in folklore goes by the moniker 'hummadruz.' It existed before the Industrial Revolution, but among many explanations from the pragmatic to the esoteric, one researcher's prime candidate was submarine communications at around 76 Hz in frequency.[54] The 'hum' was apparently common in York at the time the local engine shed was host to a squadron of 'Deltic' class diesel locos, which by a maritime connection were powered by twin Napier engines of a type used in motor-torpedo boats. York motive power depot was thought to be the culprit by 'hum' sufferers.

Superstition is no stranger in the world of professional football and Dr Paul Darby, an authority on the Oriental art of *feng shui*, was called in to lift a jinx on the unlucky south side dressing-room at Cardiff's Millenium stadium. Dr Darby scattered incense and sea salt, rang bells, chanted a Buddhist ritual and even led a horse around the pitch to banish bad spirits. He explained: 'The maze of railway lines and the Bristol Channel behind the southern stand disrupt the positive energy of that part of the stadium.' [55]

Lastly, a couple of tales regarding abandoned tracks. An ambitious plan was mooted fifteen years ago to reopen the line between Frome and Radstock, in Somerset, closed in 1988. The line's marketing title was suggested as 'The Jack and Jill Line' after the nursery rhyme couple who, according to local legend, climbed a hill within view of the railway.[56] Some of our native verses such as this have been proffered as dating back to the Neolithic and were used to teach children cosmology. Water on top of a hill sounds odd, but not if one considers either the creation of an artificial dew-pond to thermodynamically collect early morning water or a blind spring below the surface divined by water dowsing and collected via a well. Sadly, I've not seen mention recently of this doubtless struggling uphill railway venture. Like dew-ponds, mazes date back to prehistoric times, when they were known as 'Troy towns' and were utilised to stop malign spirits following anyone about to undertake a journey. Where once the original course of the ECML ran before being diverted to skirt the short-lived Selby coalfield, a Sustrans cycle path includes a large circular maze at Escrick, spread across the track bed in a shallow cutting and utilising concrete cable-ducts abandoned by British Rail.[57]

Here be dragons

The nineteenth century traveller and folklore collector William Howitt eloquently ended his account of County Durham's legend of the Lambton Worm by noting another 'mightier worm' nearby – 'the flying dragons of steam rush, with fire and smoke, and thunder through the ancient haunts of the Worm,' with the then recent and novel introduction of the Durham to Sunderland railway line.[58] Though those dragons of the railway era of steam supremacy have all but gone – vanquished by the oxy-acetylene cutters of the breakers' yards – some remnants remain, hanging on in the pockets of resistance known today as preserved lines, like some prehistoric leftovers from the age of dinosaurs.

Two such relics are 'Peggy' engines on the North Yorkshire Moors Railway (NYMR). 'Peggy' was a name used by railwaymen in the Sunderland area to denote a train engine belonging to the Lambton railway system, which worked over the North Eastern Railway between Penshaw and Sunderland staiths and South Dock, the line Howitt referred to. When the coal industry was nationalised in 1947, the Lambton system became part of the National Coal Board.[59] The NYMR now runs an annual reunion train for the enginemen of the former Lambton system, called naturally 'The Lambton Worm.' In 1996 it claimed a new record for the slowest ever round trip on the Grosmont-Pickering line of six hours and ten minutes, due to 'Peggy' No. 5 sustaining a hot axle-box.[60]

From a line which refused to die, to one which sadly expired. Particularly powerful is a serpentine earthworks depiction of the Lambton Worm. It was created by Andy Goldsworthy, is 984 feet long and easily visible between two bridges along a derelict railway cutting near Pelaw, beside cycleways created by Sustrans. Northern Arts commissioned sculptures every mile between Consett and Sunderland, so the route is known allegorically as 'The Celestial Railroad'. One cyclist was reported to have manoeuvred through the Worm maze opposite the Jolly Rovers pub without realising what it was, while another fancifully thought it had been created to commemorate all-day pub opening.[61] At Fatfield, where Worm Hill stands (the Lambton Worm did not wrap itself around Penshaw/Pensher Hill, despite widespread popular belief and two books by this author setting the record straight),[62] a Canadian called Michael Olita burrowed beneath a railway embankment for a conceptual artwork called *Earth Encounter*. His lair was signalled by a display of painted stones and he offered guided tours of his underground chamber.[63] Who says shamanism is dead? [64]

Speculating on the prehistoric leftovers theory for saurians being described as dragons throughout north-east England, Peter A. White noted that the railway pioneer George Stephenson lost a locomotive when the line at Mordon sank. More recently, and certainly not apocryphal as the previous instance might prove, in 1964 a derailed diesel locomotive almost repeated the same aquatic vanishing trick. If my memory serves me well it was a 'Class 37' which caused consternation. The point being that the locality is sufficiently marshy that it lies in a parish named Bradbury and the Isle, and would have made a splendid refuge for amphibious relics.[65] While back with George Stephenson and his fire-breathing steeds, a promoters' meeting for the Stockton and Darlington Railway was held in Yarm, North Yorkshire, in the commercial room of a hotel. It was the aptly-named George and Dragon.[66]

In 1967, John Michell, something of a modern Merlin to the magic mushrooming hippie tribe of Albion, drew attention to Chinese dragon legends and sites of monster killings throughout England. He marked the twenty-plus dragon-slaying spots on a map and found most could be joined by two straight lines running across the country. Michell believed they also had resonances in the old straight tracks, or 'leys', rediscovered in the 1920s by Alfred Watkins, and also the flying saucer sightings plotted along straight lines known as 'orthotenies'.[67] In his ground-breaking article, he also enlisted abandoned railway tracks. I include the short poetic section dealing with railways. It's hippie-era air evokes an enchantment still to be found along disused lines.

> Lung Mei as Lines of Thought. Since it appears that at certain places
> along two straight lines the dragon cult survived well into the
> Christian era, it is evident that these lines must have acted as
> transmitters of certain ways of thought. If, as it appears, these lines

are also tracks, signposts of a route through the sky, we can find an interesting parallel in a new system of lines, the hundreds of miles of abandoned railway and canal tracks which now extend to almost every corner of the country. To anyone with no knowledge of recent history these lines would be inexplicable. A person who knew nothing of railways – perhaps someone from a distant planet where overland communications of the sort we find natural here was unknown – would be unable to guess their meaning.

Yet an alien visitor might note something peculiar about these lines, these thin strips of waste country with their derelict tunnels, sheds, caverns and miniature wild places. For in their present state they form a sort of lateral sanctuary, not only for plants and animals which are found along their route and nowhere else in the neighbourhood, but also for a submerged portion of the human population, tramps, hermits, gypsies, fugitives and lunatics. In the various shelters provided by the old canal and railway works these people abound, sometimes harried by local authorities, but often left alone as an unobtrusive feature of the 'problem' which vagrants are said to present. Anyone who walks along their sanctuaries can meet them. A favourite place of refuge is the old North Wilts Canal, built to enable the skippers of narrow boats bound for the West Country to avoid the long flight of locks at Devizes, which was abandoned at the beginning of this century; it still provides shelter for outcasts from its terminus, Swindon. Groups of otherwise homeless men have settled round this great tunnel of the long derelict Hereford and Gloucester Canal. An old railway shack near Oxford is the home of a destitute fanatic whose obsession is with flying saucers. All these people have something in common. They know that others of their kind exist somewhere down the line of their sanctuary. They are linked by the forgotten paths of industrial corruption and, if left undisturbed, will eventually form distinctive lines across the country. These lines of thought could still be traced long after all other marks of the lines of physical communication have disappeared. Similalrly, apart from the curious fact of the alignment of ancient sites along their route and the dragon monuments in the churches, the only real indication of the British Lung Mei is in the persistence of the same legend of the dragon in the villages on their route.[68]

Flying saucers

Isambard Kingdom Brunel added magnificent ships to the GWR portfolio of extra-curricular ventures. So what if British Rail had ambitions for interstellar space travel? In fact, in 1996 the Patent Office revealed that in 1973 British Rail lodged a patent for a nuclear-powered flying saucer. This was not an April Fool spoof, but the 'unearthing' of an extraordinary design. It was registered by BR because the inventor, Charles Osmond Frederick, was at the time one of its employees. The venture combined highly-advanced pioneering technology with innovative adaptation of long-established scientific principles. The craft was to have been fuelled by liquefied fusionable material, with the nuclear reaction triggered and controlled by pulsed laser beams, powered by a homopolar generator. The principles had been discovered way back in the 1830s by Michael Faraday. The vehicle's thrust would be provided by charged particles from the reaction zone being deflected by powerful super-conducting magnets into the magnetic field below the spacecraft. Though the passengers and crew were shielded from the nuclear processes, the thermal energy created was dissipated to the platform containing the passenger compartment. Here lay the flaw, for the occupants would have been microwaved into cinders before the craft had left the Earth's atmosphere. In the age of the hovercraft, perhaps it wasn't such a bad try after all.[69]

On a personal note, I'm a 'repeater' UFO spotter, the most recent occasion being on 24 September 2003, as my train arrived at Westbury, Wiltshire. A gleaming circular 'daylight disc' crossed the sky and vanished into clouds. It was only in view for a few seconds, though for some reason I subsequently got it into my mind that this flat disc had filigree edging. It would seem to have been heading from the direction of Westbury White Horse and, of course, this is an area which also encompasses that Sixties centre of sky watches and strange happenings, Warminster.[70] Consulting the works of that shamanic regional journalist Arthur Shuttlewood for clues, I found that in one of his books he claims 'that most sightings and all reported landings of UFOs in Britain stemmed from guidemarks of seven white horses [carved chalk hill figures] situated west to east, from the one at Westbury to that at Uffington.'[71] This is blatant local partisanship on Shuttlewood's behalf and would appear statistically nonsensical.

Rather differently, I was astonished to spot what appears to be a classic circular craft, apparently below cumulus clouds on a sunny day in 1962, pictured in a steam railway enthusiasts' magazine. The scene is Stalbridge, on the much-lamented Somerset and Dorset joint line, at 12.45 p.m. on 27 March. The UFO can be seen to the right above '2P' 4-4-0 No. 40563 heading a Templecombe to Bournemouth West train. The UFO, if that is what it appears to be, is dark underneath and less so on the top right hand side; the middle portion a light brownish shade.[72]

Whatever is on this photograph, my taking seriously what possibly is not there shows at least how the UFO mythos exerts a powerful influence. It has even pervaded that modern malaise of creative vandalism, railside graffiti. A magazine interpreting contemporary vision and belief published a photograph sent by a reader of graffiti near a railway station in Pennsylvania. The artist has depicted such contemporary UFO themes as as foetus holding a glowing and sparkly ball, connected by its umbilical cord to a multicoloured saucer shape contained in the word 'estro'. There is also a hovering flying saucer shining a beam on to a slender silhouetted human figure, next to which is the message 'I wish I could really tell you all that's happened to me.' The editor comments: 'Is this a public expression of an actual UFO abduction, an example of how far UFO imagery has enterered street-level popular culture, or an expression of the same kind of emotional and artistic sublimation that produces "real" abductions?'[73]

On a lighter note, ticket inspector Mikel Hemmer, 31, of Pordim, Bulgaria, thought he would alleviate the tedium of working a forty-mile stretch of rarely-used rural railway by dressing up as a spaceman. 'I would pretend I was on a space mission,' he explained. 'I had a special oxygen pack and would walk slowly through the carriages as though I was in zero-gravity.' He would probably still be role-playing were it not for the train having been chosen as the venue for a top-secret defence meeting. 'We were discussing chemical weapons,' one of the delegation of high-ranking military officials recalled, 'when a spaceman walked in and asked for our tickets. We thought it was an assassin and all hell broke loose.' Mr Hemmer was sacked and took on a job as a farmhand. 'I still wear my suit,' he confided. 'It stops me getting manure on my shoes.' [74]

Cosmic insights

James Watt watching a kettle boil, Archimedes soaking in his bath or Newton contemplating an apple's descent. Accounts of great discoveries invariably feature those either in a state of idleness or leaving themselves open to the whim of inspiration or the vagaries of Lady Luck. Such epiphanies may have an element of the apocryphal, but they have benefited humanity. Misfortune, too, can be a boon. Railways have helped create towns such as Middlesbrough from nothing; a few cottages on the Tees estuary mudflats became as Gladstone put it so eleoquently 'the infant Hercules of the North,' but not before John Vaughan, while walking on the Eston Hills, stubbed his toe on a particularly heavy stone whose weight and colouration convinced him that it was ironstone, and so the Cleveland iron industry was apocryphally born.[75]

Advances in human society may be attributed to serendipity, but I believe they are always part of a great plan. Fort believed so. The superstitious would agree. Illumination, good fortune or its reverse, are part of an unconscious dimension, the belief in whose existence we parade by personal rituals, the carrying of talismans and the reading of horoscopes. From the mundane to fusion with the cosmos, we believe we can know or alter destiny. At the risk of deriding Darwinians, man is distinct from animals, for he alone exerts free will. So here follow examples of railways opening the doors of perception (and jamming a camera shutter), bringing success, relying on the god of machines, attracting meteorites and disrupting telluriuc energy.

Inspiration

It can't have been a pretty sight. An obvious n'er do well young man, scruffily dressed, his features drawn with a look of anguished creativity. A notebook into which he was writing with a bloody syringe. Australian rock singer, cult idol, author of morbid ballads Nick Cave was penning – or syringing – pained lyrics while travelling on the mausoleum-like London Underground.[76] Another great romantic songwriter, Paul Simon, is generally believed to have penned that paeon to homesickness, *Homeward Bound*, on Widnes railway station en route to a folk club engagement in Hull. Others have been heard to claim the train halts at Wigan or Runcorn, not to mention Halifax bus station, were his inspiration.[77] Belief was sufficient for a plaque – subsequently stolen – to be unveiled at the epiphanic spot. Maybe it's as well it's no longer there. It seems it was all poetic licence as Paul Simon came out with a stunted denial to writing in the song on Widnes station to interviewer Alan Frank: 'Well, no, not exactly in the station. But around that time, sure. While I was up that way.'[78] Paul Simon is now a very rich man, but author J.K. Rowling makes him seem a pauper by comparison. Creator of the Harry Potter books, Joanne Rowling was a single mother in her mid-thirties living modestly in Edinburgh when she had the idea for a schoolboy wizard while stuck on a delayed train between Manchester and London in 1990. Yet it was six years later that she finished the first book in the series, *Harry Potter and the Philosopher's Stone*, when she was desperate for money after the break-up of her marriage.[79]

Another fictional character arrived fully-blown inspirationally to Emma Barstow on a Tube station. In a few intense moments, while returning home after seeing the editor of a cheap literary imprint, the middle-aged novelist observed a figure from the French Revolutionary era. Almost half a century later she recalled:

> I first saw him standing before me – don't gasp, please – on the platform of an Underground station, Temple, where I was waiting for my Circle Line train for Kensington. Now, of all the dull, prosy places in the world, can you beat an Underground railway station? It was foggy, too, and smelly and cold. But I give you my word that, as I was sitting there, I saw – yes, I saw – Sir Percy Blakeney, the Scarlet Pimpernel, just as you know him now. I saw his exquisite clothes, his slender hands holding up his spy-glass: I heard his lazy drawling speech, his quaint laugh... '

The woman in question had been born Baroness Emmushka Orczy, a real titled lady born in 1865, and her book *The Scarlet Pimpernel* surpassed anything else she wrote. It took her only five weeks to write the novel after her strange vision.[80] Just as Baroness Orczy had visited her editor before inspiration struck so solicitously, crime fiction grand dame Agatha Christie travelled between her Devon home from Churston to London to take a book manuscript to her agent. The return journey led to the idea for a particularly well known thriller, *The 4.20 from Paddington.*[81] Not murder, but suicide, was the inspiration for Leo Tolstoy. He apparently observed the body of a young woman, who had thrown herself on to railway tracks, being carried away on a stretcher. Fortuitously some good came of the sad act as the Russian novelist suddenly had the idea for *Anna Karenina.*[82]

Media polls continually put *Adlestrop* among the nation's twenty top favourite poems. Its inspiration was Edward Thomas's train being delayed at this rural halt while journeying on 24 June 1914, though the verses were not actually written until 8 January the following year. 'I couldn't write a poem to save my life,' Thomas told his friend Eleanor Farjeon. Killed at Arras in 1917, he would have been amazed at the attention still given to *Adlestrop*. Worlds away from the rustic charm of Gloucestershire, the railway station at Perpignan became a common denominator in reconstructions of the last hours of three doomed women; two found dead and mutilated, one perhaps still missing and all connected surreally with the works of the artist Salvador Dali. The brutal killings took place near the station in the south of France which Dali had once declared to be the 'Centre of the Universe.' He would stop off here from his home across the border in Spain to send on his baggage by train, and found it particularly inspirational. Here he experienced a series of epiphanies, the most curious of which occurred in 1965. He recalled: 'My penis sprang to attention with joy and ecstasy.' The station was bathed in a quasi-religious light and 'everything became overpoweringly evident.' The station appeared continually in his oeuvre, such as with *The Railway Station at Perpignan*, which depicted a man about to sodomise a young woman. The women, as mentioned, disappeared near the station and police believe Dali artworks may have inspired the killer.[83]

Thomas Cook, a Baptist lay preacher who believed alcohol was a social evil, wished to improve the lives – and livers – of working people. This vexing problem was solved when, as he walked from his home in Market Harborough to a temperance meeting in Leicester, he allowed his unconscious mind to speak to him. He later wrote: 'The thought suddenly flashed across my mind as to the practicability of employing the great powers of railways and locomotion for the furtherance of this social reform.'[84] He organised a Sunday school outing for five hundred people from Leicester to Loughborough in open carriages and subsequently excursions to temperance meetings throughout the Midlands. There were no buffet cars and for most it was their first taste of real travel, if not real ale. A multi-million pound travel agency business was born.

It was also while walking that one day in 1840 Thomas Edmonson thought of a method of printing train tickets with the name of the station, class of carriage and consecutive numbers. The Quaker railway clerk on the Newcastle to Carlisle line had found it both tedious and irksome to have to write on every ticket he sold, but with the aid of a watchmaker called Blaycock, he was able to construct the necessary machinery. Edmonson, a bankrupt, paid off every penny he owed with his new-found wealth. He died, aged 58, in 1852. By 1898, Euston station alone was turning out sixty million tickets a year, each million weighing a ton.[85]

Another invention to transform an industry has railways to thank – or not. Some children were kept happy for hours – others driven to despair. It was a Tokyo subway train filled with noisy youngsters who set Aki Maita thinking, why couldn't they quieten down, read, play with a toy... such as a Tamagotchi. The unassuming housewife was struck by the thought that there had been a boom in small pets in Japan. She explained: 'Everyone wanted hamsters, mice... cute pets like that. At the same time there were a few pocket games which people were playing with, like Gameboy. It seemed natural to combine the two: to cross a real pet with an electronic game. That was my idea,' Aki Maita's idea became the small plastic egg-shaped 'virtual pet' which became a marketing sensation and the most popular toy in history. They also entered the lexicon of contemporary legend, such as the eleven-year old girl in Des Moines, Iowa, who was reported to have committed sucide after the 'death' of her Tamagotchi, or the woman in Sydney who allowed her three cats to starve because she was too busy attending the needs of her cyber pet. Turning full circle, a Tamagotchi was abandoned on a San Francisco subway platform with a note tied to its chain which read: 'Please look after my beloved Tamagotchi, love Laura.' [86]

And another full circle to return to pop music and railways. During the late Nineties, Josef Porta formed what born-again rail enthusiast Andy Dobbs described as a 'splendid punk-folk band, spiky-haired anarchist trainspotters whose music is well worth a listen.' [87] That band was Blyth Power, named after 'Class 56' freight locomotive No. 56134, itself named after the Northumberland coal-fired power station. Fans of the band would turn up at gigs wearing orange high-visibilty vests!

Luck

These stories all have in common being in the right place at the right time. There will be those readers who wish fate had not intervened for the boss of Creation Records, Alan McGee. According to showbiz legend, McGee missed his train back to London from Glasgow and heard a band by accident in a Scottish dive. Subsequently he signed those musicians in 1993. They were Oasis. [88]

Another case of talent spotting occurred when Shola (the name means 'dream come true') Ama was humming to herself as she waited with her mother for a train at Hammersmith Tube station in London. It was 1995, and she was spotted by Lwame Kwaten, a producer for the FreakStreet record label and a member of the British soul band D-Influence. 'This guy approached me and told me he worked for a record label and could I sing for him,' said Shola. 'So I sang there on the platform and he invited me down to his studio.' Her single *You Might Need Somebody* was a worthy platinum-seller and in 1998 she won the Brit award for Best Female Artist. [89]

Another case of a loosely rail-conected possession resurfacing forteanwise happened to bookseller Ben Beech, of Scarborough, North Yorkshire, who found in a job lot a cherished copy of a book he had won as a fourteen-year old schoolboy a decade previously. 'My mum thinks she threw it out one day for a jumble sale, although she didn't own up for quite some time,' said Ben. The book, awarded for a poem he wrote about a fish, was Roger McGough's *Waving at Trains*. [90]

Jinxes

The notion that objects or places can be jinxed or cursed belongs to all races, nations and ages. Usually the jinxed subject or spatial area has significantly been associated with some accident or violence. Cars seem particularly prone to this bad luck; the Porsche in which the film idol James Dean died having a long series of mishaps before vanishing in transit as a kit of parts on a train heading for Los Angeles. Discussing Dean's car and Isambard Kingdom Brunel's massive ship ship *Great Eastern*, the writer Colin Wilson proposed a new explanatory concept, borrowing C.J. Jung's term for meaningful coincidences and calling it 'Bad synchronicity'. [91] The *Great Eastern* had a disastrous career, beginning with the loss of two workers and eventual discovery of the skeletons of the missing riveter and his assistant. When in 1859 it was about to be launched, Brunel feared waves could drown spectators and called a halt, resulting in the ship becoming stuck on the slipway and taking three months to free. Brunel suffered a stroke, collapsed on the deck and died a week later.[92] Wilson suggested a 'thought field' or 'recording' could be imprinted on such an object or place, which when unpleasant was called a 'ghoul' by maverick researcher Tom Lethbridge.

Railway historian Philip Atkins has suggested certain stretches of railway line appear jinxed: 'A ten-mile stretch of the ECML, extending from just north of Peterborough to just south of Huntingdon, witnessed three "write-offs" in less than a year in the early 1960s. In December 1961, a collision in thick fog at Connington resulted in the first condemnation of a Gresley "V2" (60977). Also involved in that smash was another "V2", a three-month-old "Deltic" (D9012), and the "A3" No. 60078 *Night Hawk*, all of which were repaired. However, less than three months later, the very same Pacific derailed again, close to the same spot at Wood Walton, and that time it was condemned. The third incident occurred at Offord in September 1962 when "A1" Pacific No. 60123 *H.A. Ivatt* was involved in a collision, as a result of which it became the first of its class to be withdrawn.' [93]

If the definition of a jinx is an inexplicable run of bad luck, then it can be applied to diesel-electric 'Class 40' No. 40126. Two years after emerging from the English Electric works at Newton-le-Willows in 1960, then numbered D326, it was hauling the London-bound *Midday Scot* when in freezing fog it crashed into the rear of a staionary Liverpool-Birmingham train north of Crewe, killing 18 people and injuring 33. In 1963, D326 was stopped in the Great Train Robbery (see Chapter Five) and in 1964 a railman on the roof was electrocuted by overhead wires. The jinx was still active in 1965 when D326's brakes failed and it ran out of control at more than 40 mph towards Birmingham New Street station before an alert signaller diverted the rogue light engine on to a goods line, where it collided with a freight train and injured the guard. Upon eventual withdrawal, as 40126, the loco was supposedly shunned by preservationists and cut up with unseemly haste.[94]

Tom Lethbridge's 'field theory' could take the parapsychology and folklore out of the chequered career of 40126, the business aboard 37069 and 'psychic ether' of Connington; the Brahan Seer and Barnetby's clairvoyant requiredsome other explanation.

Photographic negativity

Another form of jinx has been a constant bugbear for persons attempting to photograph anomalous phenomena such as ghosts, flying saucers and mystery animals. Cameras are found to malfunction or are forgotten about, or evidence then vanishes.

Not quite in the realm of the paranormal but a special circumstance, perhaps unique, is this reminiscence. I was in York on 20 November 1976, when 'Western' class locomotive No. 1023 *Western Fusilier* hauled an enthusiasts' special from the West Country to the city and was met by several hundred rail fans. I later popped into a pub and was checking engine numbers when a stranger approached and asked if – being obviously a trainspotter – I knew the reason for the huge number of rail fans on York station that day. After explaining the reason we got talking about the golden age of steam. He had been a fireman at Borough Gardens and recalled that the depot's allocation included three 'B1' class 4-6-0 locomotives which were too long to be accommodated on the depot turntable. Consequently, to turn them they always had to run around the triangle of tracks nearby in Gateshead. He had never known the trio leave coupled together for the manoeuvre and as they were in numerical sequence, Nos. 61319, 61320, 61321, he was keen to photograph this fortuitous opportunity. He persuaded the drivers to halt at one point long enough for him to get a photograph for posterity, but when in position, he found the camera jammed. It had worked perfectly beforehand and after the rail manoeuvre was completed and the engines uncoupled for their respective duties, the camera functioned soundly again.

Discussing the perils of paranormal photography, Bob Rickard notes: 'A further stage in the hapless life of photographic evidence is the high incidence of camera malfunction at the critical moment – a detail confirmed by many a witness or investigator of UFO, mystery creature or psychic phenomena – and other calamities.'[95] Such as the triangle trio here.

God of Machines; also meteorites

Whether the 'gods' are 'superpeople' or Jungian archetypes need not detain our train of thought in this mixed traffic of a miscellany. As reported earlier (Chapter One), rail deaths do not seem high on the agenda of humanitarianism in India; a nation with more than a billion people and 108,700 kilometres of track. An insight into India's passing the buck appears under the headline '"God of Machines" in charge says rail minister' in *The Times of India* newspaper. It reported: 'India's railway minister has absolved himself of blame for accidents plaguing the world's largest rail network, saying the fate of its thirteen million daily passengers rested with the Hindu god of machines, Vishwakarma. 'Indian Railways is the responsibility of Lord Vishwakarma,' Laloo Prasad Yadav said. 'So is the safety of passengers. It is his duty (to ensure safety), not mine. I have been forced to don his mantle,' the mercurial minister said on a visit to his hometown of Patna in eastern India. Yadav's statement came less than a month after twenty people were killed and about a hundred injured as a passenger train plunged off a bridge in western India when it hit a boulder. India suffers accidents almost daily, due in part to outdated infrastructure. The rail system has a workforce of 1,600,000, making it the world's largest non-military employer. As for Yadav, outlandish statements are stock in trade for this low-caste activist who enjoys wide support among Bihar's peasants and is a top coalition partner in the left-leaning government. He began signing letters as Lalu Prasad, dropping his surname, reportedly after consultation with astrologers.[96]

Charles Fort documented many varied falls of objects from the sky and it was not long before his time that scientific opinion avowed that stones did not fall from the sky because there were no stones in the sky. Today we know them as meteorites. But could some deliberately choose railway locations? Meteorites are far from common, maybe only half a dozen being found worldwide annually. Relatively recently commuters and staff were astonished to witness a 2¼-inch iron meteorite smash through the glass roof and shear a pipe at Lewes station, Sussex. Station manager David Cates was so excited he planned to use the object as a paperweight.[97] Many

The·Line·to·Legend·Land·Nº 18

G.W.R.

The Midnight Hunter of Dartmoor

RUNNING across the southern part of the heart of wild Dartmoor is a very ancient road. "The Abbot's Way" they call it, and antiquaries hold varied opinions as to when it was made, and even as to where it led to and from. To-day,

Thus begins an account of the spectral Wish Hounds or Yell Hounds of Dartmoor. It is one of a series of folklore leaflets issued by the GWR in 1922.

years previously, 1881, at 3.35 p.m. on 14 March to be exact, a sonic boom was heard over north-east Yorkshire and a few seconds later workmen at a railway siding in Middlesbrough heard a 'rushing or roaring' sound overhead before an object buried itself in an embankment nearby. The British Museum laid a claim for the meteorite for its collection, but the North Eastern Railway company regarded it as lost (or rather found) property, and as it landed in Yorkshire, there it would stay, in pride of place at York's Yorkshire Museum. Because of its size and soft landing, the 3lb 8oz meteorite was undamaged and its smooth, swirling patterns and cone shape are due to its nose-first directional flight path. Its importance was recognised immediately, even to the extent that the hole its impact made was dug up and carefully preserved in a box.[98]

Just as Fort chronicled the appearance of material from some 'Super-Sargasso Sea,' he was just as keenly interested in disappearances. In the year after he published *The Book of the Damned*, the Labour Member of Parliament Victor Grayson vanished during a 1920 train journey from Liverpool to Hull. Equally mysterious was the inability to identify two victims of a 1928 rail crash after a Leeds to Bristol express hit a goods train at Charfield, Gloucestershire, and burst into flames. Only the bodies of a boy aged twelve and a girl around six years went unrecorded among the sixteen casualties. They were seen boarding the train alone at Gloucester by the ticket collector, who survived the crash. A breast pocket of a school blazer was found with the motto 'Luce Magistra', and a sock with the initials CSSS. Schools and tailors were canvassed without result and no one reported the children's disappearance.[99]

Long before physicists posited wormholes in space, Fort had the notion of holes in the fabric of the universe through which people and objects could vanish either forever or temporarily or even relocate. He is credited with creating the term 'teleportation.' The inspiration for his conclusions that 'there may have been a transporting current through so-called solid substance, which "opened" and then "closed," with no sign of yawning. It may be that what we call substance is as much open as closed'[100] was based upon a very strange occurrence. Visitors to the city of Bristol from Leeds in December, 1873, Thomas Cumpston and his wife were awakened in their lodgings by a noise. When Mr Cumpston got out of bed to investigate, he was confronted by a gaping hole in the floor resembling a whirlpool. Just as he was being sucked down, his resourceful wife grabbed her husband and dragged him from the eddying entropy. In a state of alarm, the couple escaped through the window, ran to Temple Meads station, where for some unrecorded reason Mr Cumpston fired a gun into the air. Still in their nightclothes, the couple were arrested for disorderly conduct. They blamed their predicament on the uncanny occurrence at their hotel, but upon checking, the police could find no evidence of the homicidal hole and dismissed the event as an example of 'collective hallucination.'

Fort recounted in his works a number of cases where ordinary men and women would apparently vanish spontaneously. The Cumpston case led him to his transient transporting agency notion, which has gained a considerable following within the paranormalist community.

Chapter Three

Wonders and blunders

The term 'health and safety' has connotations these days of the nanny state, compensation culture and risk aversion, but is an overall umbrella for this section. Health would impinge upon everything from rail crashes and wars to scorpion bites. Safety could encompass dodgy carriage doors, wrongful demolition and too-hot refreshments. Speed records, stale sandwiches and sportsman's hurt pride could come in between.

Railway safety

Before examining a number of railway accidents which have folkloric elements, spare me a moment to present a few facts to put risk and safety into context. When a suicidal motorist caused a high-speed train to crash at Ufton Nervet in 2004 there was a hysterical reaction from media, politicians, lawyers and activists to ban level crossings and make train seatbelts compulsory. This neglected to consider that such costs would be astronomical in comparison with risk and result in higher fares, which would encourage passengers to leave public transport for greater-risk voluntary travel, i.e. cars. Anyone with a brain should be able to appreciate that statistically the likelihood of death in a road accident is more than thirty times greater than on the railway.

'Mary Celeste' of the tracks

Probably the most authoritative commentator on railway accidents ever to have put pen to paper was L.T.C. Rolt, whose book *Red for Danger* is a classic. So if he says that of all British major accidents one 'remains the most mysterious' then doubtless it is. The train involved was the 8.45 p.m. semi-fast mail from King's Cross to Edinburgh on 19 September 1906, due to stop at Grantham at 11 p.m. Unfortunately it sped through Grantham at an estimated 40 mph or more and hit a crossing goods train, resulting in the loss of life of eleven passengers and a postal sorter. Those on the platform did not observe the crew, but in the south signal box Alfred Day was to report that both driver and fireman were standing motionless on either side of the footplate, each staring ahead through his spectacle glass. Rolt commented: 'The Grantham disaster produced an unprecedented crop of rumours and fantastic theories. The driver was drunk. The driver had gone mad. As the train approached Grantham the driver and fireman had been seen struggling with one another on the footplate. The driver was accustomed to join the train at Grantham, had thought he had done so on this occasion and believed that he faced a clear run to Doncaster. All these stories were either disproved at the inquiry or else the facts made them quite preposterous.'[1]

The favoured and most credible theory was that Driver Fleetwood suddenly took ill (as he had also the previous June with sciatica on the footplate) and that Fireman Talbot was so concerned in helping that he failed to realise the train's position until too late. Yet, convincing though this scenario was, it could not be reconciled with signalman Day's witness statement. What precisely took place on the footplate that fateful night '... is a question that Sherlock Holmes himself could not answer. It remains the railway equivalent of the mystery of the *Marie Celeste,'* Rolt concluded.

Also never explained to this day is the worst accident to befall London Underground, which also centres upon a driver as if mesmerised. On 28 February 1975, the 8.37 a.m. six-car train from Drayton Park entered the terminal Platform Nine at Moorgate and accelerated into the dead-end of the tunnel constructed for the Lothbury extension. Forty-three passengers and the driver died and 74 were injured. Tube expert Nigel Pennick wrote:

> At the inquest eyewitnesses told of how the driver was seemingly
> transfixed at the controls, but as the cab was smashed almost flat
> (four inches deep) by the impact, and it took a long time digging
> out the mangled wreckage, it was impossible to do a post-mortem
> on the driver's remains. Tube trains have a safety device known as
> the 'dead man's handle', which must be depressed by the driver at
> all times. If it is released, for instance, if the driver has a heart
> attack, then the brakes are applied. This did not happen at the
> Moorgate accident, and so it was assumed that the driver had not
> had a seizure. Urban lore connects the driver's 'transfixion' with
> the Lothbury extension 'apparition' of 1904, perhaps a
> remanifestation.[2]

A newspaper report, in poor taste if true, stated that a doctor trying to ease the pain of those trapped sent the message 'I want Entonox' (a form of anaethetic) but by the time the message had been passed down the chain of rescuers to the medical assistants, it had become 'The doctor wants an empty box.'[3]

After such a gruesome true tale, Pennick related a more light-hearted incident concerning the pneumatic mail tubes built in the 1860s and 1870s:

> The commercial pneumatic operation was two lines linking Euston
> station with postal sorting offices in Eversholt Street, Holborn and
> Cheapside. Close-fitting cars carrying rubber flaps were blown
> through the tunnels by air pressure from steam-driven fans.
> Although used for mail, occasionally VIP passengers were carried
> for fun, and lore tells of a Victorian lady in crinoline dress who
> leant too near the tunnel entrance, fell in and was blown from one
> end of the line to the other. The fact that crinolines had been
> superseded by bustle dresses by then does not detract from the
> story.[4]

Just as the Grantham crash of 1906 produced wild claims, the Paddington rail disaster of 1999 had a bizarre element. The drivers of both a Great Western 'IC125' high-speed train and a Thames service which passed a signal at red were killed. Yet rumours swept homes and pubs across Britain that one of the drivers had been distracted seconds before impact by a woman in the cab. The claims formed part of a ten-point dossier posted on the Internet by an anonymous train driver. It alleged: 'One of the drivers involved in the crash enjoyed the company of a second person, namely a woman, in his carriage and she was distracting him only seconds before the two trains collided.' A Railtrack spokesman responded: 'Anyone who knew the drivers would find it highly offensive. There is absolutely no evidence to suggest that anything was going on.' Gossip of a mystery woman had been gathering momentum ever since the 5 October crash which killed thirty people, including drivers Michael Hodder and Brian Cooper. Even though no extra body was recovered, British Transport Police spokesman Simon Lubin said: 'The only way it could be true would be if that person managed to get out of the wreck and has now disappeared.' At least three national newspapers hinted that the blame lay with the second person in one of the cabs.[5]

Tamworth Triangle

When is a straight line a triangle? The answer is when five people fall from trains on a straight track in Warwickshire within a ten-month period. The Press or forteans dubbed that stretch of the WCML between Lichfield and Atherstone 'the Tamworth Triangle'. Certainly Euclidean geometers did not so name it. Nor British Rail, which said InterCity doors were perfectly safe and anyway, if they were not, any malfunction was due to passengers' alcohol intake or horseplay.

There certainly were an alarming number of fatalities in the Eighties, before safer forms of door locking began to be introduced, with 212 people falling out of trains in Britain between 1979 and mid-1991.[6] Tamworth victims' families' solicitor Douglas Fraser said: 'There were five deaths in the space of ten months on a very short stretch of track in the Tamworth area. They are bizarre in the extreme, because they don't appear to have any explanation.'[7] I saw the door of a diesel multiple unit swing open after my train was a mile or so out of Hull Paragon station and the guard scurry to ask if I'd seen anyone fall out. I assume it had simply not been closed properly when the train left Hull, but would this apply on the WCML and elsewhere? The bereaved and their supporters seemed to agree that train doors were dangerously faulty, but added conspiracy theory in that should British Rail admit this, then suspect stock should be sidelined, a shortage of carriages would reduce services and in the pre-privatisation period the coaches' value would become commercially disastrous.[8]

Among the acres of newsprint devoted to the mystery, it seems there was only a single suggestion of foul play. This book will discuss a homicidal character supposedly haunting London Underground platforms; could such a sinister assassin be stalking trains. Indeed, does Tamworth have more than its fair share of weirdos? This suggestion of murder appeared in the *Mid-Wales Evening Leader*, which claimed 'fears that someone was pushing people out.'[9]

Jinxes

In returning to jinxes, in his book covering all railway accidents worldwide involving twenty or more fatalities, Peter Semmens argued that choosing twenty, rather than say nineteen, could alter any formation of 'clusters' in his data, and as such, statistics were the result of random chance.[10]

Archivist Philip Atkins noted a Yorkshire accident hot spot: 'As for jinxed areas, the Harrogate district would appear to have been unusually dangerous with three engines "written off" around there within just ten years between 1946 and 1956.'[11] However, he then went on to analyse the wheel arrangement of steam locos involved in accidents. The 4-6-0 was the most numerous but that could be explained by their statistical predominance after 1959. Few 2-6-0s were victims mathematically, yet three members of a single class of 2-6-2, Gresley's 'V2', sustained terminal accident damage. They, like many 4-6-0s, were engaged in higher-speed work. On the Southern Region there was the statistical curiosity that after 1961 apparently no examples (among more than three hundred engines) of 2-6-0 and 4-6-2 types were retired on account of accident damage. Also 1964 was a particularly bad year for loco casualties with a total of at least nine.

Lastly, as soon as International Space Station astronauts began assembling their £135M mobile transporter, designed to creep at 0.06 mph along a 91-metre track, the headline was ready-made to use. As the first railway in space broke down, sub-editors dusted off 'Euston, we have a problem… '[12]

Which was fastest?

Rail speed claims have all the hot air of exaggeration and partisanship while even revealing a great difference between we Britons and our American cousins. The role of the editor also looms large to differentiate between myth and reality. I can do no better than quote John F. Clay on this contentious matter:

> There is no disposition to adopt an attitude of insular superiority,
> nor to claim that British integrity is superior – there have been just
> as many partisans and rumour mongers in this country, but
> happily the wisdom of editors and writers has consigned most of
> the false claims to the waste paper basket, and those few that have
> got through have soon been challenged.[13]

Clay also noted that reputable American writers rarely discredited questionable national legends. 'They must have their own private doubts and indeed they usually add the words "alleged," "reputedly" or "claimed", but the correct word to attach to the more extreme claims would be "impossible".'

Folkloric claims neglect the world of reality where train resistance, laws of motion and the key factor governing the speed of a train, whatever its motive power, was and still is the power/weight ratio.

In the USA there was a famous claim for the New York Central 4-4-0 No. 999 to have achieved 112½ mph on 10 May 1893.[14] An equally widely-claimed record was that for 127 mph by Pennsylvania Railroad 'E2' Atlantic No. 7002 on 12 June 1905. The train despatcher recorded 85 sec for an alleged three miles. John F. Clay was dismissive: 'The sections on each side of the "record" did not involve any exceptional speeds and any speed curve which would have made the times remotely possible would have required such a rapid acceleration on a moderate down grade that, despite the relatively light load, an hp [horsepower] of over 4,500 would hardly have sufficed.'[13] This for a type which on test at Altoona plant managed only 1,200 hp with a controlled firing rate. 'It is well known how many pitfalls can affect accurate timekeeping of high speeds when milepost times are recorded by stopwatch from the train. When the telegraph was additionally introduced between sighting and recording, as in the making of a train despatcher's sheet, then the scope for errors was endless,' Clay concluded.

Mallard's record run

Having dismissed the spurious 127 mph claim, attention needs to focus on the rivalry between the LNER and LMS, competing for customers to Scotland and also prestige. The LNER stole the lead with its *Silver Jubilee* service between King's Cross and Newcastle. A Press demonstration run headed by one of the brand new silver-liveried 'A4s' with air-smoothed casing, No. 2509 *Silver Link*, reached a new record of 112½ mph. Not to be outdone, the LMS introduced its own *Coronation Scot* between Euston and Glasgow and on the trial run one of its new streamliners, *Coronation*, reached 114 mph. However, this was well behind the validated world record for steam of 124½ mph achieved by a German locomotive. Nigel Gresley was looking to improve his own mechanical greyhounds to outclass the LMS. A successful double-draughting experiment with his 'P2' class was then extended to four new 'A4' Pacifics, including No. 4468 *Mallard*, whose record-breaking run of 3 July 1938, was nominally one of a series of quick-acting brakes testing exercises.

Gresley wrote beforehand: 'Whilst the brake trials will be made south of Peterborough, it is proposed to run the train to Barkston and back in order that a fast run down the bank from Stoke tunnel may be recorded.' While the train was being turned on the Barkston triangle, the Westinghouse Brake Company's test team were told of the proposed speed record attempt, and offered the use of a taxi to take them to Peterborough if they wished. They all declined and were among the small number of passengers. Another indication that there was secrecy attached to the run seems borne out by the fact that engineers responsible for the track were kept in the dark, for during the crucial stretch for the record there was an annoying speed restriction at one point. At the summit of Stoke bank the train was doing 74 mph, six miles later the speed was up to 116 mph and finally just after Little Bytham a peak of 126 mph was held for a mere 185 feet.[15]

That this record-breaking run seriously damaged *Mallard* is repeated ad nauseum. Certainly Inspector Sam Jenkins on the footplate had caught a whiff from the aromatic safety device nicknamed the 'stink bomb.' Placed in the hollow crank-pin of the 'A4's' middle big end, the smell released indicated overheating had occurred. Driver Duddington was instructed to ease off and *Mallard* came off the test train at Peterborough. The forced acceleration up the bank from Grantham to Stoke summit and afterwards following that unfortunate speed restriction had overextended the locomotive mechanically. The overheated bearing has been the subject of much unnecessary controversy over the years. Records at the National Railway Museum give the engine's full overhaul and repair history, and not having been back to Doncaster Works until September of that year indicates no serious damage was done. Also former King's Cross shedmaster Peter Townend wrote definitively and dismissively: 'Big end failures were much less common than is often thought. The biggest myth is that *Mallard*'s centre big end was damaged by its 126 mph world record of 1938. It wasn't. The phial burst, as it was designed to do, alerting the crew, who stopped at Peterborough with no damage to the engine whatsoever. The smell did its job.' [16] While Michael Harris commented: 'Controversy has accompanied the incident of the overheated bearing, with some commentators alleging that serious damage was done to the big end. Others involved in the test run have clearly and unequivocally stated – after four decades since the great day – that *Mallard* suffered no more than the usual bearing overheating that was not an unknown occurrence with the inside cylinder of three-cylinder locomotives.' [17]

Scheduled for preservation since 1960, *Mallard* went back to Doncaster for what was reported to be purely cosmetic treatment. Pictures of work in progress, and the ease with which it was eventually to be brought back to main-line standard, bear out the rumours that there was a diplomatic smokescreen and much spending was hidden in the budgeting for work supposedly done on 'Deltic' diesels.

Today it matters not that a similar speed may be reached, albeit illegally, by a family car or that 'IC125' units and 'Class 91' electrics in normal running now climb Stoke bank almost as fast as *Mallard* descended it in an all-out effort. The world speed record for steam traction was a triumph and very unlikely ever to be beaten by a conventional Stephenson-concept locomotive.

One person who suspects an attempt may have been made on *Mallard*'s record is Frank Henry, who wrote to a magazine seeking confirmation. It even starts like a foaf tale: 'A friend of mine who was a fireman on the London Midland Region in the '50s and '60s told me of an "illegal" attempt to beat the 126 mph speed record set by *Mallard*. This is supposed to have happened with a Glasgow-London express headed by a 'Princess Royal' or 'Princess Coronation' Pacific. The footplate crew drove the loco down Beattock or Shap, but were reported by various signalmen, station staff and the train guard. They were replaced at the next station and reprimanded. Can anyone recall such an incident?' [18] Unsurprisingly there were no recollections and anyway their being replaced is another case of the folklorically dodgy interrupted journey.

Not so Flying Scotsman

There are also those whose partisanship stretches to regarding the ex-LNER 'A3' Pacific No. 4472 (60103 under British Railways) *Flying Scotsman* as the world's most famous loco and their favourite. Whenever it is mentioned in the media you read something along the lines of the ungrammatical 'the first steam locomotive to break the 100 mph record.'[19] It most certainly wasn't. I get equally exasperated at the GWR extremists who believe the outside-framed 4-4-0 *City of Truro*, outdated even at the time, achieved 102.3 mph, or 104 mph to some, descending from Whiteball tunnel on an *Ocean Mails* train from Plymouth on 9 May 1904. Charles Rous-Marten's stopwatch speed sequence analyses have led several eminent train-timers to doubt whether No. 3440 ever achieved even 100 mph. Its power output would have been in excess of that of a 'King', 'Duchess' or even 'Deltic'. A figure of 92 mph is just feasible. So, discounting *City of Truro*, honour of being first to exceed 'the ton' could belong to GWR 4-6-0 No. 2903 in May, 1906, when C.B. Collett, later its chief mechanical engineer and who was on the footplate, gave the speed as 120 mph, though this information was not made public until April, 1932.[19] This too is equally conjectural and general opinion looks for the first authenticated 'ton' as belonging to Gresley 'A3' Pacific No. 2750 *Papyrus*, which achieved 106 mph in 1935.

As for that other old chestnut of *Flying Scotsman* being first to travel non-stop from London to Edinburgh, three days before the LNER began non-stop runs to Edinburgh Waverley, on 27 April 1928, the LMS *Royal Scot* express was divided and ran in separate portions for Glasgow Central and Edinburgh Princes Street from Euston. The 401.4 miles to Glasgow were covered by 'Royal Scot' No. 6113 *Cameronian* and the 399.7 miles to Edinburgh by the smaller 'Midland Compound' 4-4-0 No. 1054, both non-stop.[20]

Flying Scotsman does have a world record, marking the longest non-stop run by a steam loco – at just over 422 miles in Australia in August, 1989.

Flying Scotsman may be the world's best publicised loco, a favourite in the eyes of 'folk history', but its actual fame is insubstantial.

Creation myths – or who was first?

Like infants squabbling over who won a game, the often unseemly behaviour of adults reveals them as pedantic and childish in their insults when it comes to arguing whose was the first railway or first of a type of railway. As for first railway itself there can be no winner as each contestant may make its claim on different criteria.

In discussing George Stephenson, readers will recall that I feted him on the grounds of 'folk history'. I believe the Stockton and Darlington Railway, despite certain claims to the contrary, takes pride of place for both its role in history and the public's perception of its priority. It is number one through 'folk history', public acclaim or people power precedent. Historian O.S. Nock made the same point when reflecting on the 1927 centenary, which acknowledged 'nevertheless that in strict historical accuracy it was the first only in one rather incidental respect – that passengers were conveyed in a steam-hauled train. The fact that this apparently occurred only on the opening day, and was not repeated for several years after, was equally incidental. The really important factor was that the Stockton and Darlington enterprise was the catalyst that stimulated the world development of railways.'[21]

The precursors quoted by the pedantic brigade can be summarised (though I know my thumbnail sketches will be rubbished by the finical)

The Middleton Railway – first to receive an Act of Parliament (1758) and oldest still in operation. Commercial steam entirely as early as 1812.

The Oystermouth Railway (Swansea and Mumbles) – first to provide a regular, fare-paying service on rails (1804).

The Llanelly and Mynydd Mawr Railway – first public railway. A section of 4 ft gauge line was open in 1803, two months earlier than the generally considered case for the Surrey Iron Railway, though the Welsh line's Act was not obtained until 1804.

The Stockton and Darlington Railway – first railway to use steam locos from the outset. Its predecessors being links in a chain rather than the mainspring from which all else followed.

The Canterbury and Whitstable Railway – first planned proper public passenger and freight carrying railway with regular and published timetable using own wagons with proper termini using specialised track and mechanical traction. Thus having all the hallmarks of a modern railway and preceding the Liverpool and Manchester Railway by four months.

Of course these are British examples, but the principle of parallel lines of stone blocks with grooves in the centres goes back to prehistoric times, originating in ancient Babylon around 2245 BC. I like the almost specific dating, but even that pales into insignificance amid an even older, surreal claim for Malta. 'On a corner of the Mediterranean island is a large area of stone known locally as Clapham Junction. Before the wheel was invented, Neolithic man transported rock to the sea on sleds, wearing deep ruts like railway tracks in the stone,' wrote Chris Lloyd. 'There are no animal marks, which suggests the sleds were powered by some unknown locomotive force – one archaeologist has mentioned flying geese – as long ago as 4,000 BC.' [22]

Back in the present, railway academic Professor Colin Divall, lecturing on the appeal of the past and collective identity, stated correctly: 'At least some of the time, heritage transport attractions are in the business of peddling historical myths. Insisting that we were the first, or the best, in some particular facet of transport is one way in which we forge, shape and share local, regional and national identities with our visitors.' Professor Divall then put up a defence for rail enthusiasts, concurring that for many years, they had been treated shabbily. 'A good deal of this criticism tells us more about the prejudices of certain kinds of journalists than it does about enthusiasts and their interests. And it is also clear that the public history of transport would be much the poorer without the efforts made by amateurs and volunteers over the last 50 years or so.' [23]

The issue of local identity blew up into a railway war in 1990 when Stockton claimed to be the birthplace of railways. Darlingtonians put forward a counter claim. At its pitch, this amusing display of columns of venom was stoked by sheaves of documents and maps posted in the Darlington area and sent anonymously to several supporters and railway buffs in the Stockton area. Both sides were even given equal space in a joint front page lead in a regional broadsheet to argue their respective corners in this entertaining bout of shadow boxing.[24]

Similarly, despite so much written about early railway development, the translation of steam engine into locomotive should be simple to follow. Not so. Transport expert L.T.C. Rolt cautioned: 'Unless he walks with great circumspection the student of early locomotive history is likely to become completely lost in a labyrinth of contradictory facts, conflicting claims and allegedly original drawings and illustrations which, more often than not, turn out to be conjectural. Indeed, it is doubtful whether any other major invention has been the subject of so much heated argument.' [25]

Blunders

An early form of railway rivalry was the 'Battle of the Gauge' between companies employing what we now know as standard gauge and broad gauge. In the 1840s the competing gauges met at Gloucester and cartoonists and writers such as W.M. Thackeray made fun of the performance to exchange passengers and their baggage between trains. Clearly someone had blundered.

Broadly speaking...

Isambard Kingdom Brunel had chosen the exceedingly odd gauge of 7 feet 0¼ inches (2140 mm). When persuading the GWR to adopt this broad gauge his motive was the desire to create a territorial monopoly. As all companies endeavoured to expand their spheres of influence, the GWR's independence protected it from the incursions of others. Brunel maintained that larger, wider locos would be safer, faster and could haul heavier loads. The GWR opened in 1838 and had magnificent engines. Brunel delighted in his railway and its block to through running. He scornfully referred to his rivals using 'colliery gauge'.

George Stephenson had the benefit of starting from scratch and could have chosen any width. He is said to have taken the distance between the wheels of his farm cart as a working measurement.[26] Or did 4 feet 8½ inches (1432 mm) derive from the width of horse-drawn colliery wagon ways in north-east England, where he first experimented with locos? This width is said to echo the width of the entrance gates of the forts the Romans built on Hadrian's Wall. 'A nice theory, but archaeologists have never agreed about it,' wrote Hunter Davies.[27] Similarly wagon wheels supposedly followed ruts in long-distance roads built by the Romans and those grooves were created by Imperial Roman chariots built just wide enough to accommodate the back ends of two war horses. Before that it was determined by the width of two yoked oxen. Back with the Romans, could 4 feet 8½ inches derive from the stride of a Roman soldier measuring 2 feet 5 inches and two such equalling a Roman pace of 4 feet 10 inches?

Stephenson or Brunel? Parliament understood the need for arbitration and its gauge commissioners conducted extensive inquiries and trials into the pros and cons of each system. In 1845 a standard gauge special 2-4-0 loco, known simply as 'A' or

'Great A' was built by Robert Stephenson and Company and achieved almost 48 mph between Darlington and York, later reaching 60 mph. Despite its performance being inferior to that of Brunel's contestant, the Gauge Act of 1846 standardised 4 ft 8½ in for all subsequent development, although the GWR did not convert its line to the national norm until 1892.

In the United States 4 ft 8½ in is standard, basically because the country's railroads were built by English expatriates. They were not to know then that solid rocket boosters for the space shuttle were to be made by Thiokol in Utah, and that even if their designers had preferred them to be wider, because they needed to be shipped by rail to the launch site, this meant the train had to run through tunnels and subsequently a major feature of what is arguably the most advanced transportation system in the world, was determined more than 2,000 years ago by the width of animals' backsides.[28]

An unintended gauge issue brought problems to the Hastings line in East Sussex. The situation arose when the Tonbridge-Hastings section was built in Victorian times and its builders were economical with bricks, leading to an insufficient depth of tunnel lining being used. When a tunnel lining collapse exposed the builders' trickery, the decision was made to place more bricks around the tunnel lining, rather than start again and bore the tunnel to a larger diameter. This reduced the diameter of the tunnels compared with neighbouring routes, leaving a legacy of a width restriction and specially-built rolling stock, including the 'Schools' 4-4-0s, 'Slim Jim Class 33s' and the 'Class 201' DEMUs. Passengers were consequently squashed closer together until electrification in the early 1980s led to singling the double track through some tunnels with the line running down the centre with bi-directional signalling. A less likely version has the contractor simply ignorant of the amount of lining required.

I prefer that the tunnel tale was based on deliberate deceit, but one pertaining to Sidmouth has double blunder and red faces aplenty. Cliff erosion opened to view a railway tunnel sealed since 1836 after a line was built to carry limestone to the Devon town's proposed harbour. A tunnel was driven through cliffs, a bridge spanned the River Sid and track laid to the port site. The necessary steam loco arrived by sea only for the developers to realise there was no crane to unload it. The ship was re-floated and the loco unloaded by horse and cart. In a bid to restore their credibility, the promoters arranged celebrations to accompany the first steaming. Alas, the engine was too large to enter the tunnel. It seems this further setback caused the entrepreneurs to lose heart. They lifted the rails, removed the bridge and sealed the tunnel.[29]

Deleted comma clanger

Here's one for Lynn Trusse if she updates her punctuation bestseller. East Lothian District Council ordered British Rail to rebuild the waiting-room it demolished in error at Drem on the ECML, and all because of a missing comma. Instead of demolishing the tiny station, it was marked down for listed preservation to mark its Victorian elegance. Its waiting-room was stripped of its rare fittings, windows, lavatories and roof, but the council was insisting on the station's rebuilding and the restoration of the nineteenth century drinking fountain and cast-iron fittings. A British Rail official said: 'There was a missing comma in a planning document and the station building was demolished in error. It will be reinstated.' Councillor Pat O'Brien, the council's planning chairman, said it had asked for everything to be put back where it was. The crucial sentence referring to Drem station stated that 'Drem station bridge... ' should be retained. After the event, engineers realised, it should have read retain 'Drem station, bridge... ' [30]

Poor planning

Fancy ten minutes in London after a 237-mile rail journey? Inter-City West Coast was offering a 474-mile round trip at £34, but to qualify for the supersaver day return, daytrippers had to catch the 9.22 am from Aberystwyth, arriving at Euston for 2.25 pm, and then return to Wales on the 2.35 pm train. For £37, a normal day return would give eight hours in London, presuming the 5.23 am was caught and return arrival was at 11.18 pm. Unsurprisingly not one of the bargain tickets had been sold. It's one of those stories featuring a bureaucratic jobsworth and this one is well-named. Marketing manager Bernard Pratt condescendingly said it was reconsidering the offer and might allow travellers to return on a service leaving Euston at 6.15 pm.[31] The Press had another field day when an offer had Birmingham daytrippers supposedly fuming because they had just 13 minutes in Fishguard, Pembrokeshire, before the last return train.[32]

Blame the computer

If it's not company cretin then blame the computer. Asked to suggest the route from Hull railway station to Hull bus station, the Railplanner computerised railway timetable came up with the following: 'Hull (depart 06.05)-Hessle-Ferriby-Brough-Gilberdyke-Saltmarshe-Goole-Thorne North-Hatfield and Stainforth-Kirk Sandall-Doncaster (change) -Scunthorpe-Barnetby-Habrough-Grimsby Town (change) -Great Coates-Healing-Stallingborough-Habrough-Ulceby-Thornton Abbey-Goxhill-New Holland-Barrow Haven-Barton on Humber (change) -Hull bus station (arrive 10.18 – Total journey time: 4 hours 13 minutes)'[33] Is this what is called lateral thinking?

Moved in error

To attempt a folklore comparison with the changeling motif would be more plausible than the question, does a diesel shunter resemble a main-line steam locomotive? Only if you're a driver for Allelys. When the haulier was employed to collect a British Rail 'Class 09' shunter from Didcot power station and take it to Old Oak Common for repairs, the engine taken up the M4 to London was a preserved steam giant. When the haulage company driver arrived at the power station he was told that locos were loaded and offloaded at Milton industrial estate. 'A few days earlier, Allelys had delivered *Nunney Castle* back to us from the Great Central Railway, but we left it sitting on the private siding at Milton, while we sent its tender away to Swindon for the wheelsets to be re-profiled,' said Richard Preston, Great Western Society locomotive manager. 'The Allelys driver saw the "Castle", assumed it to be the "09" locomotive he'd come for, and instead of phoning his office to check, just loaded it up and took it off to Old Oak Common. They don't look the same, do they?' Security staff at Old Oak Common saw steam locos arrive regularly for open days, special events or tyre re-profiling, waved it through, saw it offloaded and guarded it for a full day before it was transported back down the M4 to Oxfordshire.[34]

Obviously another misunderstanding brought the unprecedented sight of 'Warship' No. D821 *Greyhound* at Tyne yard. The preserved diesel-hydraulic had, it seems, been sent in error from Worksop Open Day. Instead of returning to the North Yorkshire Moors Railway, it was booked to appear at the East Lancashire Railway.

Greyhound's former stamping ground was over the Devon banks between Exeter and Plymouth. Because of the steep gradients beyond Newton Abbot, Isambard Kingdom Brunel chose the new atmospheric system of traction. Instead of steam engines in front of the trains themselves, this invention provided pumping houses every few miles along the track. These stationary engines pumped out air, which via a system of pistons and vacuum had trains travelling at up to 70 mph – and this was in 1848. They only ran between Exeter and Newton Abbot, although pipes to carry the steam were laid over part of the rougher terrain. This costly blunder, nicknamed the 'atmospheric caper' by Devonians, was abandoned because of technical problems.[35]

Soft brains and mobile phones

There are those who believe grand Victorian railway stations were built in the image of vast cathedrals to soothe nervous passengers as they embarked upon perceived perilous journeys to distant places at frightening speed. There was in those days so much spurious 'evidence' of the medical dangers of rail travel that it is a wonder anyone used this mode of transport. Doctors attested that travel through long tunnels would result in suffocation due to 'destruction of the atmosphere' and dampness in deep cuttings would expose otherwise robust people to catarrhs, consumptions and agues. As with today's health scares they were varied and plentiful. Railways were accused of aggravating epilepsy, apoplexy, respiratory and circulatory diseases, spinal anaesthesia, disease of the vertebral column, affections of the kidneys and bladder; in fact, virtually every organ was likely to be influenced to some degree. Carriages were cold and blamed for sore throats, earache, toothache, rheumatism, pleurisy and pneumonia. Just as today mobile phones are the subject of debate, for the Victorians it was alleged that reading 'cheap papers or books' on the train could be injurious to the eyesight. Grave though these health panics were, it was not until 1862 and the publication in *The Lancet* of a report on 'The Influence of Railway Travelling on Public Health' that the subject was deemed worthy of systematic investigation. *The Lancet* claimed to have purged hearsay so as to 'substitute accurate information as to the direct physical effects of railway travelling on the body.' Yet not everyone was reassured. 'His brain is now showing decided symptoms of softening' it was observed of one regular traveller, while it was not until after a Brighton to London commuter ceased travelling that his inability to sleep, numbness of limbs and great depression disappeared.[36]

That 'disease of the vertebral column' mentioned earlier became known as 'railway spine,' a quaintly-named syndrome whose acceptance began around 1860. It was applied to those who had survived railway accidents without a scratch, but suffered such vague symptoms as giddiness, headaches and 'nervousness'. At first it was blamed upon after-effects of severe deceleration caused by the accident. Civil actions arose which make today's compensation culture seem amateurish, with gobbledegook claims of chronic and sub-acute inflammation action in the spinal membranes and in chronic 'myelitis'. But there was no medical evidence of physical damage to the spine. Medical experts supported the notion of 'psychical shock' and 'profound exhaustion of the nervous system of traumatic neurasthenia' causing 'fright and alarm'. Today we would call it post-traumatic stress disorder.[37]

In Victorian times, even the passengers themselves could be injurious to the health of liveried servants of the railway companies. An article written in 1898 describes the work of the ticket-collector:

> Taken on the whole, he is one of the most hard-working, one of the most civil and conscientious functionaries that guard the doorway through which every traveller must pass. His hours are long, his troubles many, and the irascible and eccentric passengers who continually hamper his movements do not tend to prolong the extent of his natural life. Have you ever noticed how many comparatively young ticket-collectors are the unfortunate possessors of grey hair? It is the worry and monotony, nothing else, that does it. Ladies, it seems, are the worst offenders in the ruffling the temper of the innocent and patient collector. One lady, for instance couldn't find her ticket and had only a sovereign to pay a ninepenny fare. The collector couldn't stop the train while he hunted for the nineteen-and-threepence, so perforce had to jump into the carriage and accompany the lady to the terminus, only to find to his unfathomable disgust on arrival that she had been sitting on the ticket all the time. Many are the queer places in which people will hunt to find the return half of the ticket that never turns up. One collector claimed that an eccentric old gentleman even went to the luggage van and overhauled his luggage in a fruitless search. Even the booking-clerk is not without his quaint and amusing experiences. Passengers will often ask for tickets to the station at which they are booking, or to places they are thinking of, but not going to. They will get angry and stamp their feet when the clerk gently reminds them of their mistake.' [38]

As for mobile phones, apart from the only proven ill-effect, irritation, caused by people announcing into their handsets that they are 'on the train,' now that the novelty has worn off, moron-and-mobile combination tales have petered out. However, who cannot fondly smile inwardly recalling such as the high-powered businessman boarding a train while barking orders to some minion before finishing his call and sitting down immensely satisfied. His smugness being dissipated when the man opposite began to feel unwell and asked if he might borrow the mobile phone to call ahead for help. It was then that the captain of industry had to admit that his phone was a child's toy.[39] I also have on record a tale of an exasperated man who

The author (right) and Screaming Lord Sutch pose while discussing Fortean matters during the mid-Sixties. While on tour the rock 'n' roll legend visited Loch Ness and tried to lure the purported monster using British Railways' sandwiches as bait. (Richard P. R. Wilson)

threw a fellow traveller's bleeping dog'n'bone out of a train window, the 'outwardly mobile' fellow suffering phone rage.[40] More serious was the case of a businessman being rushed to hospital after a fellow train passenger in New York grew tired of his mobile phone ringing, snatched it, broke it up and forced him to eat it at gunpoint.[41] The same newspaper published an identical story, but more detailed, with shop worker Mike Pratt, aged 28, flipping on the New York underground line and forcing financier Pierre Monro, while holding a gun to his mobile-chattering victim's head, to eat his phone.[42]

Nothing medical, but to end these calls, a guard on a Great North Eastern Railway train announced there was a shortage of taxis at Wakefield Westgate station. 'So, if you have a mobile, you might like to call a loved-one and ask them to pick you up,' he suggested helpfully. 'Clearly, if you don't have a loved-one, you'll have to try the wife.' [42]

Spread of sandwiches

I wonder if comedians still make jaundiced jibes about stale, curled-up-at-the-edges railway sandwiches? It was certainly no joke for those with a discerning palate when Virgin Trains swept away its dining cars. Luxury land cruises and the preserved sector still know the value of good catering.

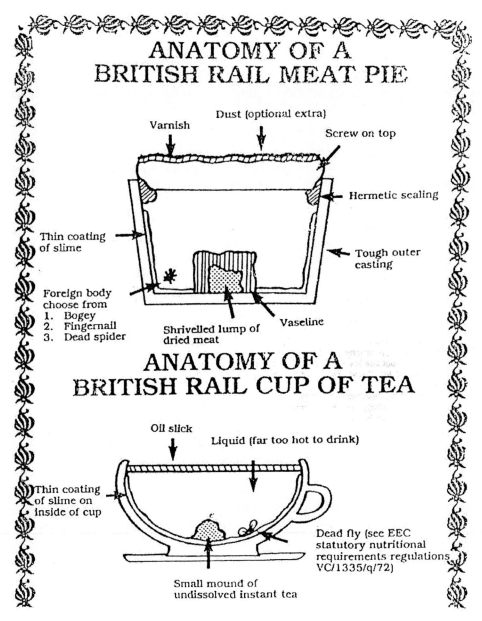

ANATOMY OF A BRITISH RAIL MEAT PIE

Caption labels on image:
Dust (optional extra)
Varnish
Screw on top
Hermetic sealing
Thin coating of slime
Tough outer casting
Foreign body choose from
1. Bogey
2. Fingernail
3. Dead spider
Shrivelled lump of dried meat
Vaseline

ANATOMY OF A BRITISH RAIL CUP OF TEA

Oil slick
Liquid (far too hot to drink)
Thin coating of slime on inside of cup
Dead fly (see EEC statutory nutritional requirements regulations VC/1335/q/72)
Small mound of undissolved instant tea

Usually it is the curled sandwich which is the butt of railway catering humour. Here from the past is an example of photocopy-lore courtesy of Loughborough Student Charities Appeal, 1987.

Another rhetorical question was asked by columnist Bill Borrows. 'Have you ever wondered why the coffee they give you in car showrooms is too hot to drink? "We're told to make it in the microwave," an employee at a major car dealership tells me. "Otherwise they spend all day sitting around drinking it. It helps turnover".' [44]

According to Robin Young this salesman's ploy is nothing new, for an earlier Victorian 'foible was to serve soup and coffee so hot that passengers on station platforms stood no chance of finishing their cups before they had to reboard the train. That way vendors could return the unfinished refreshments to the cauldron to be reheated for the next trainload of customers.'[45] Or as Roy Stevens had earlier put it: 'One of the oft repeated folklore stories is that soup was served so hot that customers couldn't possibly drink it and, when they left, the soup was returned to the urn for serving up to their next group.'[46]

Back with that comic reputation, Anthony Trollope (who wrote many of his books on trains, some of which were among the quality prose works read on journeys as 'yellowbacks', perhaps as a reward of his custom)[47] got on his high horse as long ago as 1868 about the railway sandwich, describing it thus:

> ... but the real disgrace of England – that whited sepulchre, fair
> enough outside, but so meagre, poor, and spiritless within, such a
> thing of shreds and pairings, such a dab of food, telling us that the
> poor bone whence it was scraped had been made utterly bare
> before it was sent to the kitchen for the soup pot.[48]

There is a story of some dubiousness that in late 1840 Isambard Kingdom Brunel and his superintendent of locomotives, Daniel Gooch, met and lunched in open fields outside Swindon to discuss the siting of the proposed GWR loco workshops. 'The legendary tale that they threw a sandwich to mark the spot for the first surveyor's peg makes a good story,' wrote Roy Stevens, 'but the events that followed during the next 150 years were to surpass even their imaginations. In October 1840, shortly before that picnic, the directors of the GWR had made the recommendation "that the company's principal locomotive station and repairing shops be established at or near its junction with the Great Western Union Railway at Swindon".' The interchange of engines was accompanied by a stop for refreshments and so it was at Swindon where the soup story found its genesis.[46]

Still with Swindon, as mentioned, classy dining provides income for preserved lines and the Swindon and Cricklade Railway has its 'Moonraker' service based upon a tale familiar to all folklorists. Spokesman Russell Wear said:

> The legend dates back to the days of smugglers and excise men.
> Smugglers used to store their barrels of goods in ponds around
> Swindon. When the moon was out they would retrieve the barrels.
> However, if the excise men caught the smugglers lifting the
> barrels, the smugglers claimed they were trying to catch the
> moon's reflection in the water – hence the term 'moonraker'.[49]

Allies divided

Although the role of railways in any conflict is always enormous, and wartime is always a hotbed of rumours, comparatively little in the way of folklore appears to have been generated. Thus I have been reduced to parading a motley platoon of yarns.

A correspondent thought he would share the knowledge that women 'train watchers' had been recruited furtively in Belgium during the Great War from among housewives whose kitchens overlooked railway lines. 'Information as to whether trains were carrying troops or horses was apparently recorded by the ladies in their knitting – plain for men, purl for horses. The knitting was then sent to a decoding centre where the secrets contained were, quite literally, unravelled,' wrote Henry Gumston, adding humorously, 'Might it not prove possible for your current lady readers to contribute to the "Traffic and Traction" section in a similar way?' [50]

More correspondents were discussing whether a British submarine returned from patrol with a train painted up as a 'kill'? It seems that during World War II, *HMS Turbulent* may have separately hit a goods train, electric train and road convoy after surfacing three times near enemy coasts in the eastern Mediterranean. It was also believed that on its nuclear-powered successor, 'Train Night' is still celebrated at sea with a formal dinner, when a model train graces the wardroom dining table.[51]

A photograph I have seen published a couple of times shows almost 120 American 'S160' 2-8-0s stored in South Wales awaiting the D-Day landings in a single row on the former Barry Railway branch at Treherbet in 1944. Strangely thirty years later history saw the phenomenon of Dai Woodham's Barry scrapyard with even more steam locos in brigade strength. Dai only managed to collect one former LNER engine, 'B1' No. 61264, subsequently saved for posterity. I once heard that the LNER authorities thought so highly of 'A4' Pacific No. 2509 *Silver Link* that it spent the entire war hidden in a shed at Doncaster Works. In the Sixties the pioneer 'A4' was ignominiously scrapped at the same location. Or not. As I was completing the manuscript for this book anticipation was growing that locos could be unearthed from the scrapyard at Doncaster Works. The land is to be developed for housing, and demolition could confirm whether staff buried rather than scrapped some locos. Tantalisingly Howard Johnston reported that asbestos removal 'will either finally lay the myth to rest, or reveal some devastating surprises.' He added that the dismantling process 'has long given rise to the rumours that boilers (or more) of the more "difficult" locomotives may not have been broken up at all, but buried in what was a very large site. Now, enforced excavations for house foundations will reveal all.' [52]

A readers' column also supplies a new angle to what I would have mentioned anyway. Introduced in 1941, designer O.V.S. Bulleid slipped the first of his 'Merchant Navy' Pacific class locos into the wartime building programme as mixed traffic engines. The SR desperately needed new passenger locos with rapid acceleration to keep pace with the intensively-timetabled electric train services between Woking and London. Maybe Bulleid was economical with the truth, but the 'Merchant Navies's driving wheels were only 6 ft 2 in, decidedly a mixed traffic measurement. Correspondent G. Jukes made the first-class point: 'It was during the war that the LMS built 13 'Princess Coronations' (five in 1940, four each in 1943 and 1944). These had 6 ft 9 in driving wheels and were express passenger locomotives. So was there in fact a wartime ban on building express engines which Bulleid had to circumvent? And if there was, why did it not apply to Crewe?' [53]

Here we see partisanship at work and the 'engines that won the war' has been attributed to many classes of various companies. An anonymous writer wrote: 'The "V2", however, can never be stripped of its honourable place in the history of British railways – after all, weren't they the engines that won the war!' They were certainly conscripted to perform Herculean tasks, but another unidentified partisan sneered: 'The hoary description that the "V2" was the engine "that won the war" is a romanticism designed to buck up senile LNER veterans.'

Another example of battle lines drawn has raised the spectre of political correctness. Recently the Heritage Railway Association issued new rules over Nazi uniforms. Many steam railways hold profitable World War II re-enactments, but scenarios such as the Severn Valley Railway organising mock interrogations by SS officers have been deemed inappropriate. The row began when Peak Rail's newsletter published a photograph on its front cover of a 'German Stormtrooper' posing in front of a wartime 'Austerity' tank engine. With the sixtieth anniversary of the liberation of Auschwitz recently celebrated, to which trainloads of Jews were transported, several members took offence. David Morgan, HRA chairman, commented: 'I'm very conscious that Jewish people can be a little over-sensitive sometimes. But it is totally inappropriate for people to dress up as Nazis on our railways.' [54] Yet were it not for 'alternative histories', literature would be the poorer. Would Mr Morgan and Jews wish to ban works such as Philip K. Dick's masterful *The Man in the High Castle*, in which triumphant Japan and Germany divide the USA? Peak Rail chairman Paul Tomlinson warned: 'To try to sanitise history, or airbrush out those aspects which could offend people, is not only misguided but, in my opinion, dangerous.'

Cup final prophecy

I have only three sporting items worthy of inclusion and, as with wartime conjecture, two are selected from readers' letters.

'It is a very well known piece of railway lore that a passenger looking out of a carriage window as his train passes a cricket match will never see a wicket fall,' wrote Michael H.C. Baker, after being similarly disappointed many times until just outside Aberystwyth, as the train awaited the go-ahead to pass over a level crossing, a fielder took an excellent catch. 'The batsman was clearly most upset for as he approached the pavilion he hurled his bat into the bushes beside it, followed by his batting gloves.' Mr Baker's train moved on and passed a second match in an adjoining ground where there was just time to see a delivery smote hard and straight for the bowler to catch. Mr Baker deduced: 'I therefore conclude that given all these circumstances, it is possible to see, not one, but two wickets fall – the most important proviso being that the train in which one is travelling has to be a Welsh narrow-gauge steam one.' [55]

An agreeable case of serendipity was recorded in a letter from Roland C. Bond, in charge of the inspection of the 'Royal Scot' locos under construction by the North British Locomotive Company at Glasgow. Riding on the footplate of No. 6100 on its inaugural journey to Derby on the early evening of 14 July 1927, as the loco passed alongside the Chevin golf course adjacent to the line at Duffield, its eminent designer, Sir Henry Fowler, and Mr S.J. Syme were playing close to the line. 'They waved to me,' recalled Mr Bond, 'and I returned the salute!' [56]

An earlier section dealt fully with fulfilled prophecy. Another exceptional example is scored by soccer seersmanship. As is noted by its archivist, Nigel Pennick, the prophecy was 'authentic, direct and proven.' For a fortnight before the Football Association Cup Final of 1904, an 8 ft by 7 ft poster was displayed outside the Great Central Railway offices in Piccadilly, Manchester. Below the company's name was written 'English Cup Final, Crystal Palace, April 23rd, 1904', Crystal Palace being the London venue. A drawing of a footballer scoring a goal was the main body of the poster, with the legend 'Billy Meredith Secures the Cup', and details of cheap train fares for football fans to get to London from Manchester. When the 'defeated' goalkeeper, Dai Davies of Bolton Wanderers, saw the poster he was hardly delighted. Later, he wrote: 'Some days before the great game I saw... a huge placard... showing Meredith, the Manchester City captain, in the act of defeating me, and, incidentally, scoring the winning goal. As soon as I saw the placard I made up my mind that such an event as that must be prevented if it were at all possible. During the game, however, it happened that Meredith did score the winning goal in a manner exactly as shown on the poster. The very fact of this goal being scored was the means of the City's team winning the coveted Cup.' [57]

All things bright and beautiful

My material for this sub-section could have populated a separate volume, but not wishing to be a rabid inclusionist along Noah's lines, I culled my copy with all the pragmatism of a farmer drowning kittens.

A sting in the tale

Kent's remote Isle of Sheppey harboured a colony of scorpions at Sheerness naval dockyard, with the first recorded specimens being sent to the British Museum as long ago as 1870. The quest for the British species, *Euscorpius flavicaudus*, confirmed another colony in the 1980s at Ongar railway station in Essex, and they have since been recorded at Harwich and Pinner. They could have arrived in cargoes imported from the British Empire or have lived here undetected for hundreds or even thousands of years. One source described it as the European (rather than British) yellow-tailed scorpion, 50 mm long and 'its sting can be fatal to the elderly and very young.' [58] A less hysterical approach described it as one inch long and 'harmless, capable of nothing more than a pin prick.' [59] Around 1980, zoologist Bernard Betts estimated there were about 50,000 specimens at Sheerness and may still exist. 'They can withstand more than 200 times the amount of radiation we can stand and go without water for over a year,' said Mr Betts. He was also involved in locating the Ongar colony at what was then a London Transport Underground overground branch terminus, since closed and the subject of a heritage line bid. 'There used to be a steam goods yard and underneath the platform where they stored the coal and everything else was the colony of *Euscorpius*,' he recalled. He told journalist Robert Verkaik some Press coverage stirred up bad feeling by making out that he had 'planted' tropical scorpions there. 'It was so ridiculous I didn't bother challenging the reports and a bit later a fire underneath the platform destroyed them.' However, there was to be another twist in the tale when a correspondent to a national newspaper claimed responsibility for the Ongar colony's introduction. 'After years of mystery, I think it is about time to explain how scorpions came to be found at London Transport's Ongar Underground station in Essex,' confided F. Pepper, of Leyton, east London. 'This unique colony brought a host of experts to study the insects... Now I confess. There was, just before the discovery of the scorpions, a fear that Ongar, a single-line station, might close like hundreds of others around the country had during the Beeching era. So I bought five harmless scorpions for 10p each from a Camden Town pet shop and placed them on the station in the certain knowledge that conservationists would never permit its closure while they were in residence.'[60] Perhaps this is suspicious; reminiscent of people who seek reflected notoriety by coming forward to admit crimes they could not have committed.

While on the subject of insects, I cannot resist mentioning a *Punch* cartoon of 1869 having a railway guard saying to a lady carrying a wicker basket: 'Cats is "dogs" and rabbits is "dogs" and so's Parrats, but this "ere "Tortis" is a insect and there ain't no charge for it.'

Which leads neatly to another tale of railway personnel, with parrots being station announcers during the first years of the Edinburgh to Glasgow rail line, opened in 1842. The birds were trained to announce 'Haymarket' to alighting passengers. However, by 1845 no parrots remained. The accepted explanation was that all the smoke got into their lungs and the squawkers croaked. However, the truth is that with all the whistles, bells, and so on going on in the station they found more interesting noises to emulate, and quickly didn't bother to shout 'Haymarket.'[61] Before self-enforced redundancy they spoke most distinctly, but as *The Builder* reported in 1861, other railways relied upon their porters, who were less articulate.

Fortean favourites

The Himalayas have the yeti, or as it was called when I was a lad, 'abominable snowman'. North America has the sasquatch, or as it is nowadays known with undue familiarity, 'bigfoot'. China has the yeren, or as forteans prefer, 'wildman'. Railway engineers encountered three of these manimals in Shennongjia on 3 September 1993. Giving chase, they got within thirty yards as the creatures fled into dense forest. As they observed their quarry plough through the undergrowth 'with superhuman speed and strength', their courage deserted them and the chase ended. The pursuers described the unfamiliar beasts as between 5 ft and 5 ft 6 in tall, with long dishevelled hair, slightly rounded eyes, broad foreheads and protruding chins. A sort of civilised Bob Geldof. Subsequently investigators found droppings, the analysis of which suggested the wildman and wildwoman were herbivorous.[62] Several expeditions have hunted the yeren with little success. Hair specimens analysis has led to a consensus that they are dealing with an unknown variety of primate; a species closer to human beings than the great apes. Yet some folklorists would dismiss the yeren as simply an old-fashioned fairytale ogre described in oral tradition coupled with interstitiality, that is a creature whose categorisation is a blurred identity between human and animal, a fearful contamination.

Another fortean favourite, entombed amphibia (frogs, toads, but never seemingly newts) is generally thought of as a Victorian era speciality. However, a gang carving an extension to a railway to the south of Te Kuiti, on New Zealand's North Island, discovered an occupied cavity four metres down in sedimentary mudstone. 'The frog was moist, but not exactly bouncing about,' observed bridge inspector Mr L. Andrews. Later that day in November, 1982, a drilling machine uncovered another entombed frog.[63] Closer to home but back in time, in 1835 navvies digging the route of the London to Birmingham railway cracked open red sandstone rock and discovered a toad within. It seemed 'oppressed' when exposed to the air, gasped feebly, turned from brown to black, and due to injury died four days later.[64]

Yet another more modern fortean classic genre is alien big cats. A media cynic could infer from the volume of sober reports that a commuter is more likely to spot a puma than a train. Preserved railways seem particularly prone to attracting big game. A black panther-like creature was spotted at Birstall on the Great Central Railway; operations assistant Norman Blake found footprints by the tracks near Sheffield Park on the Bluebell Railway, on which loco crews have spotted various unfamiliar large felids from the footplate; and other big cats have been seen along the Nene Valley Railway near Peterborough. Big cat experts say the beasts follow railway tracks as they have become wildlife havens which are relatively undisturbed for much of the day. Those holidaying on waterways in quiet rural areas have also been urged to watch out for exotic felids, particularly at dawn and dusk.[65] Fortean folklorists are familiar with the usual explanations to account for these out-of-place animals: circus or zoo escapes; release from captivity with the introduction of Dangerous Wild Animals Act or when grew too big to handle; even trans-dimensional semi-solid phenomena. London Zoo's Doug Richardson, on being described a big cat seen near Northolt station in suburban west London, said: 'The description sounds like a mountain lion. Railway land would suit it perfectly. It would be undisturbed and have a plentiful food supply.[66]

Alien big cat sightings have been so numerous and ubiquitous for it to be certain that the public is seeing exotic wildlife aplenty. However, for these to be flesh-and-blood creatures, the depredation to livestock would be enormous. Authors John Michell and Bob Rickard pinpoint the dilemma:

> We can not disbelieve in UFOs and English pumas, because of
> the frequency and certainty of their sightings; but neither can we
> believe in them in the same way as we believe in aeroplanes and
> foxes because it seems to be part of their nature that they can
> never be caught and scientifically studied.[67]

They then go on to suggest a solution:

> From all this we have brewed a theory, which like all our theories
> is temporarily and loosely held. It is that creatures now extinct
> which once inhabited a certain district continue after their
> extinction to haunt that district in phantom form, varied with
> occasional real, physical appearances, until the time comes to
> reveal themselves.

Having seen a black panther cross in front of a car driven by a companion in rural Northumberland, what I saw looked as solid and large as a melanistic leopard I saw shortly afterwards behind bars at Paignton Zoo. Yet I believe what I witnessed strolling from the gates of a large estate was at a liminal point between dimensions, perhaps a form of guardian, a classic space-time transient of an interstitial life-form.[68]

Chapter Four

Seasoned travellers

Commuters are the largest percentage of rail travellers. The name derives from the American term for holders of season or 'commutation' tickets, and refers to those who travel between home and workplace. The coming of the railway revolutionised transport between where one lived and one worked, with reduced-rate season tickets available to all but the very lowest paid. Thus the majority could move away from city centres and live in better surroundings and travel to work by train. In time, as this shift to the initial suburbs gathered pace, the middle classes sold up and moved farther out still into the countryside. To move vast numbers of workmen and clerical staff, high-capacity compartment coaches were designed to pack in as many people as possible with scant regard for comfort. Those from the 'residential' suburbs were offered something better and first class was introduced. Even this could be fraught for some, and 'club' carriages would be attached to offer an even greater level of luxury.

Regular travel hardens people to the vagaries of Britain's railway system. There are irritants and exasperation, tedium and light relief; in fact, all human life encapsulated as part of life's rich tapestry and the journey that is life.

Nevertheless, few will have encountered such oddities as the man who delayed by ten minutes the 14.24 Exmouth to Barnstaple train at Eggesford on 28 February 2002, when he refused to alight, produced a voodoo doll and placed a curse on the guard.[1]

This section begins with more reasons for delay, followed up with sexual encounters, alcoholic intervention, mischief and coming to harm.

Some excuse!

Accumulations of modern true stories on a theme can stake a claim to be justifiably folklore as much as collections of ancient dragon slayings or perennial Shrovetide customs. These can often be no more substantial than amassed filler paragraphs on a popular topic which by journalistic quirkiness responding to perceived corporate ineptitude are garnered by fortean-minded clipsters and add up to a thematic matter which strikes a chord with the public. A good example is excuses for train delays. The more the media highlights ludicrous reasons for trains running late, the more operators' lame excuses become the topic of conversation on the railway itself, in pubs, offices and homes. These irritations are shared sympathetically and it rarely matters whether the cause of delay is beyond human control – railways still get the blame. These being, anyway, further examples of the interrupted journey scenario.

Being an avowed Portugophile, my favourite for passengers being delayed by the non-running of their train at Swansea was: 'The driver is sunning himself on the Algarve and there is no one else to drive the train.' Of course, more sober railwaymen acknowledge problems and rather than irritate with frivolity adopt a positive approach. Railtrack North West produced leaflets explaining the facts about 'leaves on the line' and how it was getting to grips with the problem. Railtrack bosses at the headquarters in Euston Square, London, made sure there would be no leaves jibes when they chose an artificial tree. A spokesman confirmed the executives traumatised by fallen leaves found the tree a welcome relief, but said that 'it is also terribly environmentally friendly, as we can put it in a box and use it year after year. It is considered rather modern and hi-tech, which reflects our building. We have had all sorts of people coming in to admire it.' Really? 'It is painted acid green, with an angel on the top wearing Doc Martens.' [2]

Many of my favourite excuses, however, feature fauna rather than flora. You've got to admire the sub-editor's 'Last-minute itch causes driver to scratch service' headline when a female driver refused to go beyond Hastings after fleas left her covered in tiny bites. So the 9.59 from Eastbourne, East Sussex, to Ashford, Kent, stayed put until pest control experts had gone in and made sure the cab was mite-free. [3] Another unfortunate driver left passengers stranded for several hours near Leipzig, Germany, during 2000, after he swallowed a hornet and was stung in the throat. [4] Meanwhile, another case of infestation was reported by *The Times of India* in 2003 when an express was detained at Shoranur after cockroaches invaded the air-conditioning. The Gujarat-bound *Thiruvananthapuram Happa Express* had to be stopped at the station after the passengers, mainly tourists, demanded that 'stringent' action be taken against the beetles. After an eight-hour ordeal insecticides were sprayed to rid the insects. [5] Another kind of bug afflicted a computer at Gobowen station, Shropshire, which was thought to have fallen victim to the millennium bug when it began printing tickets with the date 1 April 1980. [6] Hordes of caterpillars halted the operations of the New York Central Railroad for 35 minutes on 2 June 1953. These and excessive numbers of army worms suddenly appeared for days before and after global geomagnetic field activity. [7] Meanwhile in Australia it was millipedes, when train operator V/Line in Victoria told passengers: 'We have had a plague of millipedes. When they are crushed by trains, they form a sticky liquid which causes wheels to slip on steep grades. We apologise for delays.' [8] Similarly Japanese passengers were held up for two hours after a train stalled after running over an army of millipedes at Hansu. [9] More such 60 mm long bugs hatched due to freak weather conditions and caused a train to slip to a standstill near Osaka. [10] On the Ghan railway, in Australia, delays were caused by termites eating wooden sleepers and whole sections of track were repeatedly swept away because they were built over dry riverbeds. The notorious delays became part of Outback legend with trains regularly arriving not hours but days late. There were stories of food supplies having to be dropped by parachute. One train driver, during a two-week delay, set off into the Outback with his gun to shoot wild goats for the passengers to eat. Such delays came to an end in 1980 with the completion of a new standard gauge line laid on concrete sleepers over more solid foundations. [11] When heavy rain coaxed snails from under cover on to rails of the Casablanca to Fez line, in Morocco, they brought an express to a slippery halt and blocked the track for several hours. Mysteriously, they often congregated at the exact same spot on the line.[12]

Mice were blamed for delays of around twenty-five minutes when Great Western train services through Swindon, Wiltshire, were hit by mice eating through signalling cable in 1997.[13] Similarly, kamikaze rats gnawing cables and roasting in a blaze of glory regularly stopped Thameslink services in central London during 1998 before the wires could be securely boxed. In July that year a snake slithered up a pylon and was electrocuted, causing a power surge that halted twenty-three trains carrying 12,000 commuters in northern Japan.[14] While to save it coming to harm, a packed commuter train had to stop for twenty minutes near Farnham, Surrey, because a badger was asleep on the line. Staff woke it and the beast shuffled off.[15]

Humans can be just as blameworthy. Central network bosses claimed delays were caused by passengers getting on to the trains too slowly.[16] Even when on a train trouble can be caused as when four trains were delayed for 100 minutes due to a man on a stag night dropping his trousers in front of a female passenger at Hucknall station. Police attended, but a Railtrack Midlands memo dated 12 August 1996, reported that no arrest could be made due to being 'unable to identify the bottom concerned.'[17] That part of one's anatomy was also featured in a news item regarding a forty-year-old railwayman in Italy facing criminal charges for train delays because of frequent attacks of diarrhoea. On one occasion, a train had to wait thirty-three minutes for the man to return from the toilet and he faced a £3,000 fine and up to a year's imprisonment if found guilty.[18]

A train driver thought he was averting an al-Qaeda attack after he spotted a man in camouflage gear on the trackside at Wimbledon, south-west London. He believed the man to be carrying a rocket-propelled grenade launcher, but police found the man was carrying a didgeridoo. However, no one told the driver the suspect was handling one of those Australian aboriginal instruments so beloved of Rolf Harris, and when he spotted the man on his return journey he called the police again. Consequently Bedford to Brighton trains were delayed by thirty minutes.[19] Delays can also affect narrow-gauge systems as model railway village owners Rory and Jean Jones found to their literal cost. The annual summer opening was halted when insurance cover was refused by Royal and Sun Alliance with the 'heightened threat from terrorism' being blamed. A new insurer was found but the Southport attraction started a week behind schedule.[20]

Still on the subject of international tensions, four anti-Iraq war protesters standing on the WCML at Oxenholme to hold up a Glasgow to London service decided to beat a hasty retreat when they discovered the train was carrying Glasgow Celtic supporters on their way to a UEFA Cup game at Liverpool.[21]

An article in *Steam Railway* told of a late-night Manchester to Blackpool train being delayed. The tale from the railwaymen's mess-room at Bolton told of the train with compartment stock having quite a 'reputation.' One evening the communication cord was pulled between Salwick and Lea Road, and the train lurched to a halt. Looking down the train, it was noticed that one of the doors was open, so the fireman and the guard both walked towards it and were startled to find a woman who was completely naked. When challenged as to whether it was she who had pulled the cord she confirmed that she had, with the explanation: 'Yes, he won't give me my money!' At the next station, Preston, the police were waiting. The train crew never did find out whether she got her money for services rendered, but it put a new twist to the expression 'train in revenue-earning service'. [22]

Almost lastly, a truly bizarre Good Samaritan scenario featuring 'Coronation' class loco No. 46233 *Duchess of Sutherland* which was waiting to return to York when an inaccessible hydrant at Hull station led to a road tanker being hired. The driver, believing he was doing everyone a favour as it was a steam train, filled his tanker with hot water. When transferred to the tender, far from saving the crew time and effort to boil the water, his action had the effect of destroying the fine pressure balance required to make the injectors 'pick up' and it was not possible to get water into the boiler. Only when steam was noticed rising from the tender was the error realised, but by then it was too late and the train returned diesel-hauled, leaving the support crew to pump out the wrong sort of water and refill the tender with the correct cold sort.

To close, one which neatly segues into the next section and has all the hallmarks of dubious lusty legend. When the famous *Orient Express* failed to be able to set off from the Austrian town of Innsbruck in September, 1984, engineers were summoned to examine the loco. Nothing amiss could be found and it was thirty minutes before railway officials found a girl and her boyfriend having sex in one of the compartments. The account claims to explain: 'They were so "wrapped up in each other" they had failed to notice the girl's foot tangled around the communication cord, thus applying the emergency brake. The train finally moved off – arriving at its destination some seventy minutes late. ("We regret to announce... ").' [23]

Goes like a train...

Having contemplated writing a book along just these lines twenty or so years ago I began making notes and collecting possible material; the cuttings categorised under 'sex' became voluminous, but mostly repetitive, sordid or dubious, and patently unsexy. I jettisoned column after column of sex on trains, sex on tracks, even fetishists or the desperates' preference for alfresco nookie on station platforms. To spare Sir Richard Branson's blushes I binned clippings of Virgin Trains' waitresses with 'Bristol' printed on their blouse fronts and Virgin Trains' buffet sales of Otis Spunkmeyer's muffins. Who would embarrass the railway announcer who left his microphone on when he rang his wife and started talking dirty to her or the crews who would swivel the headlight designed to allow gentle buffering up at night to bank trains up the Lickey incline, but would shine it on courting couples in the narrow lanes alongside the West Midlands main line.

Twenty years ago Bluetooth was unimaginable, still less its perverted use; being a radio technology, with about a ten-metre range and utilised by mobiles, which has spawned 'toothing', an unsavoury practice whereby commuters can arrange impromptu sex sessions with strangers in train toilets.[24] Train sex below the English

Channel is also a modern craze; flashing, streaking and nudity timeless. In fact, any craze or exploit can be deemed a form of folklore. Whereas there is a yawn-inducing reaction nowadays to dubious claims of aircraft mile-high sexual antics, its rail-borne equivalent has become the Mile Low Club in the Chunnel of Love, with couples sneaking into toilets for a tunnel trembler at the deepest point – 377 feet below sea level. According to a front page splash in a not-too-discerning tabloid, Jason Ellis and Karen Woods boarded 'Le Shuttle' for thirty-five minutes of locked loo passion. 'The rocking of the train added to the experience,' said romantic computer consultant Jason, 'and meant nobody outside knew what was going on.' [25] Another tabloid extolling the underwater frolics on Eurostar trains had office worker Louise Simmonds proudly boasting that she and her boyfriend had quickies in both directions. Understanding Eurostar spokesman Jim Rowe said: 'Our main concern is making sure that none of our passengers are upset or offended. We'll allow more or less anything within reason.' [26] While yet another downmarket newspaper claimed the four-minute Tube trip between London's Finsbury Park and Tottenham was highly recommended for rapid nookie. [27]

However, nothing under the sun is new, and as far back as the nineteenth century the randy fraternity were making love. The train trysting attracted such popularity that several of the more inventive European brothels provided chambers decorated like railway carriages which shuddered and vibrated mechanically when they were occupied, and for added realism also resounded with chugging and whistling sound effects.[28]

Compulsions, as noted elsewhere in this book, are a fortean sideline and flashing is one of the more upsetting examples, yet often with humorous consequences. For instance there was a pervert who exposed himself to a woman while travelling on the Metro network in Paris, who fled when his victim, a transvestite, flashed back.[29] The coming to harm motif applies to chef Alain Erbault, who cooked his goose after flashing at two girls in Dijon, France. He tried to flee with his pants down, but fell under a train.[30] Streaking may now induce yawns, but surely red-blooded males would have enjoyed seeing a girl dash naked up the *Orient Express* until colliding with a waiter, striking her head on a table and lying dazed and covered in soup. But would such a prestigious enterprise have a ticket-collector to escort her back to her room? Adding to the improbability of it ever happening, the girl is not properly identified, the company would not confirm the occurrence and the diary lead item ends with the obviously fabricated anonymous elderly gentleman who was so impressed he vowed to book another trip on his return to England. Always beware diarists.[31]

Staying with nudity, here is a type of interrupted journey story with an undertone of someone high-ranking being slowly stripped of their pre-eminence and dignity. It is the supposed tale of celebrated Edwardian beauty Lady Bingham, who while travelling to London from the West Country, suffered an indignity which became the talk of society for some time. According to legend, her ladyship was joined in the carriage by a stranger, who to her embarrassment began to stare at her. Eventually he commanded in a low voice, 'Take off your veil.' Nervously Lady Bingham complied. 'Now take off that hat.' She did so. As the journey continued she was instructed to remove her overcoat, coat, waistcoat, blouse, skirt, petticoat, camiknickers, corset, brassiere and boots, while her tormentor stared unsmilingly. Allowed to sit naked for some time, the man then pointed ominously to the luggage rack and told her to climb on to it. 'Now don't move from there,' he instructed. Andover, Basingstoke, Woking, Weybridge passed as Lady Bingham lay naked, cold and scared for an hour and a half. As the train drew into Vauxhall, the man left the carriage silently, stepped out on to the platform, blew Lady Bingham a kiss and was never seen again.[32]

Railways and sex are occasional bedfellows. We even use the expression 'goes like a train' for a female with a strong sex drive and 'pulling a train' for a girl enjoying multiple-partner intercourse (particularly in a Hell's Angels situation).

Social lubrication

Brunel gets everywhere! In desperation, I once called at what may well have been the grottiest pub it's been my misfortune to imbibe within. This tawdry tavern, opposite Bristol's magnificent Temple Meads station, named insultingly 'The Isambard Brunel', had by my next visit on 15 June 1996, been renovated and renamed 'The Reckless Engineer'. I was with a party of fellow enthusiasts, members of the InterCity Railway Society, and we were quaffing merrily as a prelude to a meal in the restaurant next door, when in came a stripogram, who after reading some ribald verse, yanked down the shocked birthday boy's trousers and whipped his naked bum. Being a Freemason and birthday celebrant *par excellence*, Brunel would certainly have enjoyed this modern ritual of incantation, flagellation, initiation and humiliation.

Any interrupted journey has about it something of a liminal quality, from *The Ancient Mariner* to *Adlestrop*. Nigel Pennick sent me a clipping with 'FOAF?' appended. Judge for yourself:

> Harking back to the days of 'Oh Mr Porter', British Rail placated
> delayed passengers one night last week the old-fashioned way.
> When the 7 p.m. Charing Cross to Ashford pulled up short in
> Marsden, a guard announced that a goods train had blocked the
> line ahead: 'You might as well go to the pub – I'll come and fetch
> you when we're ready to pull out.' Dutifully, the commuters
> trooped out. Two hours later, the train's hooter blew. Scarcely a
> grumble was to be heard as they made their way back to their
> seats. They don't teach customer relations like that at BR charm
> school.[33]

Similarly, the person who penned the following alcohol-enhanced incident prefaces it with 'we don't vouch for the complete accuracy of this story, but it sounds a good one.' Again, judge for yourself.

Fifty 'exuberant' youths (they used to call them hooligans) decided upon a smashing night out in Andover. The plan was to catch a train from Whitchurch, Hampshire, create mayhem on the way, and then board the last train of the night home. However, they had not bargained on the guard of the outbound train, who apparently tipped off station staff for some revenge later on. For the homeward run, the few legitimate passengers were ferried home by taxi. The gang meanwhile boarded the train, and were horrified to see it race through Whitchurch without stopping. It came to a halt at a station eight miles away. The unlucky 50 doubtless came to their senses when they realised they had a long walk home. And it was a freezing cold night to boot. Fair dos? [34]

Describing a trip on the ECML, starting for Edinburgh at 7.40 a.m., Brian Hollingsworth praised the 'IC125' itself, breakfast and 'incidentally, a third nice thing about BR is that the drinking hours which apply elsewhere in Britain do not apply on trains so one can "down the first pint" long before the more permanently situated pubs and bars are allowed to open.' I wonder if the author continued in the buffet, as crossing the marshy fens north of Huntingdon, he uncourteously observed: 'Fenland people are widely supposed to be born with webbed feet – confirmation, if true, of the theory of mankind's aquatic origin, so well set out in Elaine Morgan's fascinating book, *The Descent of Woman.*' [35]

I regard the ability to down that first pint of the day long before the sun reaches the yardarm as most civilised, but on sporting occasions the ability to drink on trains is often curtailed, particularly on 'footex' specials. But there is also nowadays on pleasure railways the 'beerex', also a commonplace attraction at diesel galas with real ales. The Cottage Brewery Company created a 'Millennium Series' of keg-busters such as 'Deltic Diesel', 'Mallard IPA', 'Stanier Black 5', 'Johnson Single Bitter' and 'Windsor Castle Ale'. What better way for a 1999 monthly countdown of beers named after milestones of British railway history? [36]

A bar which I would really like to visit forms the interior of a former 'Metrovick' which is an ingredient of the Hell's Kitchen pub, opposite Castlerea station on the Dublin to Westport line. The gutted diesel locomotive has seating in what had been the engine-room. It is housed below a glass canopy and a signal positioned alongside at stop gives the impression of the loco having smashed through a pub wall. Another semaphore signal outside the pub indicates that the pub is open for business when lowered. Being inside the loco must be like the enchantment of entering a fairy rath and losing all sense of time.[37] So clink your glass with your fellow traveller to frighten away the Devil.

Mischief

Best to get the disgusting out of the way first, particularly as the tale's monitor referred to the central character as 'something of a legend at his local station.' For Rajiv Kumar, of Madras, India, was sacked for breaking wind to the famous da-da-da-daaa opening of Beethoven's *Fifth Symphony* in D minor. He had previously played spoons over the public address system, organised belly-dancing in the ticket office and snake-charming in the toilets.[38] His bosses labelled it a disgusting deviation from the timetable.[39]

Another 'trouser trumpet' entertainer was zany Paul Oldfield, of Macclesfield, a.k.a. Mr Methane, whose repertoire included the Crystals' classic *Da Doo Ron Ron* and

The postcard reproduced here shows a South African signalman named Wylde, who lost his legs in an accident on the Port Elizabeth main line in 1877. When he saw a baboon for sale in the local market he bought it for a pet. It became devoted to his master and was soon trained to fetch water, sweep out the shack and hand a special key to passing engine drivers, who used it to adjust points farther up the line. He would rush to the signal-box and get the key from a peg on the wall whenever he heard an approaching rain. Eventually 'Jack' learned to work signals on his own and became so proficient that he was able to carry out the whole operation while his master remained at the shack. He was never known to make a mistake. The partnership continued for nine years until 'Jack' died of tuberculosis. Apparently as recently as the early 1970s another baboon named 'Jock' was also working as a signalman near Pretoria, earning 1s 6d a day and a bottle of beer every Saturday night.

who defended his act by saying: 'Some prudes find it a bit offensive, but most people think it's hilarious. I believe it's an art form.' He justifies inclusion here as having quit his train driver's job for showbusiness, training on baked beans, sprouts and pickled onions.[40]

British Rail staff were hunting pranksters who neatly repainted all the blue and white station platform signs at Maidstone Barracks in Kent to make them read Maidstone Bollocks.[41] A witch-hunt closer to home was on to find the culprit who allegedly confounded passengers at Euston station awaiting a tourist train to Sellafield organised by British Nuclear Fuels. The departure board read: '8.30 Sellafield Site: We're glowing there.'[42]

Coming to harm

Long, long ago I worked out never to believe any brief paragraph in a newspaper which cited Johannesburg, South Africa, as its source. Typical of the unlikelihood of any veracity is the claim that at least fifteen people were crushed to death when guards used electric prods on crowds trying to board packed commuter trains in Tembisa, a black township near Jo'burg.[43] No less likely was the tale of Stanley Lemon, who was arrested on a subway train in New York after he zapped a fellow passenger with a cattle prod. The businessman told police he bought the device to stop other commuters reading his newspaper.[44]

However, for sheer weirdness, I have a true story. Trainee caterer Mark Smith left a train at York and in front of horrified travellers, slashed his wrists. It was the twenty-year old's tenth such protest over a twenty-month period. A charge of disorderly behaviour was dropped at York magistrates' court when Smith agreed to be bound over to keep the peace for twelve months. Of his most recent protest, he said after the hearing: 'I just like travelling on trains and I only do it when I'm annoyed with British Rail. I want to ensure their services are kept up to scratch. I was on a day trip to Newcastle but got off at York when the journey became a bit uncomfortable.' Smith was dripping with blood when British Transport Police were called to the station travel centre. They found a number of razor blades hidden in his socks. He was seen by a psychiatrist, who diagnosed there was no need for treatment. However, a psychologist would doubtless have seen this self-mutilation and scarification as a form of magical protection for himself and other travellers who suffer discomfort; a blood sacrifice for the betterment of society in the face of an uncaring monopolistic monster.[45]

Literary losses

Lawrence of Arabia claimed to have left the first draft of *The Seven Pillars of Wisdom* in an attaché case in the waiting-room of Reading station in 1919 while changing trains and spent the following three months rewriting the 250,000-word work from his preliminary notes. Another writer forced to start again from scratch was Ernest Hemingway, whose first wife, Hadley, travelling to meet him in Lausanne left a suitcase containing the drafts of virtually all of his early stories and a novel in progress on a train in France when she left her seat to get a drink in 1922. Charles Dickens also had a close encounter with the lost-in-transit authorial sprite in 1864 when his Folkestone-London train became derailed. Despite his carriage hanging precariously from a bridge, Dickens escorted his female companions to safety before returning to salvage a bottle of brandy and the half-completed manuscript of *Our Mutual Friend*.[46]

My favourite tomes-and-trains tale must surely be apocryphal. Matt Thorne noticed that a fellow passenger was reading a copy of *Tourist*, his first novel. As they were alone, Thorne plucked up courage to comment: 'Excuse me, that's my novel you're reading.' 'Oh, I'm sorry,' said the woman. 'I found it on that seat over there.'[47]

Breaking the ice

The genesis of any familiar phrase is fraught with optional explanations. Twelve unusual facts about the *Irish Mail* ends with the belief that the term 'breaking the ice' originated on this train, which began its life in 1785 as a horse-drawn coach travelling between the Swan with Two Necks pub in Gresham Street, London, and the Eagle and Child, Holyhead. Soda-acetate foot-warmers were provided in cold weather, and when cooled, station porters shook them to regenerate the heat. This interruption led to an exchange of comments between passengers who up until then had maintained a frigid silence.[48]

London termini

London is richly endowed in having so many excellent stations. These cathedrals of the nineteenth century with their Victorian Gothic splendour tell tales from the vengeful Boadicea to verbose Betjeman, Victorian civilisers to vomiting civil servants. Here are the termini where the railways lived up to their stations in life.

Kings Cross. Best known folklorically as the final resting place of Queen Boadicea (or Boudica or Boudicca to pedants), buried under Platform Ten. How the freedom fighting head of the Iceni tribe, who rose against the Roman imperialists, torched Londinium and rammed the Roman noblewomen down on to stakes through their vaginas, and was finally defeated in AD 61, came to be laid to rest here is a mystery to me.

It is nowadays most famous for Platform 9½. from which departs the steam train for Hogwarts School of Witchcraft and Wizardry, and would-be travellers must take a run-up at a point exactly between Platforms 9 and 10.[49] This is depicted in Warner Brothers' blockbuster film, *Harry Potter and the Philosopher's Stone*, but when dozens of police and security guards stopped anyone watching the filming of J.K. Rowling's best-selling book, parents described the crackdown as 'heavy-handed'.[50] Actually, Platform 4 stood in for the secret Platform 9½ and trains packed with extras used Platforms 3 and 5. Strangely a Platform 0 is planned to create extra capacity, and although theoretically a nonsense, Platform 0s already exist at Cardiff and in Japan.[51]

Euston. Far more amusing than the hunt for the fabled whereabouts of the stones from the Doric arch which adorned the entrance to the original station, is a tale of free food. Commuters were pleasantly surprised to be offered 1,000 bacon sandwiches by a Hannibal Lecter look-alike, being part of publisher Heinemann's launch of *Hannibal*, Thomas Harris' sequel to *The Silence of the Lambs*. Smacking of publicists' fashioned apocrypha, in front of the publisher's stand, a young couple stood, eyes tight shut, in a passionate clinch, when the spitting image of Sir Anthony Hopkins approached and tapped them on the shoulders. As their faces froze in startled recognition, 'Dr Lecter' hissed: 'Would you kindly stop doing that on the station, please. You're making me feel... rather hungry.'[52]

In fact, it was at Euston that William Henry Smith founded his first station bookstore in 1848. A year later the association between trains and reading was cemented by the foundation of Routledge's Railway Library, which offered cheap, accessible paper-bound novels for sale to passengers. These books, so-called 'Yellowbacks', were the genesis of paperback books.[53]

Words in another context, became unintentional fictions when British hospitals began sending medical notes to India to be typed and the Association of Medical Secretaries claimed to have discovered a number of 'worrying errors in notes transcribed by sub-continentals from the voice recordings of UK surgeons, such as the patient diagnosed with "Euston Station tube malfunction", instead of "eustachian tube malfunction".' [54]

Paddington. Poet Laureate Sir John Betjeman described Paddington as 'the strongest personality of all the larger London stations.' This grand creation was Isambard Kingdom Brunel's temple to the long-distance passenger train and the concourse is still known as 'The Lawn', a name deriving from a grassy sward once lying between Brunel's temporary station and Praed Street.[55] Elsewhere I argue the case for railway travel being a great source of inspiration, but Paddington specifically caught the eye of master painter L.S. Lowry. Sitting in an Oxford-bound train in 1962, a trolley pulling baggage trucks on the opposite platform attracted his attention. The 74-year-old artist, by then an establishment figure after being elected to the Royal Academy, made a quick sketch. The drawing formed the basis for *On a crowded station platform, Paddington* which is today valued at around £250,000. It is an unusual example of a picture of the capital by Lowry, who specialised in northern industrial scenes. Lowry was subsequently honoured by having a WCML electric locomotive, No. 86239, named in his honour.[56]

Liverpool Street. Somehow London's busiest terminus seems irredeemably associated with what can be colourfully termed 'technicolour yawning'. An authoritative history of the City and its re-emergence as a force in international finance is somewhat marred by the image of the trader heading home from Liverpool Street on one's 'Vomit Comet'.[57] Or as restaurant critic Matthew Norman pondered: 'Why anyone in their right mind would want to raise the spectre of Loadsamoney days, when traders celebrated their new-found wealth with vomiting fits on Liverpool Street station each Friday night, I'm not absolutely sure.' [58]

The City looms large as a reason why Royals rarely used Liverpool Street as a departure point for Sandringham due to ancient and time-consuming formalities which had traditionally to be enacted whenever the sovereign entered the limits of the City of London. Consequentially, King's Cross was usually preferred. However, by the more enlightened Sixties regulations had been relaxed for all but formal occasions.[59]

Waterloo. Every so often some Europhile numbskull suggests we rename Waterloo (or Trafalgar Square) to avoid offending French tourists or businessmen. Are travellers arriving at the station from across the Channel insulted to be reminded of Wellington's victory over Bonaparte in 1815? It's hypocritical anyway as Paris has a station called Austerlitz, so perhaps the Austrians should complain to the French as it commemorates Napoleon's victory in 1805.[60] As for the actual Battle of Waterloo

– in Belgium, incidentally – and the name is Flemish, not French – there's the sensitive question of who beat Napoleon. Was it the British and their Dutch-Belgian troops or the Prussians? When this very question was put to the Duke of Wellington after the battle, he made no bones about the answer: both. He added: 'There was glory enough for all.' [61] In fact, those French moaners would do well to contemplate Waterloo's Victory Arch, made of Portland Stone, which commemorates the London and South Western employees who lost their lives in the First and Second World Wars.

Waterloo International. Next to the main-line station, this 1990s £400m addition is covered by a 400-metre long glass canopy below which passengers enter or leave Eurostar services to or from Paris or Brussels (ironically close to the original Waterloo). The more apprehensive travellers doubtless ponder the possibilities of Channel tunnel collapse and propinquity with salt water and stray marine life. Their fears will not be assuaged by a vast new sculpture depicting... fish.

Victoria. This terminus name has obliquely entered everyday language after a go-between paid off prostitute Monica Coghlan with £2,000 from best-selling author Jeffry Archer at this station. An 'Archer' is now the betting term for a £2,000 wager.

St Pancras. Currently undergoing a £600 million transformation to become terminus for the Channel Tunnel Rail Link, it will expand from six to thirteen platforms. More bad luck? Its 300-room Midland Grand Hotel failed to conceal the noise and dirt of the railway below and it closed in 1935. It became offices. They shut. High-speed train Project Rio from Manchester was *the* railway success story of 2004. The Strategic Railway Authority snuffed it out.

Chapter Five

Crime and punishment

With speed of transit and ease of access, railways allow the criminal fraternity opportunities to travel for pursuance of their nefarious activities and a means of a quick getaway. Here are Great Train Robbery villains feted as latter-day Robin Hoods; mystery gas-attack assailant flaps; the Kray Twins' relocated InterCity legend; a chilling Tube tale which comes true; fanatical apocalyptical sect; homicidal boxcar Hell's Angels types and loitering Venusian; plus the usual stupid, ingenious, humorous and bizarre human suspects.

The Krays

It might seem obvious for a crime chapter to begin with the Great Train Robbery, but why? Its exponents were not 'A' list villains and the criminal status of the only one whose name is remembered today, Ronnie Biggs, was dismissed not so long ago by his persecutor, former Detective Superintendent Jack Slipper, as nothing more than 'a teaboy, second class.'

No, let's start at the top and they don't come any classier or crueller than the notorious Kray twins, who travelled by rail. At least they did for one infamous visit to Newcastle upon Tyne in February 1967. Here the myths of that Geordie excursion have been hyped and twisted out of all recognition and the truth is more bizarre than the legends of Tyneside club land. Our story even begins with a rail link, for a man found shot dead in the back seat of a Mark 10 Jaguar under a railway bridge in the early hours of 5 January 1967, was Angus Sibbert, renowned as the one-armed bandit king of the north-east. Two men were tried and convicted for the crime, but it was the Krays who were first approached to carry out the killing. The mobsters declined through loyalty to one of their own former East End friends, Paddy Hallett, Sibbert's £300-a-week bodyguard. Things got ugly when the Mr X who had ordered Sibbert's demise took exception to Hallett's giving evidence and he was viciously attacked on the night of 17 February 1967. The next morning Hallett rang the Krays in London and said he needed help.

Without further ado, the Krays arrived at Newcastle Central at 7 p.m. that night. The first myth of this fateful reunion was that Superintendent Jack Vinton met the twins and escorted them across the bridge and put them straight back on a train south. 'We divvn't need you sort here, bonny lads,' he explained. 'We've enough criminals of wor own.' Another version of the run-you-out-of-town scenario portrayed Vinton as having found the pair in La Dolce Vita, a famous night-club of the time, and summoned a waiter to present them with a railway timetable, open at the relevant page, on a silver platter.

A more modern belief transformed the real reason for the visit into a bid to take over the lucrative fruit machine business in the workingmen's clubs, but the police told them straight-facedly that in that case they would have to appear before the committee of each and every one of the four hundred clubs in the region. A compilation of this and other such myths provided the basis for the classy cult film of 1971, *Get Carter*, starring Michael Caine. (Not a lot of people know that).

Back to the social call on Hallett. After leaving their bags at a hotel, the Krays paid their respects to old chum Paddy, his Geordie wife and children. Meanwhile, burly gentlemen with barely-disguised hardware were arriving from throughout the north of England and Scotland. By 10 p.m. they were busy trawling the clubs, searching for the man who had ordered both Sibbert's killing and Paddy's stabbing. According to one version they found Mr X, and Vinton suggested the rivals got together privately to sort out their grievances. The upshot of which was that Hallett was compensated for the slashing and the Krays paid for the trouble they were put to. The Krays returned on the 11 a.m. train the next day.[1]

A Krays' associate, Eric Mason, recalls either a separate and earlier visit to Newcastle or a garbled version of the trip already detailed. Whatever, a party of seven arrived by train, having been invited by American singer Billy Daniels, who was appearing at La Dolce Vita. Daniels joined the Krays' party after his show, as did Angus Sibbert, later to be gunned down after leaving the same club. According to this alternative train of events, accumulated legend avers that a rival team of heavies, already running protection rackets on Tyneside, feared the Krays were muscling in to extend their underworld sphere, and sent them packing with the threat never to return. Ex-mobster Mason said: 'Newcastle was an excuse for quite a pleasant couple of days socialising. It was purely a social call. Every city in Britain claims to have run the Krays out of town. The Krays were never interested in extending their interests beyond London.'[2]

Captain Cutlass

In a reverse move, north-east port Hartlepool can claim to have a lesser-known legend than its world-renowned claim to have hanged a monkey during the Napoleonic wars, believing it to be a French spy. In the early Sixties a local reporter hyped a provincial gang of minor criminal misfits and sold Hartlepool as 'Little Chicago' to a headline-happy national newspaper world. The Turquoise Gang's leader liked to be known as Captain Cutlass, and in the reflected glory of the lurid glare of disproportionate infamy, announced that he was going to London to sort out its underworld empires and leaders. The swashbuckling Cutlass travelled by train only to find London's criminal fraternity did not like the cut of his jib. He allegedly got no farther than the barrier at King's Cross station before being unceremoniously turfed back on the next train to Teesside. Last I heard, he had emigrated and become a millionaire scrap dealer in New Zealand under his real name of John Padgett.

The Great Train Robbery

Only the coshing of the have-a-go driver marred the Great Train Robbery from producing a gang of bona fide folk heroes. By any yardstick it was a superbly audacious crime.

There was a certain grandeur about the plot to halt a southbound mail train in the Buckinghamshire darkness on 8 August 1963, at a signal tampered with to show a red aspect. Ingenuity netted booty to the value of £2,631,648 – a huge sum 38 years ago (worth around £33M today). For many it captured the imagination, while others sympathised with 57-year-old driver Jack Mills, struck over the head when he refused to follow the gang's orders. Mills was awarded £250 by the Post Office and returned to work on less onerous duties. He died in 1970 of leukaemia and pneumonia, while the coroner felt impelled to emphasise that his death had nothing to do with the coshing. Yet the belief persists that it did. Also worth emphasising is that the robbers did not carry any firearms, yet received savage sentences and Ronald Biggs still languishes in jail.

At the time, most of the nation could recite the names of each and every one of the fifteen-strong gang. Today only that of Ronnie Biggs (and for older people, maybe Buster Edwards) is remembered. Biggs, sentenced to twenty-five years for conspiracy and thirty years for armed robbery, was sent to Wandsworth jail, from where he escaped after serving only fifteen months of his sentence. He fled to Australia and then moved to Brazil, from where he defied justice for years before giving himself up to UK authorities. Earlier, Detective Superintendent Jack Slipper flew to Rio de Janeiro in 1974 and arrested Biggs, but the fugitive beat off extradition because of a loophole in the law – he had a son, Michael, by lover Raimunda.

The extradition issue was put to John Mills, son of driver Jack, who in June 1997 told a newspaper: 'I've never given up hope of seeing Biggs returned to Britain to finish serving his sentence. He should be made to pay the price.' [3] But by the October he had mellowed to saying Biggs deserved punishment, but that he would still be a 'bit sorry' if Biggs was brought back.[4]

Eddy Robinson made the headlines when he opened a Great Train Robbery theme pub adjacent to Darlington Bank Top station in County Durham. Rail bosses and union leaders were supposedly furious over the name 'Buster's'. Inside, cuttings recalling the robbery adorned the walls. Coincidentally, Ronald 'Buster' Edwards was a club owner himself at the time of the robbery. When second-man David Whitby left the locomotive cab to query the red light, Edwards bundled him down the embankment and pinioned him to the ground. Railtrack spokesman David Potter was quoted as saying the pub name was 'offensive and in very bad taste.' Pub boss Robinson denied causing offence and countered: 'It's just like calling a pub after Robin Hood or Dick Turpin. They were robbers but are part of folklore.' [5] Phil Collins' portrayal of Edwards in the film *Buster* made the criminal almost cuddly; such is the celluloid transformation which seduces our perceptions. A special rail-connected irony is that I last heard that Edwards ran a flower stall at London's

Waterloo station and the heist was planned at the Ship and Blue Ball pub in Boundary Street, a stone's throw from Liverpool Street station.

Yet Robinson has a valid point, with footplate men themselves to back him up. Virgin 'High-Speed Train' driver Alf Manktelow was joint owner of new 7½-inch gauge Talyllyn Railway 0-4-4T steam locomotive *Robert Snooks*. According to Alf, Snooks was the last highwayman to be hanged in Britain. Buried on Boxmoor Common, alongside the WCML, he was a legendary figure among generations of Midland region crews, especially those based at Bletchley and Watford. 'When I first moved on to the footplate,' said Alf, 'I was quickly made aware that I should doff my cap when passing the site of the highwayman's grave.'[6]

Robinson was also sympathetic to Biggs' plight: 'I appreciate justice has to be seen to be done, but Ronnie should only return if he can strike a deal over his sentence.' In fact, in a media coup, *The Sun* newspaper brought Biggs back to Britain in a blaze of publicity, the broken fugitive having suffered two strokes and a minor heart attack. Scandalously this seriously ill man remains in prison to this day.

But to close this episode, Biggs, when asked to contribute to an art exhibition on the theme of stars' bodies at Salford Museum, Greater Manchester, sent his fingerprints.[7]

The Venusian Train Robbery

Railway stations are places where you encounter some weird people, and I don't mean trainspotters. Venusians, for instance.

Roosevelt railroad station in Sao Paulo, Brazil, was one city location where Aladino Felix had such a rendezvous and was to develop something of a criminal interest in railway practice.[8] Felix had been one of two men to encounter five saucer-shaped objects hovering over the mountains near Parana, Brazil, in 1952. Felix revisited the spot on the following few nights and on the third a craft returned, landed and he was invited aboard. The saucer captain, a being who looked ordinary and human, persuaded him they were Venusians with friendly intentions. In March 1953 his chum the captain turned up on his doorstep in a cashmere suit, white shirt and blue tie. Thus began a long series of visits during which the man discussed UFOs, their mechanics and a master race to come. Felix's notes of these conversations were published in a book, *My Contact with Flying Saucers*, under the pseudonym Dino Kraspedon. As with most contactee literature it was generally dismissed as the ravings of a crackpot.

His real identity remained a mystery until in 1965 Kraspedon surfaced as self-styled prophet Aladino Felix. When he warned of a disaster about to take place in Rio de Janeiro, a month later floods and landslides claimed six hundred lives. In 1967 he was on television soberly predicting the assassinations of Martin Luther King and Robert Kennedy. From hare-brained author he was elevated in status through the uncanny accuracy of both his major and minor predictions. When he began foretelling an outbreak of violence, murders and bombings in Brazil, it was not thought odd when a wave of bizarre terrorism began. In Sao Paolo an army headquarters, newspaper office and American Consulate were among the bombing targets. There was a wave of bank robberies and an armoured payroll train was held up.

Eventually the Brazilian police rounded up eighteen gang members. Their bomb expert turned out to be a 25-year-old policeman, Jessee Morais. As the truth emerged, it was learned they had planned to assassinate top government officials and eventually take over Brazil. Morais had been promised the role of police chief in the new government and guess who was the ringleader – Aladino Felix!

Arrested on 22 August 1968, the flying saucer prophet and revolutionary declared: 'I was sent here as an ambassador to Earth from Venus. My friends from space will come here and free me and avenge my arrest. You can look for tragic consequences to humanity when the flying saucers invade this planet.' [9]

Remember Mr Felix next time you're accosted by a weirdo on the platform. He might just be a spaceman or someone wanting you to help hold up a bullion train.

It's a knockout

In 1991, the travel pages of a national broadsheet passed on a warning which would strike a chord in seasoned folklorists. On the surface it read as a cautionary tale for tourists abroad.[10] Diane Pepper reported that she had met two girls on a train travelling across northern Italy via Venice and Ljubljana, who shared a compartment alone. They placed their money and passports in their bumbags and used these as pillows to sleep, heads facing away from the door. They awoke in the morning to find their passports and bumbags on the floor, with all their money missing. They failed to see how anyone could have sneaked in, removed the bags under their heads, gone through them and then scooted without disturbing them.

Helpful after the event, the Italian guard produced a card in English, French and German explaining that they had been the victims of an international gang of thieves, well known on that route. Apparently, the criminals used some form of knock-out spray, aimed through the vent in the door, rendering the passenger temporarily unconscious while they rifled through belongings.

Two days later a tabloid presented a condensed account with Pisa, Italy, as the crime scene for thieves spraying chloroform into train sleeper compartments and then robbing unconscious passengers.[11] In 1992, a gang robbed seventeen Britons on a French train after spraying gas into their compartment. Dubbed 'The Sleeper Gang,' they stole £1,630 from one family before robbing a further twelve Brits before stopping the Boulogne to Avignon overnight train and fleeing. Victim Mark Atherton, of Westhoughton, Lancashire, said: 'We were all out cold.'

The scam, if real, had relocated to eastern Europe by 1997, where overnight passengers were being warned against thieves prepared to gas them with ether and use knives to rob them. Two years previously a spate of such robberies had been reported in Poland and Russia and reports suggested the problem was recurring.

Jennifer Cox, of the guidebook publisher Lonely Planet, said: 'Robberies using gas were common two years ago and the signs are that they are becoming more common again.' She had heard such travellers' tales from Russia, Romania, Hungary and Bulgaria.[12]

Sounds plausible unless you are versed in phantom gasser lore. Over forty-three bizarre days in 1933–4, towns in Botetourt County, Virginia, USA, were exposed to incidents where an unknown person or persons sprayed a peculiar, nauseating gas into people's homes, causing several forms of symptoms. Though the attacks may have been genuine, there was speculation that the gasser might have been imaginary. Escalation spread to neighbouring Roanoke County. Ten years later Mattoon, Illinois, experienced an almost identical outbreak from a phantom anaesthetist.[13] Michael Goss' excellent study tells us much about mystery assailant 'flaps.' Another researcher, Willy Smith, set out to debunk the mass hysteria hypothesis despite twenty-five claims over eighteen days without motivation and no one being apprehended or identified.[14]

The Press also continues to publish news items of British truckers gassed in their cabs. These are always abroad (xenophobia?) and the most recent development has not theft but smuggling of asylum seekers (the latest bogeymen) as the *modus operandi*.[15]

The invisible killer

When a Japanese cult launched a nerve-gas attack on the Tokyo subway, observers could be fooled into thinking it was entirely novel. Not so.

Though utilising a 'harmless' bacteriological agent, *Bacillus subtili yar niger*, travellers on the New York subway were surreptitiously subjected to tests by the US Army in June 1966. The exercise was designed to assess the vulnerability of American subway systems to bacteriological warfare. The selected substance was darkened with charcoal and then sprinkled on the platform, while more small quantities of the germ were sprayed from the street through gratings to be sucked into the station. At one stage, a train was covered by a cloud of the agent, but passengers alighting merely brushed their clothing, glanced at the grating as culprit and carried on as normal.[16]

Before the millennium, many apocalyptic cults flourished and, perhaps, the most dangerous one was the Japanese Aum Ahrinrikyo ('The True Teachings of Aum'), whose nerve-gas attack on 20 March 1995, occurred at Kasumigaseki, the hub of a rail system carrying five million people a day.

Folklorists have had a fascination for apocalyptic movements through the ages and their appeal. We used to happily celebrate Guy Fawkes and fellow conspirators' thwarted efforts, but these days terrorism has no mitigating aspects. And gunpowder is one thing; nerve-gas is something else. German scientists discovered sarin accidentally in the Thirties. Its deadly qualities made it even too dangerous during the Second World War, though they had manufactured it in quantity. It can be made in the form of two liquids – clear, odourless and almost harmless – but mixed, a pound can easily kill 10,000 people, particularly in a crowded, confined space such as a rush-hour underground station.

The cult's leader, Shoko Asahara, claimed an improbable alliance of Freemasons, Jews, Americans and the British royal family were preparing a nuclear attack on Japan in order to create a wartime prosperity. The Aum cult knew nuclear weaponry was expensive but a biological alternative would be cheap by comparison.

Kasumigaseki was chosen as its exits are across the road from Japan's parliament, near to police headquarters and the finance and trade ministries, and quite close to Emperor Akhito's palace. Around 8 a.m., five two-man Aum teams boarded different crowded subway trains, all scheduled minutes later to converge at Kasumigaseki. As their trains arrived, they placed lethal bags on floors or parcel racks, punctured them with umbrella tips, alighted hastily, took antidotes and scuttled off to Aum safe houses. Their aim had been to disrupt or perhaps avoid a planned raid on their Kamikuishiki mountain headquarters, perhaps learned through infiltrators, planned for 22 March. A horrified world saw passengers staggering from the exits, choking and vomiting. Eleven died and 5,000 ended up in hospital.[17]

And everything comes full circle. Just as the US military performed its experiment on the New York subway in 1966, almost thirty years later, one month after the Japan horror, a secret mock attack with nerve-gas was staged on the American city's subway system. The conclusion was that with present or foreseeable technology, there was no defence against sarin. You have been warned.

Maniac on the platform

Collector of and commentator on contemporary legend Mick Goss was serendipitously able to overhear a remarkable new urban belief tale on London Transport's Circle Line in 1985.

One woman was regaling her companion with a scary scenario where a homicidal psychopath had taken to pushing young female strangers under subway trains. Goss named him the 'Maniac on the Platform'.

Apparently, the serial murderer would stand among the crowd on Tube platforms behind his intended victim and as the train swept out of the darkness would stealthily give her a firm shove, toppling her beneath the train. At this point in the narrative, the teller raised her palms to chest level, miming the pushing action with grim determination. Her action was to emphasise the thrust was deliberate and not the jostling seasoned Underground travellers are accustomed to. She even did an action replay, hissing in duplicate to emphasise the true horror: 'This is deliberate! He does it deliberately.'

But that was not all. His *modus operandi* selected no specific station but the equally random victims were always girls. There was no description of him because no one could identify the perpetrator of the crimes who melted away undetected and, of course, these had been hushed up by the authorities so as not to spread alarm or encourage copycat killings.

And there's more. The narrator announced that the story was true because she 'actually knew' someone to whom it happened. Well, not quite, she clarified. Her friend knew this doctor whose daughter was about to be married and it was she who was making an unintentional journey when it happened.

There is no need here to get bogged down with urban lore analysis: suffice to say we have the usual authority figure (doctor) to give the tale an element of assumed veracity and on top of the horror, her unfortunate whim to travel elicits pathos, even the maudlin. Many are apprehensive of Tube travel, feel claustrophobic, fear assault and are anxious of encountering the insane. The Maniac on the Platform is the latest in a long line of subterranean bogeymen: muggers, beggars, tramps, bombers, soccer hooligans, molesters, druggies, cultists and other assorted weirdoes. Despite tens of thousands using the London Underground daily, it is still a focus for all manner of rumours and anxieties.[18]

Since Goss's 1985 eavesdropping there have been several cases of persons temporarily or permanently deranged attempting to push random victims under oncoming trains on the Tube. Two are known to have succeeded and one victim died subsequently.

Almost certainly neither assailant had come into contact with the Maniac on the Platform legend, never mind being influenced by it. What is significant is that the rumour had achieved reality; life imitated art, fact rewrote fiction. Folklore terms this process 'ostension'.

My source for the first of these heinous crimes actually begins 'A maniac ... ' and tells how an attacker pounced on a stranger from behind, without exchanging a word, pushed him into the path of a train, fled from the platform, vaulted a ticket barrier and ran out of the station. He was chased from Finsbury Park Tube station in north London, but escaped in the side streets. Meanwhile, his unnamed victim had slipped through a gap in the tracks into an inspection pit as the train rumbled over him and survived, though suffering burns from contact with the live rail. Detective Chief Inspector David Shiperlee, of the British Transport Police, said: 'He acted like a complete madman. The victim was pushed violently from behind just as a train came in. By sheer good fortune he wasn't killed. Why it happened is a complete mystery. There was no conversation between them.' The thirty-year-old victim had been on his way to church with his brother. Both he and his attacker were black.[19]

In another horrifying incident, in what the judge was to call a 'ruthless and deliberate' crime, during the evening rush-hour at Mile End Tube station on 13 September 2002, Stephen Soans-Wade, 36, grinned before hurling stranger Christophe Duclos into the path of a fast-moving train. In the pandemonium which ensued, the deranged junkie calmly walked up to a London Underground employee and said: 'I am waiting for the cops. I was the one who pushed someone on to the tracks. Voices in my head told me to do it.' Frenchman Duclos, 37, suffered multiple injuries and died in hospital three days later. Soans-Wade, a loner from a County Durham housing estate, who had fled from an abusive father and racialist insults at school (his mother being Anglo-Indian), developed alcoholism and an escalating heroin and crack cocaine addiction, before coming into contact with mental health services in east London. The Old Bailey was told he was determined to get into hospital 'at all costs' after claiming that demonic voices were ordering him to kill. The court heard a long catalogue of street crime, violence, medication and sectioning. There was alarm that medical negligence failed to protect the public from a man with an astonishing history of mental problems. Yet psychiatrists diagnosed a personality disorder, but believed that he was not mad.

On the fateful day, Soans-Wade claimed he was suicidal and asked to be readmitted to St Clement's, Bow. He vanished before doctors could see him. After roaming the Underground he spotted Duclos. He later told doctors he was plagued by voices instructing him to kill and chose the Frenchman because he was alone and wearing black. Soans-Wade, who had admitted manslaughter on the grounds of diminished responsibility but denied murder, showed no emotion as the unanimous verdict was delivered.[20] Judge Martin Stephens jailed Soans-Wade for life on 24 February 2004.[21]

Previously on the national rail network, five-times-married mathematics genius Dr Anthony Bowl, with an IQ of 150, smiled as he was sent to Broadmoor in 1987. His obsession with blondes had led him to shove forty-year-old Margaret Pucci under an express at crowded Wimbledon station, south London.[22]

In November, 1999, 41-year-old Alan Casey said he shoved a man under a train at Hatch End, Middlesex, in order to save the world.

I have on file more flesh and blood cases from around the world, including another blonde pushed under a subway train in Manhattan, New York, USA, by a schizophrenic, and a mentally-ill Laotian who believed he was a reincarnation of Bruce Lee, who sent an old-age pensioner to his death on the Paris Metro. Toronto suffered six cases over six months in 1997–8 until a man was arrested, charged with aggravated assault and ordered to undergo psychiatric assessment

Goss, in his ponderings, mused: 'Or perhaps the Maniac was born in some thriller writer's brain.' [23]

When Goss wrote those prophetic words in 1985, Tobias Hill was fourteen years old but grew up to publish a literary thriller in 1999, *Underground*, being the story of a Polish Underground worker, Casimir, who discovers that a murderer is pushing young women in front of trains. One of his potential victims is a beautiful but disturbed waif called Alice. Her overground life is spent involved in petty crime and clubbing; her underground life is sleeping rough in the cavernous Kensington Town subway station which closed in 1924.[24] Incidentally, Hill's earlier book *Midnight in the City of Clocks* is a sequence of poems about Japan, London and urban myths.

Another closed station, British Museum, was the setting for a mid-Seventies feature film *The Death Line* (also known as *Raw Meat*) starring Donald Pleasance. Its plot centred upon an earth fall which trapped both male and female Victorian navvies in the abandoned station. However, they were not sealed in sufficiently to stop them developing cannibal tactics through to the present, when they would snatch the last passenger of the day from Russell Square station platform, and dragging them back to British Museum via side branch tunnels. Their only language was the words, 'Mind the doors.'

Enjoy your next Tube trip.

Freightening

With friendly 'bulls', hobo slang for railroad security guards, older hoboes even get a helping hand in US marshalling yards. These were itinerants who over twenty years or so criss-crossing America could cover all its 200,000 miles of track. They regarded it as a right to roam.

In a chilling article on how this unconventional lifestyle of camaraderie turned sour, Nancy Nusser wrote about Hippy John, whose philosophy was: 'It's freedom from the rules everyone has to obey.' Taking to the tracks around the time of the anti-Vietnam War movement, she notes that 'riding the rails had acquired a mythology all of its own and hoboes were seen as rebel spirits conducting life in the best traditions of pioneer libertarian America.' [25] But just as the Sixties coin had love-and-peace hippies on one side and violence-and-worse-violence Hell's Angels on the other, the homeless hoboes of today have to contend with a psychopathic subculture.

Crusading police officer Bob Grandinetti, of Spokane, noted a rapidly escalating carnage of bodies turning up on the tracks. In the late Eighties it was presumed the severed limbs resulted from railroad accidents, but by the mid-Nineties the tally was in the hundreds. In the face of official indifference into what he inferred was a nationwide gang killings epidemic, Grandinetti found out by winning hoboes' confidence that it was the work of the FTRA. The letters appeared as sinister graffiti on bridges beside railway tracks and he learnt it stood for the Freight Train Riders of America, which he discovered was founded by a Vietnam veteran, Daniel Boone, and had developed into a 2,000-strong federation; its members identifiable by different coloured bandanas to denote their area of operation. As many as three hundred killings of hoboes have been attributed to the group composed of primarily white men with racist sympathies, along with a massive food-stamp scam and drug running.

When, in 1990, Barry 'Brakeshoe' Schwartz wanted to attend a meeting of the Hobo Club in Beverley Hills, a bus driver refused to allow him on as he was too scruffy, so he paid fifteen dollars to take a cab ride. Barry doubtless felt honoured to be rejected, for during the week he pursued his career as a video-maker, while spending the weekend in down-and-out gear jumping freight trains and 'hanging out.' [26] The likes of Barry have jobs, families, cars and good credit; they just enjoy being leisure-time tramps. Around 4,000 of these train-hoppers attend regular meetings and benefit from a *Hobo News* newsletter on rail travel. The yuppie weekend glamour is decried by railway companies as setting a bad example to youngsters injured by train wheels, nicknamed 'salami slicers' by the association.

Folklorists would see all this as an extension of gypsy wanderlust within the white-collar community and Sheri Doyle completed her thesis at the University of California while on such travels, concluding that hobo culture is a serious anthropological phenomenon and part of a distinguished tradition, even if boxcar riding is only at weekends.

More ticket-less travel

Borderline folklore definitely, but with sheer invention, mob intervention and bogeyman aspect, the cross-border smuggling of humans is worth a mention. Immigration officials estimate thousands of Channel Tunnel trains could have been used for the dangerous but lucrative trade of bringing bogus asylum seekers into Britain. The migrants, who begin their journey in such places as Milan, are sewn into the canvas sides of freight trains by using 'invisible' stitching. Organised by Italian gangsters, the illegal immigrants can barely move during the 48-hour trip and pay as much as £15,000 each. Willesden freight terminal is the main destination and one group of fifty refugees were caught there trying to escape. Inspector Dave Farrelly, of the British Transport Police, said: 'Some people have been seriously injured while trying to escape from the trains. On some days we have reports of evidence of three wagons a day being used.'[27]

Milan features in another tale, as does the belief in aphrodisiacs. Customs men, who boarded a train from Brussels to Milan at the French border, believed that they had caught two cigar smugglers, but found the 24 smokes were actually far more valuable tigers' penises. Far East trade sees dried big cat willies as a sexual stimulant, but exporting them is illegal.[28]

The next item can be taken with a pinch of salt – or curry powder more appropriately. Those chroniclers of commuter woes, Margolis and Morris, say that in the Indian state of Bihar, 'ticketless travel is especially popular, and foreigners on trains there often find themselves the only ticket holders.' But then they quote the sorry state a peasant from Bihar found himself in. With all the hallmarks of a contemporary legend, we learn Ramchandra Kasiram was jailed after being caught without a ticket. The improbable story tells how officials lost his papers and so he was never called to trial, spending 29 years 'on remand' in prison. In another twist, it was only after he had been eventually released that civil liberties lawyers learned of his plight.[29]

This next story may be true or apocryphal, but I like its wit and brevity. American humorist William Edgar ('Bill') Nye was travelling by train with poet James Whitcomb Riley when he spotted an appraoching ticket inspector. Prankster Nye, who was looking after the tickets, stunned his friend by claiming to have lost one of them and instructed him to hide under the seats. Obeying under protest, Riley hid, only for Nye to hand the official both tickets. 'Who is the other ticket for?' asked the puzzled inspector. 'For my friend,' said Nye, beckoning to his pal's presence under the seat with one hand, while tapping his head to indicate his companion's lunacy with the other.[30]

A £3,000 fine was imposed on German train fare dodger Dominic Ess, who claimed the harshness of the punishment resulted from the judge having discovered Ess was having sex with his daughter, and so the fine was reduced to the customary £60 on appeal in Munich.[31] Ticket collector Yomi Tamoto, 52, was sacked from his railway job after thirty years' service after being caught on a train in Tokyo without a ticket.[32]

Nearer to home, ticket inspector Arthur Harriott, 39, made Prime Minister's wife Cherie Blair pay a £10 penalty fare for travelling without a ticket. Harriott claimed his subsequent sacking was because the high-profile incident had damaged the company's image, but Thameslink claimed his dismissal was for 'other incidents' which were 'classified.' Harriott observed sanguinely: 'I have gone from hero to zero.'[33]

Mixed behaviour

Compulsions

Fortean favourite fetishism finds itself well at home on the railway network. The strange ways of 29-year-old Lars Hagman came to the attention of Bedlington magistrates in Northumberland, who banned him from every bus and train in Britain. Hagman would stalk passengers by sitting behind them and stroking their hair. After a year-long spree he was taken to court for pestering a terrified sixteen-year-old and placed on probation for eighteen months and ordered to seek medical help. He also admitted taking photographs of the back of girls' heads on buses for eight years.[34]

Down Under, an unnamed 29-year-old woman on a train in Melbourne in 1998 heard a snipping sound behind her only to discover her ponytail was gone. Police identified the suspect and when they searched his house found eleven ponytails, but not that of his most recent victim. The equally unnamed 34-year-old man admitted approaching various women and offering up to one thousand dollars for their hair.[35]

A defence solicitor told Horseferry Road magistrates that 25-year-old student Jonothan Rosewood claimed voices in his head told him to kiss women's bottoms. The schizophrenic sex pest who stalked total strangers heard the JP's voice telling him he was banned from the entire London Underground network.[36]

Letters complaining about late trains rebounded on jobless Robert Buckner, 37, known as the Erotic Poet. A note to Connex contained such strong language that the railway company called in police. Buckner, said to have very high IQ, was sentenced at Maidstone crown court after a jury previously found him guilty of sending an indecent article through the post. The jury heard that he had been cautioned by police for a similar offence. Judge David Griffiths warned him: 'If you do this sort of thing again you will be back before the courts and suffer the consequences, which will be jail.' Buckner responded: 'What I wrote is pornographic and I deliberately wrote it so the reader would think it was a fair letter to start with, but then halfway down find the abuse.'[37]

Drug and alcohol abuse

When nineteen-year-old Bob Gould Simpkins staggered on to the tracks between Saltaire and Bingley stations, West Yorkshire, forcing two trains to stop, British

Transport Police invoked an ancient law. His escapade, while acting under the influence of the drug LSD, led to a charge of obstructing an engine from the Malicious Damage Act of 1861, one of several Victorian laws introduced to deal with railway trespass and damage. Prosecutor Richard Hodgson said that in the past few people would have survived the offence to be taken to court. Simpkins was sentenced to fourteen days in a young offenders' institution.[38]

Streaking is a contemporary tradition and Newcastle United supporters Alan Heavey and John Tolan ran naked through first-class carriages on a London to Edinburgh night express chanting 'Toon Army.' They admitted being drunk and disorderly and were fined £100 and £200 respectively.[39]

Ineptitude

As he left a store, burglar Jan Huese spotted a huge model train set in the toy department. Giving in to temptation, Huese was still playing with it when staff at the Berlin shop arrived to open up and he was handed over to police.[40]

A man who planned to bomb railway lines was jailed for nine years at the Old Bailey. His counsel told the court that James Shaw had a pathological interest in bombs and hates everyone. He added: 'He hates everyone equally. That is his problem.'[41]

Ingenuity

Starting with the fine line between ineptitude and ingenuity, it seems luggage racks worth £120,000 had been ripped out of trains on the London-Tilbury-Southend line and used at barbecues in Essex gardens. The racks are virtually useless, explained a spokesman, being made from aluminium, which melts, and have a poisonous coating.[42]

Discovering that a ban on Easter Day trading did not apply to railway stations, a wily magistrate – of all people – put a mock steam engine in front of his garden centre and opened up as usual. However, Arun district council took the owner to court, where he was fined £7,500, later reduced to £5,000 on appeal. Magistrates heard that when inspected, the 'train' consisted of a converted milk float with a platform beside it and curtain rails for track.[43]

When an Exeter to London Waterloo express raced past her home in Basingstoke, a housewife spotted a young man sitting on the buffers. After telephoning her local station, emergency messages were flashed ahead, but the train whizzed through Hook with the young man giving a regal wave to passengers on the platform. Transport police finally apprehended him when the train stopped at a red light. He resumed his journey aboard the train, handcuffed to the guard's van. 'Actually, I often travel this way,' he explained.[44]

A lawyer stuck in a Moscow traffic jam made a hoax bomb call to hold up his train.[45]

Humour

When music hall singer Percy French missed a lucrative booking due to the inability of Ireland's West Clare Railway to run even an approximation of its timetable, he put his unplanned overnight stay to good use. His song, *Are ye right there, Michael?*, poked unmerciless fun at the West Clare, but the company was not amused when the song became highly popular and sued. Luckily the jury was formed solidly of West Clare customers and they found in French's favour. Their judgement was that the song was not only fair comment, but if anything, was flattering to the West Clare.[46]

A correspondent asked why the standard gauge on a railway is 4 feet 8½ inches. In addition to academic – but conflicting answers (see Chapter Three), Bob Irwin shrewdly pointed out that it is the distance between the neck and ankles of a damsel in distress.[47]

Bizarre

Forteana with more than an echo of coincidence draws together cases of westbound passenger trains, travelling at night through desert on track owned by the Southern Pacific Railroad, where both trains were derailed on a bridge diverted into a river bed. Both involved tricking the signalling system by maintaining an electrical current between the two split rail ends, where inside spikes were pulled from eleven ties. Apparently photographs of the two wrecks were all but indistinguishable. The most recent sabotage was in Hyder, Arizona, on 9 October 1995, where one of the crew was killed and more than a hundred injured. FBI investigators found that two weeks before the Hyder crash, a specialist railway magazine, *Southern Pacific Tramline*, had run a detailed account of a Thirties sabotage at Harney, Nevada, on 12 August 1939. Despite a list of Arizona subscribers, there were no firm leads and notes found near the scene, with a diatribe against the siege at Waco, Texas, and Ruby Ridge, Idaho – both flashpoints in militia folklore – signed by the 'Sons of Gestapo', were thought to be a deliberate red herring. However, during the 1939 investigation some suspicion was cast upon Nazi sympathisers, but this time attention focussed on Amtrak employees as there was a plan to close part of the Southern Pacific, with the prospect of redundancies.[48]

Still in the USA, a train crew made an emergency stop at Darien, Connecticut, at 2.30 a.m. as they believed they had run over a body. Directing their torches to the track, a naked man lying in the space between the rails jumped up and attacked the three crew; one being bitten twice on the leg and cut on his face while a second had his face bitten. Artay Drinks, 20, of Bridgeport, ran into woods but was arrested about an hour later and booked on assault and trespass charges.[49]

Statistics

Away from contemporary legend and the light-hearted, latest statistics reveal crime on the railways has soared over recent years. Figures compiled by the British Transport Police show that the total number of crimes reported on trains, stations and railway property rose from 107,769 in 1998–9 to 123,463 in 2003–4. Sadly the

Court Poaching.

The illustration from the author's book of humorous local episodes depicts how collaborator Paul Jermy visualised my response to the poacher's phonecall.

detection rate fell from 30 to 21 percent, but more pertinently crime elsewhere has been falling, which shows a particularly worrying trend.[50]

Court Poaching

To wind up this chapter of court proceedings, here are some sentences drawn from the author's previous book of local episodes.

A splendid walkway now exists northwards from Hart Station, created upon a former railway line where once coal trains ran in abundance. As the pits closed, the line's role diminished and unemployment rose throughout the district. Within south-east Durham crime also increased. Going back to the mid-Sixties, when I was a junior reporter, I recall that the bench of Peterlee magistrates sat in Hartlepool on at least one occasion (the reason for this lost in my memory). The justices of the peace from Easington district were very different from the staid, middle-class Hartlepool contingent. Very down to earth.

When a case enfolded regarding the sorry plight of a man caught with a gun, poaching along the Hart to Haswell railway line, there was an almost unbelievable laughter in court at one point. The hapless miscreant was discovered about his nefarious deed and a chase began. After a pursuit of some distance along the tracks, the wrongdoer was confronted by the pursuer's father, a farmer with a pitchfork, who decided to use his agricultural implement as a weapon and stabbed the chap with the prongs. As mirth subsided in the courtroom, I was astounded by the casual and candid way in which the chairman of the bench nodded to me in the press box, saying something like: 'This'll make a cracking story in the Mail tonight, son, won't it?'

And so it did.

And so good was it, that when lobbying for the walkway in the early Eighties, I recalled the court case in print to leaven the serious side to finding a useful purpose for the disused stretch of land. On the evening the article appeared, I had just turned in when the bedside phone rang around 11 p.m.. It was the literally injured party calling. Rather than being annoyed that this minor criminal episode in his life had been resurrected, he wanted to tell me that it had been spotted in the *Hartlepool Mail* and he and his mates had spent the evening toasting his reactivated celebrity. Drinking to the memory very fully, judging by the law-breaker's slurring and riotous carousing in the background.[51]

Chapter Six

Going loco

Names loom large in railway circles. Right from the start individual engines were named, a practice which doubtless originated from the days when horses drawing mineral wagons had named like Beauty, Jonty and Dobbin, and which has continued to this day, with commercial forces much in evidence as locomotives are named after customers or local heroes. The value of publicity similarly led railway companies to give crack expresses individuality by naming them. From nicknames for classes to claims of gender bending, all is grist for the enthusiasts' mill. Then there are the impostor engines which usurp identities and seekers after supposedly abandoned motive power lying buried by legend. Lastly the monarchy and the duchy.

A girl named *Russell*

Breaking a taboo? Ignoring a convention? Folk got hot under the collar over a sex change at the Welsh Highland Railway, when a steam loco named *Russell* was referred to as 'he' throughout an appeal leaflet. Locomotives, ships, cars and other such inanimate transport objects have by accepted custom always been regarded as female. So should the Hunslet 2-6-2T, built in 1906 and subject of a £30,000 restoration appeal, be referred to as a 'she'? Some WHR members argued that all locos should be female regardless of the gender of the person after whom they are named. Mark Seale, a WHR volunteer, said: 'This is no laughing matter. All steam engines are "she", whether they are called *Flying Scotsman, Princess Elizabeth* or *King George V*. Steam engines have been feminine ever since they were invented. No one's sure why.' James Hewett, chairman of the West Highland Railway (Portmadog), countered: 'For goodness sake, this thing is called *Russell*. The engine was named after a man and it is just silly to call him "she"! Calling *Russell* "she" is as daft as the man who called his son "Sue" in the country music song. When did you ever hear of a Jill Russell terrier? And what about Bertrand Russell? Or Russell Crowe? No one with half an ounce of sanity would ever get it wrong with them, so why make a mistake here?'[1] Er, what about film star Jane Russell? Page 3 girl Corrinne Russell? Oh, bugger being Devil's Advocate, it must be male!

In an attempt to defuse the situation, the WHR launched an online poll to try to resolve the matter. Voting was close throughout, with both 'he' and 'she' edging ahead at different times, but at the last minute as voting closed, the 'he' vote snatched victory by 78 votes to 77. The option to vote for 'it' came in a poor third at just 18. James Hewett commented: 'I don't know if this argument will ever be completely settled, but I reckon we're safe to carry on calling *Russell* "he." Anyway, he's such a special locomotive, we're happy for him to be the exception that proves the rule!'

A man named Jane

A fascinating case exists of a loco changing from male to female and back to male. This occurred through what folklorists term a 'mondegreen' or, as writer John Michell more descriptively named it, 'aural simulacra'. After arriving at Steamtown, Carnforth, for preservation in the early 1970s, a former British Gypsum steam engine carried the name *Jane Derbyshire* for twenty years. Original owner Dr Peter Beet was told that this was the name it carried during its industrial service days. But Dr Beet's son Christopher, who became its owner, learned the saddletank was actually named *J.N. Derbyshire* after Job Nightingale Derbyshire, chairman of the British Plaster Board in 1935, and that the erroneous plates were the result of a simple verbal misunderstanding! The loco and original plates were reunited in 1991.[2]

Buried treasure

It is a century since Furness Railway 0-6-0 No. 115 was going about its business when a chasm, caused by haematite mining subsidence, appeared beneath the track and swallowed it whole. This occurred at Lindal, near Barrow-in-Furness, on 22 October 1892. The hole was filled in, the line rebuilt and with an absence of oxygen to cause corrosion, the loco still lies there waiting for some enterprising souls to raise it. Being about two hundred feet down we are not talking of raising the *Titanic*.[3]

There are also unsubstantiated claims for more locos buried around Garsdale, Goathland, Wembley, Blackheath, Cambridge, Hartlepool and maybe your backyard.

There is the reputed loss of a loco on the Whitby to Pickering line, now the North Yorkshire Moors Railway, almost exactly midway between Goathland and Newtondale Halt, discernible by a change in the local vegetation. The identity of the unfortunate engine, which overturned while running bunker first, has been posited as a North Eastern Railway 0-4-4WT. National Railway Museum expert Philip Atkins, compiler of a record of engines which met violent ends, has written that all of the class have been accounted for, either being broken up or rebuilt as 0-6-0Ts. So what if anything lies beneath the Fen Bog soil?[4]

Paul Walshaw was taking part in a pub quiz when a question asked was: 'What is buried under Wembley stadium?' The answer was: 'A steam locomotive.' The question-master claimed the stadium was built on a tip and during construction one of the locos used in transporting material met a mishap.[5] David Kinsella confirmed the tale, believing a small tank loco took a tumble and was not considered worthy of repair and consequently buried. Doubtless the current redevelopment of the site will prove or disprove the errant machine's existence. Mr Kinsella also claimed that buried at Wembley are the remains of a giant tower begun by the Metropolitan Railway to challenge the Eiffel Tower in height by 150 feet. As few visitors attended the opening of the first level and money ran out, it was eventually dismantled and also buried.[6] I recall a *Quatermass* television programme many years ago suggesting exotically and wryly that Wembley was called the 'sacred turf' not through footballing glory or locomotive bereavement, but for some earth mysteries reason.

For sheer tenacity in following a rumour of a lost loco, the prize must go to Terry Sykes and Helen Smith. They followed the local lead given by railwayman Dick Fawcett, who found a loco chimney sticking out of the ground in the mid-Thirties. Local folklore at Garsdale contended that after a driver's error, his steed toppled down the embankment near Dandry Mire viaduct, and after attempts to recover it failed, the engine was covered with ballast and rubbish. On their third attempt, the plucky pair located the chimney. However, their hopes were dashed when a magnetic detector, loaned by Thorn EMI with two technicians, failed to locate anything large and metallic. Undaunted they set about removing the chimney for display and were surprised to find that it had been upside down. 'So it looks like the story of the engine is true, but as it toppled down the bank the chimney stuck in the clay and broke off,' the seekers wrote. 'The engine was almost certainly then recovered, leaving the chimney half buried and protruding.' They believe a man called Dick Fawcett dug down to the flange at the bottom and thought he had reached the smokebox top. 'In conclusion there never did appear to be enough room in the embankment to hide even a small locomotive, and to think that the Victorians were incapable of winching a small engine back up a 20-foot embankment is also underestimating their undoubted skills. But we badly wanted it to be there so we pursued it to the end. To the Victorian perpetrators of the joke, many, many thanks.'[7]

No work of railway folklore would be complete without mention of the hover train. Invented by Eric Laithwaite (1921–97), his development of the linear acceleration motor in the 1940s as the means of propulsion was coupled with the notion of magnetic levitation to give frictionless motion. A test track at least 3½ miles long was constructed at Earith on the bank of the Old Bedford River; coincidentally where in 1870 a contest was held to prove or disprove whether the Earth was flat or globular!. Magazine correspondent Colin Brown wrote: 'There were rumours in the area that both the track and a train overturned into the river due to subsidence, as the water table is only a few feet below ground.'[8] Despite the cost of running magnetic levitation, in addition to the unknown effects of a powerful magnetic field on human beings, a working 'maglev' system was in use between Birmingham airport and the railway station six hundred yards away between 1984 and 1991.[9] As is so often the case, Britons such as Laithwaite are world beaters at inventions, but sadly our leaders lack the will to exploit them.

On the subject of watery graves, it would be interesting to learn more of an ancient iron ore train supposedly dragged from Frogmore Lake, a huge flooded Victorian quarry in Westbury, Wiltshire, where for decades frustrated anglers had broken their rods on an uncatchable monster of the deep. When a JCB was brought in it hauled out a train and solved the mystery.[10]

Next two Scottish tales: Ludditism and health zealotry. Delivering his Royal Society 1985 lecture on 'The Development of Switched Reluctance Drives,' Professor P.J. Lawrenson showed a slide of Robert Davidson's battery-powered locomotive of

1842, which the inventor demonstrated on the Edinburgh and Glasgow Railway. It operated by way of a motor in which electromagnets attracted an otherwise inert rotor. Apparently 'the idea of a loco that did not depend on coal or the exertions of a fireman evidently raised fears for jobs, pits and communities,' wrote an anonymous contributor to a railway magazine, adding 'tradition has it that Davidson's machine was destroyed by "angry workmen".' [11] More recently, redundant 'Class 27' diesel-electric loco No. 27043 was allegedly wrapped in polythene and dumped. Records claim it to have been buried at Paterson's Tip, Mount Vernon, Glasgow. Its bizarre disposal on account of asbestos content does not answer why it alone met this fate as it was, and still is, quite simple to remove such contamination from same era locos. It is not recorded whether its burial was ceremonially accompanied by weapons and food for the hereafter as is traditional. Or fuel and a length of track for its diesel Valhalla.

After publishing the Garsdale account in *Folklore Frontiers*, I received a letter from Nigel Pennick recording a local event: 'The buried train story exists in Cambridge, where the lake – once a gravel pit – on Coldham's Common is said to contain a locomotive. This story amalgamates lost lands legends with buried locos. The loco was said to have been used on a narrow-gauge line used to haul gravel in the pit (unlikely). During a tea-break, the workers noticed a nearby stream flooding over the side of the deep pit, and fled from it. Water filled the pit, and the loco, as they say, "remains there to this day." Highly apocryphal.' [12]

This led me to suspect that, perhaps, every town has its lost loco legend. Somewhere down the line, I heard long, long ago as a boy that a narrow-gauge loco had derailed at West Hartlepool's waterworks site and it lies beneath the artificial, grassed embankment in Lancaster Road. Also the landscaping at Ward Jackson park was detritus brought by rail wagons when the town's docks were excavated and money raised for the destitute founder of West Hartlepool (he died before he could receive the cash) was used to beautify the area for all townspeople and create a memorial to Jackson himself. Cracks in the tarmac were claimed to be evidence of where the wagon ways had been buried.[13]

Just as natural history records the demise of species daily and cryptozoologists hail the discovery of unexpected wildlife worldwide with uncanny regularity, so rail enthusiasts keep finding unsuspected railway systems worked by steam in China and forgotten boilers in extraordinary places. A remarkable survivor was a boiler, still with its chimney intact, found on the tiny Hebridean island of Soay, population six. Apparently it had been transported from southern England via Mallaig to produce steam at a shark oil factory run by Gavin Maxwell, author of *Ring of Bright Water*. [14] Photographic evidence of that and another 1860s abandoned boiler at the head of the Rhondda valley discovered by a photographer capturing frozen waterfalls in 1986, leave no doubt. However, a truly disputable claim attaches to the boiler of 'O2' No. W32 *Bonchurch* – believed to have been scrapped in 1965 – lying still intact at a secret location on the Isle of Wight. Upon withdrawal in 1964, the barrel, firebox, smokebox and backplate fittings of the ex-London and South Western Railway 0-4-4T were allegedly purchased by a former railwayman and have been kept safe ever since. The highly-polished backplate fittings were even said to be displayed around the living-room fireplace of the owner's home! It was said the owner had bequeathed the boiler to the Isle of Wight Steam Railway. When news of the unexpected windfall was broken to island railway officials they were highly dubious. One retorted: 'It's absolute nonsense. I watched most of the "O2s" being cut up and the boilers were simply hacked apart in the frames. I don't believe anything like this survived.'[15]

What's in a name?

Harking back to the gender of locomotive *Russell*, how many people know that armoured tanks can be 'male' or 'female'? Researching the fate of a memorial tank presented to West Hartlepool for raising a record sum per head of population for the 1914–18 war effort, I learned that the chosen veteran was a female Mark IV tank named *Egbert*.[16] I expressed puzzlement at the gender attribution, only for a reader to explain that the male tank, used to flush the Germans out of the trenches, was armed with two six-pounder guns, while the female tank was used to despatch them when flushed out and she was provided with two machine-guns on each side.[17]

Of course, many other 'sub-animate' objects are given names. Public houses were an early example and their names a rich source of interest – both nomenclature lore and their wares. Houses, from the palatial to humble, too. When made redundant from *The Times* library, my friend and mythologist Anthony Roberts named his new abode in the West Country, 'Gondolin'; after a Tolkien character I first assumed, until realising it referred to unemployment benefit! Davy Crockett named his rifle 'Old Betsy', blues singer B.B. King his guitar 'Lucille' and King Arthur had his sword 'Excalibur'. Stagecoaches carried names so naturally steam locomotives required separate identities. I understand it is unlucky to rename a ship, so with some British diesels on to their third and fourth names, what does that tell us or foretell? In fact, often the same nameplates have switched machines several times.

Nicknames

Nicknames for locos and types arose from the dawn of railways, firstly given by railwaymen and later by enthusiasts. Shed staff christened a spectacularly unreliable LNWR mixed-traffic type built between 1902 and 1904 'Bill Baileys' after the music-hall song popular at the time because they were unsure when one was despatched with a train whether it would ever return home.[18]

Doubtless there were types given slang terms by drivers but I have been unable to identify one. I did, however, find an alternative genesis to the definition 'hikers' for the 'B12' individuals fitted with an ACFI feed-water heater apparatus slung in an ungainly fashion on the boiler, which made them look as if carrying a rucksack, hence the name, but optionally some firemen claimed the term referred to the length of the walk they had to take between tender and fire-hole door.

Culloden has already been mentioned twice and it features in a tale of how Peter Drummond's Highland Railway 0-6-0s became known as 'Barneys'. The story goes that when almost new, one of these locos was being driven on a down goods by a particularly idiosyncratic driver. On approaching Culloden Moor station an adverse home signal forced him to make a sudden emergency stop. His brake application was sufficiently sharp as to derail and pile up much of the train. The driver being named Barney.[19]

In addition to railway staff, trainspotters got in on the nicknaming act. When the streamlined 'A4' class became redundant on the East Coast Main Line, members of the class were transferred to St Rollox depot for the three-hour Glasgow to Aberdeen trains. To the enthusiast fraternity they were 'Streaks', but to the Scottish drivers they were the 'Big Yins'.

Compared with descriptive or derogatory names for each and every diesel and electric class, steam had a sparser and less-imaginative nicknaming vocabulary. The LNER produced the obvious 'Antelopes', 'Footballers', 'Directors', 'Hunts' and 'Shires'. The GWR created the even more self-evident 'Kings', 'Halls', 'Granges,' 'Manors' and 'Castles,' even with the disparaging reference to gas turbine No. 18000 as *Kerosene Castle*. On the LMS there were 'Semis', 'Mickey Mouses', 'Flying pigs', 'Jinties' and 'Crabs'. On the SR, chief mechanical engineer Oliver Bulleid created Pacific classes with somewhat box-like streamlining, and appearing during the war years of austerity, his 'Merchant Navy' locos became known as 'Spam cans'. This name of the popular food derived from shoulder pork and ham, led to the later and smaller 'West Country' and 'Battle of Britain' classes also gaining the 'Spam can' epithet. As for the BR 'Standard' classes, the '9F' numerically followed the genuine former War Department 2-8-0 and 2-10-0 classes, but was not a wartime austerity design, yet was often referred to as 'Aussie blink'.

Helpfully, *The Railway Magazine* produced a dictionary of acronyms, initials and nicknames,[20] which followed a detailed earlier survey of modern traction nicknames.[21]

As for wagons, those in departmental use for Network Rail have official designations such as 'Sturgeon', 'Herring' and 'Plaice', but it has been unusual for such vehicles to gather nicknames. An interesting exception, the Thrall Europa build of BYA-coded steel carriers, has attracted the descriptive names 'Pig sty', 'Air-raid shelter', 'Anderson shelter' and 'Gypsy caravan'.[22]

A case of railwaymen themselves earning a nickname relates to the Birmingham depot of Saltley. A commemorative china mug was issued to mark its history between 1854 and 1991, and on one side was the explanation: 'Saltley men worked trains north to Carlisle, south to London, east to Peterborough and west to Bristol, and in the early days to Swansea. One day a driver, M. Paul, joking said: "Saltley men are like seagulls – they go anywhere, do anything, and ― ― on everybody!" The nickname has stuck to this day and is known throughout the land "The Saltley Seagulls".' [23]

Just as the term 'Saltley seagulls' required explanation, what and where was the 'Aintree Iron' mentioned in the song *Thank You Very Much* performed by The Scaffold? Newspaper readers came up with various options. A prosaic railway derivation suggested that it referred to the gravitational marshalling yard built by the

LNWR at Edge Hill, Liverpool, in the mid-1870s. The yard, which by 1894 covered a 200-acre site with a capacity for 6,800 wagons, handled all the goods traffic to and from Liverpool docks. Neil Burgess claimed the 'Iron' in the song was an abbreviation of the 'Gridiron' relating to two sets of sidings at the departure end of the yard, where trains were held before being despatched. However, Stephen Bold heard Scaffold lead singer Mike McGear, brother of Paul McCartney, define 'Aintree Iron' thus: 'Brian Epstein, the Beatles' manager was resident in Aintree. He was well known for his homosexuality. "Iron hoof" was rhyming slang for "poof" – hence the "Aintree Iron".' [24]

In name only...

Before the 1948 nationalisation some truly dreadful names were bestowed upon locomotives. Who in their right minds chose the terrible *Tramp, Vandal, Toad, Frog, Gog, Flirt, Belted Will, Bang Up, Snake, Slaughter, Nettle, Problem* and *Terrible* itself?

Some elements in today's society would find offensive names which were perfectly suitable when originally applied. The animals rights lobby would deplore a return of 'D49' fox hunts; conscientious objectors the names of regiments, warships and RAF planes. In fact, owner John Cameron used its original name *Osprey* in preference to the better known and longer-serving *Union of South Africa* in deference to anti-apartheid protesters. Today we name locos after valued industrial customers and more admirably school safety trophy winners. Whereas the SR honoured King Arthur and his court, Cotswold Rail feted the late Joe Strummer of The Clash. Even a fictitious place of learning has been created in the form of 'Class 26' No. D5325, *University of Drumuillie*. Inspiration for the magnificent red-backed nameplate on one side only was doubtless inspired by 'Class 47s' named *University of Edinburgh* and *University of Stirling*. Strathspey Railway wags creating a fine *blason populaire* 'because many of the railway's staff have degrees from this academic institution. Drumuillie is a village near Boat of Garten with a large sawmill; the connotation of course being "two short planks".' [25]

A most surprising choice for Manchester Metrolink tram No. 1016 was *Erotica G-mex 2004*; the dictionary defining erotica as pornography. Modern traction locos had been named *The Times, Financial Times, Brighton Evening Argus* and so on. What next? *Playboy? Razzle? Readers Wives? Asian Babes?*

Unrecorded elsewhere is the bid by managing director Stuart Bell to have a High-Speed Train power-car named after the *Sunderland Echo* and being rebuffed. A negative scoop I was told to keep quiet about at the time.

Modern traction has been particularly blessed with mythological and folkloric names. When the Western Region of BR named a block of its 'Class 47s' there came locos named *Thor, Odin, Cyclops, Amazon, Titan* and so on. Later, unofficial names were hand-painted on many 'Peaks' allocated to Yorkshire's Tinsley depot, including *Taliesin, Griffon, Phoenix, Pegasus, Centaur, Unicorn, Scylla* and *Vampire.* With No. 45052, the application on 9 September 1987, of the name *Satan* failed to find universal approval and due to apparent local objections it was changed to *Nimrod*.[27] A similar, but official, policy applied with post-privatisation open access operator Fragonset Railways (later FM Rail), whose roster of hire engines included *Hydra, Minotaur, Chimaera, Poseidon, Dionysos* and again *Vampire.*

Names chosen from mythology – *Satan* apart – have a long and noble history. Revivals of names carried by famous engines of yore have also proved popular. Heritage sites, cities, counties, famous personalities and countless other subjects have been bestowed upon locomotives. Undoubtedly the most confusing and protracted series of namings and non-namings applies to 'Class 60'. Seven managers convened to establish coherence within name categories for the hundred-strong class of heavy freight engines. Among the rules stipulated was that for those named after eminent figures of the past there were to be proper Christian names, no nicknames and no titular additions. The second loco off the production line quickly broke the cardinal rule when No. 60002 appeared not as *Lancelot Brown* but *Capability Brown*; admittedly the manner in which the landscape gardener was best known.

Railway literature is peppered with informed sources claiming name selections which failed to materialise, whose guesses were as worthless as those of spotters' platform end rumour. An as near as definitive round-up of modern traction naming apocrypha was commissioned by a certain magazine editor who reneged and the compilation has been published elsewhere by this author.[27]

Place names and mockery

It is widely believed locally that the name 'Eaglescliffe' owes its existence to a signwriter who could not spell. The confusion between the village of Egglescliffe and its more modern adjacent development arose from a painted 'a' on the railway station instead of a 'g'. Yet the booklet *Brief Notes on the Parish Church of Egglescliffe* states that the corrupted name of Eaglescliffe is first found in the church registers of 1639.

I have references to several railway station mis-spellings (correct names in parentheses): Crewe Kerne (Crewkerne), Folkstone (Folkestone), Handborough (Long Hanborough) and Bletchingdon (Bletchington). There was also briefly a road on a new housing development recognising York's railway heritage, but the dyslexic signwriter thought George's surname was spelled 'Stephhenson'!

A splendidly unlikely tale attaches to the unremarkable south London halt Vauxhall, but supposedly famous in Russia. In 1840 a fact-finding delegation visited London to observe our pioneering railway network. Given a tour of a station near Westminster, they took careful note of the name of this new structure, and assuming Vauxhall to be a generic name for station, subsequently named all Russian stations Voksal.[28] Alternatively, the first Russian railway station had a pavilion called a *vokzal* that became used as a general term for station.[29]

All drivers have signal-box staff they love to hate and West Coast Main Line locomen reputedly now refer to Crewe as 'The Crucible' in honour of the Sheffield venue where snooker tournaments are staged. This is because through running – for which British Rail spent millions on realignment – is almost impossible. Trains have to have a red before they can have any other colour signal.[30]

Crewe is a personal favourite and so is the through route between Paddington and Devon, known for some reason as the 'Berks and Hants,' from which I see absolutely nothing of Hampshire and only the southern fringes of Berkshire, which begs the question of how such geographical ineptitude attached to the term?

Older readers will remember seeing on BR locos the lion and wheel emblem which first appeared in 1949 and was mocked as the 'unicycling lion'. A completely modified totem version was introduced in 1956 and was lampooned as a 'ferret and dartboard,' heraldically correct only when facing the coaches or wagons, so on one side of each tank engine or tender the ambiguous beast was facing the wrong way. Also, the still familiar double-arrow logo was introduced as long ago as 1964 as part of the new BR corporate image, and remains an easily-recognised symbol on station signs and tickets, being mockingly known as 'barbed wire' and 'arrows of indecision.'

Substitutes and subterfuge

The conspiracy wing of steam buffery will have you believe certain iconic locomotives are impostors; for one reason or another substitutes. There is something about the switch reminiscent of the changelings of fairy lore, where a human baby is taken in exchange for a sickly elemental infant; the railway equivalent being an impostor of greater mechanical integrity selected for preservation in preference to the real but damaged or under-performing machine.

A folktale equivalent is the provenance of the body of St Cuthbert. When he died in AD 687 he was buried on the Farne Islands. When eleven years later his grave was opened, the body showed no signs of decomposition. As Viking raiders threatened desecration, the inviolate body was removed and for seven years trusted men carried the coffin around the north of England. Finally, in AD 883 they settled at Chester-le-Street, but a hundred years later another scare from more marauding Danes set them travelling again. The body was examined in 1104 and 1537, on each occasion remaining in perfect condition. But in 1827, St Cuthbert's coffin was opened and found to contain a skeleton, although the vestments and other relics remained. Legend avers that due to the risks attached to Roman Catholic relics and saints during the Reformation, St Cuthbert's body was concealed at a hidden site and a substitute placed in the supposed grave. It is said his true resting place was known only by three Benedictine monks, who have always passed on the secret to three successors.[31] A gypsy friend once told me 'Cuddie's' body lies at Finchale Priory.

The name *Saint Cuthbert* was dedicated to a 'Class 47' diesel-electric loco, No. 47702, in 1979. In the 1950s name *Oliver Cromwell* was applied to Standard 'Britannia' No. 70013. Condensing the Lord Protector's history of necessity, Cromwell's head was impaled on Westminster Hall from 1661 to 1688, when it was toppled during a storm. After a chequered career, a Mr Wilkinson bought it in the

mid-twentieth century and donated it to Cromwell's *alma mater*, Sidney Sussex College, Cambridge. This relic was buried at a sacred site, the location of which like that of Cuthbert's body is now handed down orally to successors.[32] Earlier, Michael Behrend noted that the coffins of Cromwell, Ireton and Bradshaw were stored overnight at the Red Lion, Holborn, before public exposure and mutilation of the bodies. 'It was rumoured at the time that Cromwell's body had been secretly replaced by another,' wrote Behrend, 'the true remains of Cromwell being buried in Newburgh Priory, near York. So maybe that isn't his head in Sidney Sussex chapel!'
[33]

A tale of two 'Halls'

The clearest evidence of an identity switch came as a great surprise to the owners of a former GWR 'Hall' rescued from Barry scrapyard. What for almost 27 years had languished at Tyseley, as No. 4983 *Albert Hall* was found instead to be No. 4965 *Rood Ashton Hall*, supposedly finally cut up at Swindon Works on 21 April 1962. As the rebuilding of 4983 progressed, the Birmingham Railway Museum restoration team uncovered mounting evidence that when 4983 and 4965 were in the works together their identities had been swapped. Tyseley chief engineer Bob Meanley found that many components more or less permanently fixed to the frame all bore stampings proclaiming 4965. Items of the motion also bore 4965 stampings or had been cut through with a chisel and restamped 4983. When a collection of photographs of the two locos was examined in minute detail clear differences on the frames appeared. For instance, the Tyseley 'Hall' had only one row of rivets along its cab-side whereas a comparative 1962 shot of *Albert Hall* showed it to have two sets of rivets. When the record cards of the two 'Halls' were examined some anomalies surfaced. Bob Meanley surmised: 'It's possible the true facts will never be verified, but from the many pieces of evidence we do have, I'm in no doubt that during late March 1962, someone at Swindon decided to mix up the pieces of two engines – both obviously defective – in order to make one good 'un. Logic persuades me that there was some costly defect to the frames of *Albert Hall* – it is known that a number of engines had suffered cylinder damage due to loose and incorrectly-fitted pistons around this time and this could have been the case with 4983. It is also possible that *Rood Ashton Hall* had been taken on to Swindon for a classified repair and that expensive work on the boiler had been deemed to be necessary. In these circumstances, it would be totally logical to take boiler No. 2800, which had given less than nine months' service from a major repair, and refit it to a set of frames which were in reasonable order. While the normal practice was to allocate the engine's number to the frames, in this instance the Board of Trade regulations governing the overhaul of boilers and classification of repairs may have influenced the situation. Changing the boiler from one engine to another would have required the declaration of a "heavy general" repair, demanding further work be undertaken on a boiler that didn't require to be done. The solution was pretty simple – just change the engine number! Once this skulduggery had taken place, it would have been a simple matter to despatch the remnants of the two engines to "C" shop for cutting and to show *Rood Ashton Hall* as condemned and cut up. The clerical work would have been retrospective, and simply recorded by a trusting clerk remote from the chicanery which had taken place on the shopfloor.'

The real thing? Doubts have been expressed that '9F' No. 92220, Evening Star, seen here at Hexham, is an impostor. (Paul Screeton)

He added: 'I don't doubt that someone in the works back in March 1962 made the decision to mix up the bits of two engines, safe in the knowledge that the railway was far too busy with dieselisation to worry about a little bit of subterfuge. They had, after all, turned out a repaired engine, whose number didn't really matter as long as it worked – and anyway – the evidence was going to be on the scrap pile shortly, so they were perfectly safe. Or so they thought!' [34]

Commenting on the identity of Tyseley's 'Hall', Reg Appleton recalled a visit to Woodham's scrapyard on 30 March 1963, when he discovered five locos carrying more than one number, either on the motion or on the timber bulk between the bufferbeam and the front end. The first number quoted being the preserved number: 4115 (4157); 4253 (4278, also 7242); 5029 (5000, also 4075); 5900 (5977); 5972 (5994). Appleton asked whether once the brass number plates had been removed, could anyone be certain of the identity, and also mused that maybe alternative numbers were given to suit accountancy-driven withdrawal. [35]

Last but not least

The greatest amount of correspondence regarding the possibility of a substitution relates to the last steam locomotive built for BR, '9F' class No. 92220 *Evening Star*. National Railway Museum archivist Philip Atkins found it 'incredible' that an element of doubt remained as to the true identity of the loco in the museum's custodianship. Noting it was withdrawn in March, 1965, when tragically just five years old, he noted reports hinted that its demise was the result of minor accident damage, although claiming no photographic evidence had ever been presented.

Atkins added that the boiler is definitely the one originally fitted and has probably never been lifted off the frames since the engine was new in early 1960. He added: 'In support of the "accident theory", the National Railway Museum at York holds an *Evening Star* nameplate which is distinctly bent!' [36]

Readers responded with photographic evidence of the damaged loco at both Severn Tunnel Junction and Ebbw Junction depots, where the smoke deflectors appeared undamaged and without nameplates. So could the bent reserve/original nameplate have been damaged during removal? A truly apocryphal tale with a foaf element also emerged. Here is Gareth Evans' claim in full: 'You might like to know that during my service at BR's Cardiff Division HQ in the '60s, a management trainee told me an extraordinary story that had been related to him while he was doing a stint at Cardiff East depot, where *Evening Star* was shedded. He was told that the "9F" had indeed been rammed against the buffer stops by a "Class 08" diesel shunter and had suffered front-end damage. However, because steam locos were being rapidly withdrawn, it was considered uneconomical to repair No. 92220, so it was quietly cut up and its nameplates and other fancy bits transferred to another "9F", which had already been painted in lined-out Brunswick green livery.' A less-than-impressed editorial footnote cautioned: 'Your letter certainly puts the cat among the pigeons, Mr Evans, but it suggests the identity swap was carried out fairly soon after the incident. If so, that doesn't explain why there were numerous sightings of 92220 with bufferbeam damage for many months afterwards, and indeed as late as February 1966. Surely the damaged loco would by then have been carrying the original identity of the impostor? – Ed' [37]

Philip Atkins had earlier raised the 92220 question in *Steam Railway* and the subsequent post bag elicited interesting points, some naturally conflicting. The location of the accident which caused the buffer-beam damage was variously attributed. Radyr fireman at the time Brian Jenkins related that while being driven light engine to East Dock depot it collided with a heavy lorry entering East Moors steelworks on one of the many ungated level crossings in the area. Apprentice Keith Walker was told by East Dock fitters the damage was sustained in the Tyndall Street-Adamstown marshalling yard, about one mile north of the shed and caused by a heavy-handed shunting manoeuvre. A third account by a W.J. Mayo, then a rolling stock assistant at Paddington, claimed that while held for possible preservation, 92220 went 'walkies' through the rear wall of Ebbw Junction depot. Richard Pritchard produced a photograph of the engine being restored at Crewe Works in 1967 showing the right-hand smoke deflector and part of the running plate apparently replaced along with the buffer-beam and buffers.[38]

Royal doubts

Similar doubt has been expressed as to the authenticity of preserved ex-GWR 'King' No. 6000 *King George V*. It was 'confined, under conditions of strictest secrecy' in the Swindon Works stock shed for six years, then overhauled at Newport, Gwent, and loaned to Hereford cidermakers Bulmer.[39]

Throughout its incarceration, photographs of the 'King' reveal removal of all identification. Correspondence on the matter includes a letter from Malcolm Quirk regarding a proposition by the then shedmaster at Bristol's dieselised Bath Road depot to have staff contribute a small amount each week to acquire 6000 for static display. Mr Quirk added that the plan fell through when it was revealed 6000 would be unsuitable owing to its having cracked frames. An alternative suggestion to exhibit No. 6006 *King George I* fitted with *King George V* name and number plates instead was deemed unsuitable as this was not the original loco. Surely the cracked frames issue raises the question of its eventual suitability for overhaul to mainline running, and anyway the Bath Road scheme was for a cosmetic job, not to produce a 'runner'.

The presumed impostor in this case is generally believed to be No. 6018 *King Henry VI*. After withdrawal at the end of 1962 it was returned for service for several months on special duties. Holiday camps proprietor Billy Butlin and Western Region management agreed to provision of a loco for display at Minehead. A 'Coronation' was offered for £800 less by the London Midland Region and the 'King' project was aborted, although correspondents recalled seeing a kit of parts, but with the frames in gleaming black exhibition finish. E.S. Youldon wrote that 6018 was cut up 'with such haste that the event passed unnoticed at the time by outsiders.' He added that reports appeared later that year in both *Modern Railways* and *Railway Observer* regarding a swap with 6000 and that 6018 was scheduled to work a theatre special in September, 1963, but both speculations 'were without foundation, as by then 6018 was no more – but for a long time the notion persisted in some quarters that it was tucked away somewhere at Swindon.'

If a film were made, Richard Gere could play the boss of Bulmer's heroically getting the notorious steam ban lifted and 6000 back on the main line. Or would it be too similar to his role in *Sommersby*?

Churchill's double

Further doubts have arisen as to the identity of the loco which hauled Sir Winston Churchill's funeral train. Our national hero, wartime leader and author of the memorable phrase 'railways are the agents of civilisation', had expressed the wish to be buried in the little churchyard at Bladon, Oxfordshire, which necessitated a rail journey for his coffin. He died on 24 January 1965, and the train carried his body on the 30th. Detailed plans for the railway's role had been drawn up years in advance under the top-secret codename of 'Operation Hope-Not.' [40]

Fortuitously, perhaps even deliberately, air-smoothed 'Battle of Britain' No. 34051 *Winston Churchill* survived. A debate not only as to the challenged identity of the funeral train loco, but its movements around the dates of death and despatch, rumbled within the pages of *Steam World, The Railway Magazine* and *Steam Railway*. Particularly noteworthy was correspondent D.S. Gowen, who claimed the true engine was unable to work the special because 'it lay inside Feltham shed minus pistons, rods and nameplates, with cabside numbers painted out, whilst sister No. 34057 performed the day's duties. Only the coupling rods stamped 34051 gave its identity away, and the fall of light on the repainted cabs.'[41] David Percival was later to note that a picture of No. 34057 at Feltham on 30 January showed it in exactly the same position and condition as when he photographed it on 24 January, 'which seems to disprove the "exchange of identity" theory.'[42]

As I penned this section, a newspaper I read regaled a Cotswold legend. The tale goes that the infant future Elizabeth I spent a night at Butler's Court, Bisley, where she was found dead. Fearing the wrath of King Henry VIII, those in whose safekeeping the child had been left sought a replacement local red-haired child. Unable to secure a suitable girl, a boy impostor grew up in her place. No wonder we refer to England's 'Virgin Queen.' Maybe the infant future George V died and was switched? Also they say all babies look like Winston Churchill...[43] Whatever, it would seem loco 34051 was selected for official preservation simply because of the popularity of Britain's wartime leader and funeral train role, but is the National Railway Museum's loco the real 34051?

Missionary zeal

Not the place you would expect to find a platform for railway folklore, but a football fanzine kicked off a new season of loco name debate. Darlington's *Mission Impossible* was on the right track when a knowledgeable, but doubtless over-zealous enthusiast, resurrected an old chestnut. Robin Coulthard pointed out that during the 1930s the LNER decided to build a later batch of its 'B17' tender locos for its semi-fast trains out of London Marylebone for the Great Central section. Earlier examples had been named after stately homes and allocated to the Great Eastern lines, but this series was to be named after football clubs within the LNER's sphere of operation, as a token of recognition of the contribution soccer fans made to its passenger revenue. All the batch of twenty-five were to be built in Darlington, County Durham; fourteen at the company's North Road works and eleven at Robert Stephenson and Hawthorn's Springfield works.

Locomotives began coming off the North Road assembly line in the spring of 1936; the first four being named after that year's FA Cup semi-finalists: Arsenal, Derby County, Huddersfield Town (on LMS territory, with LNER having running rights) and Sheffield United.[44] A later article gave the first four engines, Nos. 2848 to 2851, the allotted names in the sequence *Huddersfield Town, Derby County, Sunderland* and *Middlesbrough*. In reality they appeared in the order *Arsenal, Sheffield United, Grimsby Town* and *Derby County*.[45] Another source suggested the accessibility of Wembley stadium from GC metals was the reason for the 'Footballer' series of 'B17s' and that No. 2848 was released to traffic on 3 March 1936, three days after the sixth round of the FA Cup had been played and officially named *Arsenal* a few days later, thus acknowledging the team not only as cup favourites but also outstanding club of the decade.[46]

Coulthard repeats the story that skilled tradesmen at North Road were unhappy at crafting engines to the greater glory of top clubs when their hometown team, 'The Quakers', was omitted on the pretext that it was in the Third Division (North). When polite representations to management failed, a night shift conspiracy made a 'pirate' set of plates bearing the name *Darlington*. In the end management yielded and a 'B17' was turned out carrying official club nameplates. Coulthard correctly notes *Darlington* was originally numbered 2852 and had originally been earmarked the name *Sheffield Wednesday*. In 1959 the loco was taken out of service and cut up at Doncaster in 1960 (I can believe this – I saw it there during its dismemberment).

The tale was taken up by journalist Mike Amos and his 'Backtrack' column in Darlington's *The Northern Echo* chronicled quite a saga. A Mr J. Bates, a former North Road employee, challenged the story. 'Apart from anything else, he says, he's almost certain there wasn't a night shift.' Another reader sent a photocopy from Ken Hoole's book on the works' history carrying a photograph of engine No. 2849 carrying a *Darlington* nameplate and claiming that the loco had been nominated the name *Sheffield United*.

As an acquaintance of Mike's, I contacted him to remind him that when a High-Speed Train power-car was named *Darlington* in the mid-Eighties, Mike himself recounted the hoary legend. On that occasion he claimed the night shift took in *Manchester City* one evening and next morning sent out the same loco with gleaming *Darlington* name. 'Impressed both by their initiative and their handiwork, the LNER offered to provide an engine for their nameplate so long as they got their *Manchester City* back.' [48] Actually No. 2854 had been allotted the *City* name and it did not appear properly until the second batch of 'Footballers' and on No. 2871.

I have also come across a reference in an anonymously-penned regional railway book which generally repeated the apocrypha, but claimed workers made *Darlington* plates and put them on No. 2852 overnight. LNER directors were impressed and the officially-designated *Sheffield Wednesday* plates were switched to No. 2861. That said, the item was illustrated by the builder's number plate for No. 2849. Confused? Remember Hoole had an official photograph of 2849 with *Darlington* plates, which suggests that somewhere within this partisanship scenario there may be a grain of truth.

Grandfather's axe

It is generally assumed that a loco's frame gives it its identity. Yet to speed throughput of overhauls, not only did various works have extra boilers (there were thirteen manufactured for the numerically-small class '47xx' numbering nine examples), but a spare float of frames existed for a number of classes. For instance, when the ex-LNER 'B16s' were being rebuilt, war-damaged No. 925's frames were incorporated when No. 922 was modified, then 922's frames were used in the next rebuild, and so on, so it could be reported that two engines were seen on the same day at Darlington bearing the same number; an un-rebuilt example entering the works and a rebuilt one coming out.

As with many enthusiasts, I pride myself in recording only locos I have definitely spotted. But if counting what you've seen by frames only, my underlinings between 'Black Five' Nos. 45003 and 45460 are meaningless (and many other classes'

Thundering with smoke belching through Seaton Carew, near Hartlepool, nominally it's 'A3' No. 60103 Flying Scotsman, but how much of the original remains – or who cares? (Paul Screeton)

numbers). Apparently three separate sets of frames were provided by Crewe Works in 1943, one of which was for 'Black Fives' and was probably built new to the then-latest design. It was first fitted to No. 5226 in July, 1943, while its old frames were presumably repaired and fitted to No. 5027 and so on until some 280 changes later in January/February, 1958, No. 45055's frames were fitted to No. 45114 and 45114's old frames became spare.[50]

You will remember the proverbial story, either known as 'Grandfather's axe' or politically incorrect as 'Irishman's shovel'? Either way, it goes like this: 'It's still the same axe my grandfather used. It's had three replacement handles and two replacement heads, but it's still the same one.' How much of certain locomotives remained after numerous trips to works and re-buildings is a frequent topic discussed in railway circles. The original 'Patriots' were nominally rebuilds from 'Claughtons', but only a fraction was used – sufficient to satisfy company accountancy.

Railway hobbyists pride themselves in seeking out accurate historical facts. However, some situations raise more questions than answers. Digging too deeply into loco identity is a case in point. It is akin to asking whose body will it be when the Rapture comes if you have been eaten by cannibals! Roland Kennington, when chief engineer for preserved 'A3' No. 60103 *Flying Scotsman*, stunned listeners when asked how much of the loco was original. Lecturing to members of Stevenage Locomotive Society, he stated succinctly: 'None of it.'[51]

Discussing its ongoing overhaul, he explained that in the late 1920s, Doncaster Works was receiving 'A3s' back with frame cracks, so to save time and get the loco back into traffic as quickly as practicable spare frame sets were assembled. Hence *Flying Scotsman* would possibly have different frames and anyway former owner Alan Pegler purchased a spare boiler and middle cylinder when he bought the engine from BR. Even if all its component parts had been successively cannibalised from fellow classmates and replaced, it would still be the same loco. It is said the human body replaces all its tissue every seven years, and it still remains the same body, so why not a steam or diesel loco? As I understood it, when Pegler purchased *Flying Scotsman*, the spare boiler had been saved from withdrawn classmate *Salmon*

Trout. I now understand the loco has a 250lb 'A4' boiler, while the unique $19^7/_8$ inch outside cylinders give a nominal tractive effort of 39,745 lb, compared with the normal 35,455 for an 'A3.' I thank Keith Farr for these facts, which caused him to ask succinctly: 'But is "the old girl" still an A3?' [52] Probably not. Hybrid certainly. Some genetically modified spawn of Frankensteinian engineering.

Transfer fever and Cornish kings

Wish-fulfilment hopes are common to most hobbyists, whether it be the return of avocets or ospreys for birders or the transfer of a gifted player to one's fanatically-supported football club. When 'Deltic' locos were being steadily eradicated from the ECML, a commentator wrote knowledgeably that 'it is likely that more of the class will be withdrawn from service before long, in connection with which it is strongly rumoured that 20 "Class 50s" will be transferred to York shed from the Western Region during early June.' He then gave a plausible and detailed case for the relocation strategy. 'This would be done to coincide with the Mk3 sleeping cars which are due to be introduced on King's Cross-Edinburgh/Aberdeen services around that time. Also, the "Class 50s" have a greater fuel capacity – 1,100 gallons compared to the 870 gallons of the "Class 47" – thereby giving a wider operating potential which the Eastern Region is seeking. If this reallocation takes place the present Gateshead-allocated "Class 47s" Nos. 47401–20 would be transferred to Plymouth Laira to balance the deal. At this stage it is not possible to say which "Class 50s" would be transferred, but it is understood that a block of 20 would be involved rather than "scattered" numbers in the class.' In reality it was all wishful thinking and no transfer took place. [53]

When an enthusiasts' magazine reported a rail tour would take the first ever 'King' class loco into Cornwall, readers related 'a number of "folklore sightings" of "Kings" in the Duchy – but all of them hearsay, unsubstantiated by any first-hand corroboration.' They included a claim by commercial photographer the late Tom Corin that he saw No. 6000 *King George V* in 1935 passing the loco depot at Long Rock, Penzance, on a special working; a suggestion that in 1938 the GWR ran two clearance trials with 'Kings' in Cornwall (the first to Trerule, the second to Doublebois); and a report said to come from former shed staff at Laira that during the 1941 bombing blitz on Plymouth, among the locos driven across the Royal Albert Bridge each night to 'safe' stabling areas, either in Shillingham tunnel or on the stub of the pre-1908 route at Wearden, were 'Kings.' Yet no reader could provide photographic evidence and the only eyewitness account came from a six-year-old boy's sighting at Saltash in 1938 recounted 60 years later. [54]

This human trait to doubt in the face of lack of clear photographic evidence and dubious and uncorroborated eyewitness testimony is natural. It is central to most fortean phenomena where ambiguity is redolent. Sighting reports, whether they be of the Beast of Bodmin or mainline 'King' passing Bodmin Parkway station, become secular versions of religious miracle stories.

Chapter Seven

Urban myths roam the rails

From foundation sacrifices to treasure hunts, strength tests to weak bowels, concealed slums to left luggage, dodgy signals to fare dodgers, contemporary legends have travelled the length and breadth of the railway network. There is even a major cluster of tales associated with the Settle to Carlisle section, and as has been seen, Isambard Kingdom Brunel gets everywhere. Sex, suicide, social class, xenophobia, troublesome technology and the scribblings of the desperate diarist are all here.

With or without foundation?

When contractors blasted the magnificent Thorpe Thewles viaduct striding across a Teesside valley they reawakened an ancient legend. With the headline 'Blast explodes horror myth', a regional newspaper laid the ghost of the rumour that a horse and cart had been buried in the foundations. When explosives expert Walt Parsons and his squad finally lowered the last remaining pillar of the railway viaduct a team moved in to check for the remains of the overworked horse where it collapsed and died during construction of the 70 feet high column 102 years before. Mr Parsons said: 'If they had left something like that in there it would have been a major structural fault and I just don't believe it. The engineers then were too skilled for that.' Demolition contractor Maurice Jackson commented: 'We can find no trace of anything. It's just a heap of sandstone, brick and concrete. However, we'll keep looking. They might be in the two abutments at the start and finish which still have to come down.' However, nothing more was heard of this bizarre legend of the rail artery which for reasons lost in the mists of time was known locally as the Cuckoo Line.[1]

A similar tale was told of a horse and cart having fallen into a hollow pier of Glenfinnan viaduct during construction. When in 1990 engineers using special cameras inspected the inside of the piers of the structure about halfway along the scenic route between Fort William and Mallaig, which opened on 1 April 1901, there was no sign of horse or cart. Hearing of the fruitless investigation, 75-year-old Ewen MacMillan, who had lived in the area all his life, insisted the story was sound. True tale, wrong location. He said: 'My father and an old farmer who worked next to the viaduct told me the story about 70 years ago. I was fascinated and the story stuck in my head ever since.'[2] The search should have been made at eight-span Loch-nan-Uamh viaduct. A project managed by the Institution of Civil Engineers with Weeks Laboratories of Glasgow was appointed to bore holes through the 5 feet thick walls of the central pillar to photograph the 11 feet by 30 feet cavity inside.[3] However, the test drilling proved it to be solid. Undeterred, the latest radar techniques were applied and a scan taken through the concrete wall showed the remains of the cart with the horse above it. Prof Roland Paxton, a specialist in civil engineering at Heriot-Watt University, said: 'Probably the cart was being backed-up to the edge of the hole to tip rubble, went too far and plummeted down, pulling the unfortunate horse with it. There is evidence that the horse's neck was broken. Iron-shod wheels about six feet in diameter, wood and individual bones have been identified.' A Railtrack spokesman commented: 'It's great news that he has finally discovered the truth behind the legend. It is fitting that the story has been verified on the centenary of the Mallaig line.' [3]

That the horse in the foundations legends has existed at three locations at least may be of special folkloric significance. There is a rich lore of various objects being buried under or within buildings with the intended provision of ceremonial or even arbitrary prophylactic against harm, be it human burials as foundation, or substitutes such as horses, cats, oxen, skulls, dolls, witch bottles or some other object deemed to have magical or geomantic significance.

In the first geomantic approach to the subject of foundation sacrifice and allied practises – in fact, a subject so little studied as to have no broad term extant to describe it – pioneering cartographer of the subject Nigel Pennick notes that 'foundation rituals are still common, and are often accompanied by considerable sacred or masonic usage, with the deposition of coins, time capsules or documents, and on dates considered appropriate by the canons of astrological geomancy.' Pennick even claims the Great Wall of China, a German military hospital built underground on Jersey during World War II, the elevated section of the M4 motorway in west London, the Moscow Metro and Brunel's Box tunnel have lore that they conceal the remains of slave labourers or navvies who died during their construction.[4]

Pioneer urban mythologist Rodney Dale reckoned the earliest and grandest tall story of people in walls is that of the Chinese emperor Chin Shi Huang-ti (246–210 BC), who during building the Great Wall entombed one million people within its 1,500 miles. Dale also pointed out that there was an old belief that mortar was strengthened if mixed with blood. Ala-ud-din Khilji (AD 1296–1315) when constructing the walls of Delhi sacrificed thousands of victims expressly so their blood and bones could be mixed with mortar. The King of Ashanti, as recently as 1881, sacrificed 200 girls so as to use their blood in the walls of a new palace in Accra.[5]

But never mind 1881, when in 1990 the Channel tunnel rail link was the great engineering project of the century, a diarist printed a barmy account of feared foundation sacrifice. It would be criminal to paraphrase, so here it is in its unexpurgated awfulness:

> 'Deep in the Mexican rainforest an anthropologist pads between
> Indian villages. Arriving at one she is surprised to find everyone
> hiding. An old woman appears: "You have come for the heads?"

she asks, fearfully. "Heads, what heads?" the anthropologist replies. The woman runs off. The anthropologist goes to the capital and finds that a Frenchman has been looking for 300 heads of people to work on a project. She goes to another village, still deeper in the forest. The same happens. "Don't take our heads", says the chief. "No, no", says the anthropologist, eager to set minds at rest. "They're not wanting heads. They want people to work on a project." "No, no", says the woman. "You're wrong. They want 300 heads to bury in the foundations of a great bridge over the water. They are refrigerating them and sending them there." The anthropologist considers this: "Are you sure it's a bridge? Could it be a tunnel, the Channel tunnel between England and France?" "Yes, yes, that's it. They are taking our heads for the Channel tunnel." [6]

From mythical modern head-hunters back to the horse, which may have particular significance, being one of the key sacred animals in the Elder Faith; associated with the Celtic goddess Epona and Woden/Odin. The Folk Museum in Cambridge holds several horse relics recovered from old buildings and no fewer than forty horse skulls were found laid in neat ranks under the floor of a seventeenth century Suffolk house. Until the evidence of both horse and cart at Loch-nan-Uamh, I suspected such tales to be garbled folk memory of a ceremony where a horse, whose death was most probably natural rather than sacrificial, was buried in the foundations, perhaps with a libation of homebrew beer over it for luck and to protect the structure from unwanted spirits or energies.

The Settle and Carlisle line has such a rich geography of lore, including a buried human body. [7] Legend avers an engineer killed a woman and dumped her body in one of the shafts being excavated at Dent Head viaduct. The immense piers were set on a bed of concrete and once poured in, all trace of the victim was erased. By the time the details of the crime became known, the viaduct was almost complete. Being impracticable to seek any trace of the body in the foundations, all that could be done was to fix a commemorative plaque high on a pier. [8]

On the subject of crime, a related strand of legend relates to the notions of notorious East End gangsters being 'hardened criminals' encased in cement holding up motorway flyovers. [9]

There is also the vexed question of whether viaducts were built on wool. Stability would be essential and this was established at Ribblehead on the S&C by sinking shafts to the bedrock at about twenty-five feet and dressed limestone conveyed by tramway from nearby Littledale was placed on six feet of concrete. The wool story was nevertheless attached to Ribblehead and nearby Dandry Mire viaduct. A geography teacher told my class that Yarm viaduct, spanning the Tees, lay on wool foundations. We never questioned the veracity, though it sounded so unlikely that it has stuck in my mind for forty-five years. Writer W.R. Mitchell speculated that wool could have been used to prevent seepage of water into the shafts or perhaps Ribblehead was built with money earned through wool, i.e. built on Bradford wool

Yarm viaduct – in the background – was built on wool, or so claimed the author's geography master, Roger Simpson. A Fina oil train crosses behind 'Class 60' No. 60021. Yarm has plenty of other folklore, including the joke played upon strangers, who are challenged to visit Yarm Castle. After failing to find it, they are led to a wall – in the foreground – with a fantasy miniature castle atop. (Paul Screeton)

merchants' brass.[10] To add to the mystery, the line now preserved as the North Yorkshire Moors Railway was constructed by George Stephenson to service the area's once-thriving mining industry. One account claims that 'it still runs in places over the original rafts of sheepskins and wattles laid down by his engineers.'[11]

Lastly, the term 'sacrifice' is commonly used to honour those who died for the benefit of others during wartime. Literally or metaphorically it was said that there was a body under every sleeper on the notorious Burma to Siam railway, where 16,000 lives were lost during the 1939–45 War. Earlier the notion attached to the line developed to Russia's ice-free port of Murmansk, built by prisoners-of-war between 1915 and 1917. Challenging the Burma-Siam line's 'uniqueness', correspondent H.F. Ashbrook noted that mortality on the Murmansk railway was so high 'that after WWI it became part of German folklore that there was the dead body of a prisoner lying under every sleeper – undoubtedly something of an overstatement seeing that this line stretches for about 900 miles.'[12]

The wise men of Derby

An august journal with the ability to spot a myth, *New Scientist* recalled British Rail's testing of the Advanced Passenger Train in the 1970s. Engineers wanted to know what effects an impact with a migrating duck might have upon a train travelling at 150 mph. *New Scientist* continued: 'So they hired a dead-bird firing facility from an aircraft testing site and put a mock-up of the APT cab in the firing line. They set the firing speed to 150 mph and launched the bird. The result was stunning: the bird went through the windscreen and straight through the metal bulkhead behind it. The dazed engineers began to analyse their data: how thick would the windscreen have to be to withstand this, they wondered. They called an expert. The expert took one look at the data and another at the devastated cab and asked what they had used as ammunition. "There weren't any dead ducks around so we used a chicken," came the reply. "Um... do you think we should have defrosted it first?" '[13]

Later that year *PC Dealer* magazine picked up on the tale, but it featured experiments to see if Eurostar train windscreens could stand the impact of birds flying into them. The US Federal Aviation Administration loaned Eurostar a special 550 mph gun that fires dead chickens at planes to test them. Eurostar technicians fired the rooster at the train, but were amazed to see it fly through the screen, embedding itself in the rear wall of the cab. They asked the FAA to inspect the gun and after a thorough examination, the Americans advised the Eurostar men: "Next time thaw the chicken out first!"' [14]

Lads' magazine *Front* located the myth in the US with scientists keen to test a gun used to validate military jet windshields on a new high-speed train. When fired, the chicken smashed the shatter-proof shield to smithereens, blasted through the control console, snapped the engineer's back rest in two and embedded itself in the back wall of the cabin. The disastrous results, along with the windshield designs, were sent to Rolls-Royce, begging the British boffins for suggestions. Rolls-Royce responded with a one-line memo: 'Defrost the chicken.' [15]

Of course, not all journalists can recognise even so obvious an urban myth. 'Exclusive,' trumpeted a piece by the credulous Peter Welbourn. 'British Rail cried "Fowl" when it let a glass company use its testing facilities to try out a new toughened product. For the firm brought along an oven-ready chicken to fire at a pane placed by a train carriage.' Welbourn continued: 'But scientists – who'd also borrowed a high-speed catapult used to simulate aero engine birdstrikes at nearby Rolls-Royce – forgot to THAW OUT their purchase. And the frozen pullet-bullet blasted a huge hole clean through the carriage after shattering the glass!' Welbourn claimed BR in Derby joked: 'It wasn't the breakthrough they'd hoped for' and had a spokesman for Rolls-Royce commenting, 'it might have worked with a fresh chicken, but it was just like a cannonball.' [16]

My favourite version appeared on a page specifically for jokes, which puts it more into perspective. Here Deputy Prime Minister John Prescott arranged with NASA for a demonstration of a special gun designed to blast dead chickens at aircraft. In front of invited rail chiefs and the press, the chicken he had bought was fired at a driver-less new high-speed train, smashing the windscreen, tearing through the driver's seat and making a hole in the cabin wall. Prescott protests to NASA that the gun was too powerful, only to receive a terse reply: 'Next time, sir, please defrost the chicken.' [17]

There is something touchingly comical about all this, with the serious intent completely eclipsed. It could even be an update of the Middle Ages cycle of tales known as the 'Wise Men of Gotham'. In this Nottinghamshire village, rustics attempted such foolish feats as drowning an eel, raking the moon from a pond and building a hedge around a cuckoo to lengthen spring. The phrase 'reason in their madness' springs to mind. The undoubted sincerity in the stupidity led Frank E. Earp to attach 'wisdom and a state of near-divinity' to the simpletons' archetype; going so far as to link the cycle with shamanism! [18]

The story also encapsulates Murphy's Law. This is generally believed to state: 'Whatever can go wrong, will.' This, however, is a corruption of what Edward Murphy Jr., an engineer on the United States Air Force rocket-sled experiments, actually said: 'If there is any way to do something wrong, somebody will find it.' His axiom followed an experiment involving sticking about a dozen biometric sensors on to the torso of a 'human' crash-test dummy and a technician contrived to install all of them back-to-front, resulting in a popular crowd-pleasing second attempt.[19]

Watch out, here comes another crash test...

Crash! Bang! Wallop!

In a bid to calm fears about the consequences of a rail-borne nuclear flask being involved in a high-speed collision, the Central Electricity Generating Board sent a 240-tonne empty passenger train hurtling at 100 mph into a 48-tonne flask wagon. The 140-tonne diesel loco, 'Peak' No. 46009, was almost totally destroyed and the flask found to be completely intact. The dramatic demonstration was held on 17 July 1984, on a test track in Leicestershire. I see a train of such flasks pass our house weekly and never worry of health concerns or crashworthiness, although a neighbour suspects his leukaemia has been caused by this service to Hartlepool power station. Anyway, the CEGB had estimated (how?) the probability of a serious accident to a flask to be as remote as one in ten million years.

Now for the legendary titbit. According to the tale, a team from an American locomotive builder was present that day at the Railway Technical Centre in Derby. Their hosts were keen to see the nuclear flask test crash and a television set was turned on at the appropriate time. As the dust subsided, a British Rail official present allegedly remarked deadpan to his guests: 'That, gentlemen, is our standard acceptance test for freight locomotives.' [20]

Who hung the monkey?

> Question: 'Is this where they hung the monkey?
>
> Answer: 'Why, have you lost your father?'

As referred to in the introduction, this is an example of *blason populaire*. It is an expression for a distinct form of local tradition, a jeering slogan or jibe, a semi-malicious taunt levelled by the inhabitants of one town or region against those of another. The most popular and widespread belief regarding the legend attached to the older Headland part of Hartlepool (later amalgamated with West Hartlepool to form a single Hartlepool borough), is that during the Napoleonic Wars, a monkey was washed ashore and mistaken for a French spy. Chattering away in a tongue foreign to its captors, it was decided that as a precaution it should be hanged. The folk in Gotham would have been proud!

The actuality or otherwise of the event need not detain us. What is known is that travelling player Ned Corvan, who died in 1865, probably visited Hartlepool before a planned music-hall show seeking a local theme to give his act topicality. Upon hearing someone shout 'Who hung the monkey?', or similar, he had his foundation. Also at that time there was intense rivalry in the Hartlepools between two competing railway companies. The Hartlepool Railway and Dock Company having as its engineer a well-respected man called Stephen Robinson. At that time there was a very popular play called *Jack Robinson and his Monkey*. Perhaps the Headland residents proclaimed, 'We have Jack Robinson on our side of the water. The fellow planning the other dock is a monkey.' In the play the monkey's name is 'Mushapug' or 'Pug' for short. In no dictionary of that time was the word 'pug' used in connection with a species of monkey. However, in his song Corvan calls it 'Pug' as in the play. Also the song draws in fishermen, an occupation which would seemingly gain nothing from either railway undertaking. Yet during the pamphlet war a fisherman is pilloried for wearing a new suit, and it may be that he was bribed by the Stockton and Hartlepool Railway Company to give evidence in London in favour of the West Dock.

As the author of the definitive book on the monkey-hanging, I am frequently asked if I believe the story. What, if anything, really happened? Was a monkey hanged as a French spy in Hartlepool? Well aware of relocated folktales (the legend is not peculiar to Hartlepool) and the tradition of a Gotham-style stupid/commonsensical community motif, there is still the absence of any reference to the event, either as historical fact or folklore, in any contemporary writings. That speaks volumes. Yet we have Corvan's song with railway subtext. That is solid enough.

In the final analysis, I fear I can do no better than to answer the question exactly as I did in my book. 'It is a fallacy of conventional scholarship to distinguish between these aspects (history and legend) with rigorous discipline and distinction. For folklore is the psychic life of a people and cannot be separated artificially from shared events. Legends may seem like lies but they always have an element of truth. Even when exaggeration and embellishment are applied, even to the extent of deliberate falsification and invention, such "lies" of a people are not wholly gratuitous. They refer to some strata of communal reality where underlying fears, deficiencies, desires and dreams require exorcising or compensating. Their falsity makes them real; their power makes them true. In this way a self-definition of a community is created: a collective identity occurs just when and where it is needed. It can be a truth without tangibility.

'So who hung the monkey, O!'

'We did.'[21]

Spin doctoring

Spinning a yarn? Saluting the Settle and Carlisle line's centenary, Peter E. Baughan was discussing Garsdale, though he preferred the earlier alternative name Hawes Junction, 'It was, and is, a place where the Pennine winds achieve an almost malevolent violence: the turntable used to be stockaded to prevent the engines from being twirled around,' he wrote, although the ostensible purpose of enclosing the turntable with discarded upright sleepers was to keep the pit free from drifting snow.[22] Yet still the tale lives, and interviewing retired General Secretary of the National Union of Railwaymen Sid Weighell, Brian Page claimed the 'massive' (it wasn't) turntable at 'Garsdale Junction' (it isn't) would 'when once set in motion with a loco in place the wheel would turn for hours – driven round by the fierce winds.' (it wouldn't) 'There was no way you could stop it and no way you could get the engine off, not until the wind had died down. They built a shelter round it in the end,' added Sid Weighell.[23]

Someone who should know better than to peddle uncorroborated piffle is Peter Semmens, former Assistant Keeper at the National Railway Museum. Writing on immediate post-war developments his focus fell on the newly-introduced Bulleid light Pacifics in the West Country, with their 'spam can' flat streamlining. 'There were, of course, problems with them in Devon and Cornwall, too, one of the class getting itself blown round for several hours on the turntable at Ilfracombe during a gale! It was impossible to hold it against the force of the wind on the air-smoothed boiler casing until someone drained the tender, which unbalanced the turntable,' wrote Semmens.[24]

Back at Garsdale, Anthony Lambert swallowed the story and described an engine spinning like the sails of a windmill, only to be halted when ballast was thrown in the pit.[25] While putting a slower spin on the Garsdale story, Stanley C. Jenkins had a freak of nature taking place where 'the wind took charge of it and the locomotive was turned slowly round and round on its axis until somebody shovelled stones and cinders into the turntable pit.'[26] While yet another account has a specific culprit, but no exact date or authentication. This is Peter Brock's version: 'Turning on Garsdale's turntable could be difficult in stormy weather in view of the absence of a windbreak, and there was a case on record when Kingmoor '2P' 4-4-0 No. 40602 spun round like a windmill for three hours before the Helm Wind dropped. This even took place in 1949.'[27]

Because this myth is so ingrained, so seemingly plausible and so silly, I'll print a rebuttal in full: 'Did Garsdale turntable really revolve at 70 mph? Of course it didn't! In fact it didn't revolve at all as described – it couldn't possibly have done so!' concluded Eric Youldon, of Exeter. 'Assuming the tender presented a greater wind resistance on one side of the pivot than the engine did on the other, it is possible that a strong wind could have taken over – but for only a limited part of a revolution. As soon as the tender side came round into the face of the gale from the other side of the pivot, the movement would have been arrested and the locomotive stabilised in a neutral position – just as with a simple weather vane,' wrote Mr Youldon. Using simple physics, he pointed out that the only means by which the loco could have rotated continuously was if the wind was also rotating continuously. He continued: 'As with all such yarns, there must have been something to start it off, and I suggest that what happened was this: the engine was being turned, but when it neared the run-off point it became side-on to the wind. Wind force took over, and continued to push the engine until it stopped too far around. It therefore had to be pushed back again – but the same thing happened, and perhaps went on happening until assistance arrived. It is not difficult to imagine that by the time the event was recounted a few times, it reached the proportions we are familiar with, and once the story was taken seriously it was best for those involved to stick to their exaggeration.[28]

Yet more wind

In addition to the turntable tale, Ribblehead viaduct became the subject of much fanciful meteorological speculation. Battered by westerly gales roaring up Chapel-le-Dales, it is said the wind could bring trains to a standstill and blow tarpaulins off trucks to waft them away like autumn leaves (a windfall in a literal sense to any local farmer around when they fell to earth) and the doubtless exaggerated claim that cars had been blown off wagons and smashed to the ground.[25]

Former editor of *The Dalesman*, Bill Mitchell, observed that the parapets deflected the wind from railwaymen crossing it – 'they did not have to crawl as some writers have fancied.'[29] Nevertheless, the wind can be awesome and the anemometer kept at Ribblehead station recorded 92 mph in November 1961.

More than once have I come across the wild claim that on one occasion a track ganger had his cap blown off, only for it to sail under an arch only to rise again and land back on his head, but the wrong way around. He is even quoted as concluding his narrative with the observation, 'Thorr can't have ivverything.'[30]

A tale which challenges townies' image of country folk as simpletons should not be dismissed because of its doubtless apocryphal nature. One woman who lived by the S&C allegedly regularly lined up a row of empty bottles on her garden wall. In the days of steam haulage these proved irresistible to crews, who would take pot shots at them with lumps of coal. The innocent fun unwittingly kept her stocked up with fuel throughout the winter.[31]

With its dramatic scenery and poignant history, it is no wonder the railway between Settle Junction and Carlisle attracted so much folklore. It was 'the line that refused to die' despite Machiavellian machinations and statistical manipulations which have been vindicated by privatisation. More than 22,000 people – and a dog – submitted objections which led to the longest public inquiry into a rail closure proposal in UK railway history. Before the S&C's reprieve announcement on 11 April 1989, it was used as a test bed for two initiatives. The first was 'closure by stealth' which had ramifications for all other 'uneconomic lines'; the second had it being touted almost until the last minute as a precursor for the overall rail privatisation. The British Railways Board tried to find a private buyer to develop the line as a tourist attraction, but before it came to nothing, the *Sunday Express* published an unconfirmed story that in addition to five other serious inquiries, an unnamed fifteen-year-old Saudi Arabian prince had entered a bid. During the systematic rundown of the S&C, British Rail claimed the magnificent Ribblehead viaduct was on the verge of collapse. At one stage, BR estimated that to replace this principal structure would cost between £4.5m and £7m. In the event the bill was only £2.5m and it is now busier than any time during the past thirty years.

Finally, five hundred of the younger generation were in ecstasy when they descended on the base of Ribblehead viaduct for a 24-hour rave party. Arriving in around 150 cars and despite residents' complaints (what, all two of those living there?) about loud noise, police were generally content at the lack of serious incidents.[32]

The fare dodger and other folk

An urban legend concerns a German tram where a black youth sits next to an elderly white woman who loudly voices her racial prejudices to other passengers. When a ticket inspector appears, the woman gets out her ticket for examination. Before it can be clipped, the youth snatches it from her and eats it. When the inspector asks to see her ticket, she relates what has happened. Disbelieving her, the inspector ejects her from the tram for having no valid ticket. This incident formed the basis of the film *Schwarzfahrer*, directed by Pepe Danquart, shown at the Cannes Film Festival.[33] Light rail buff Nigel Pennick has pointed out that this cinematic legend omitted the well-known fact that in Germany if one travels without a ticket one is fined around £40 on the spot. It seems to point to its origin in earlier days, when a fare-dodger would just be thrown off. The whole film relied on a racist pun on the colour of the youth, and the German colloquialism *schwarzfahrer* or 'black traveller', for a passenger who rides without paying. In the USA, the film's title was *Black Rider*, a more literal translation. When the film received the French equivalent of an Oscar at Cannes, it was discovered that the story had a forerunner in an earlier version made a few months earlier in Bielefeld by Bettina Middeke. Here the film was set on a bus, running on the fictitious route 90 between Werther and Bogolzhausen. The story was the same, with an old woman complaining in racist language about the black youth, with the same result. Pennick commented: 'It appears that the story dates back over 30 years and was set in a number of different cities. In earlier times the youth was a Turk or Yugoslav "guest worker" rather than black. But the story seems well entrenched now as an urban legend. In early 1994, the Koln (Cologne) transport undertaking's company magazine, *Intern*, reported a local newspaper report that this incident had just occurred on line 3 of the Wien (Vienna) U-Bahn underground railway. I have not heard of this story attributed yet to a British bus, tram or underground railway system, but as the film has appeared here, doubtless we will.' [34]

The story has been related in other magazines, with nit-picking over where Danquart filmed the story and the correct translation of *schwarzfahrer*, plus the fact that the tale has been doing the rounds since the mid-Sixties, where originally the young man was a migrant worker from Italy, Yugoslavia or Turkey.[35]

Another dodgy tale concerns a couple who tried to avoid buying a rail ticket for their three-year-old daughter (charged at that tender age?) by putting her in a suitcase, but were caught out when the case was stolen. The parents, from Vitebsk, Russia, admitted they were remiss in not paying attention to the case while stopping off for 'a few drinks' after arriving at a Moscow railway station. Police later found the child wandering the streets lost and alone.[36]

The Railway Children

No book on railway folklore could ignore Edith Nesbit's adventure story *The Railway Children*. At one point the youngsters save a baby aboard a blazing barge. Before the fire there is a conversation between the barge master's wife and the children which I suspected to be a *blason populaire.* In the book the narrative goes: ' "You mustn't take no notice of my Bill," said the woman; " 'is bark's worse'n 'is bite. Some of the kids down Farley way is fair terrors. It was them put 'is back up calling out about who ate the puppy-pie under Marlowe bridge." ' [37] I thank Nick Brown, of York, for drawing my attention to an account of the communities mocking one another. Just as visitors would tease Hartlepudlians with 'Who hung the monkey?', a favourite insult of 'Who ate puppy pie under Marlow bridge?' was hurled by Eton schoolboys at Windsor bargees who passed them on the river. According to the legend, some time during the nineteenth century a cook in an Eton household noticed that food was constantly missing from her larder. She determined to get her own back on the thief and so, when a litter of unwanted puppies had been drowned in the house, she put them all in a large pie dish, covered them with a golden crust and put them on the larder wall. Two hours later it had vanished and the next day the remains of the pie were found beneath Marlow bridge. It was assumed that bargees had stolen the pie and, finding the contents far less pleasant than their usual stolen fare, had abandoned it on their journey.[38]

Persons of a certain persuasion have read a sexual subtext into the admittedly sex-mad Edith Nesbit's book. The author enjoyed an open marriage, was always surrounded by young male admirers and had affairs with the likes of George Bernard Shaw.[39] The Freudian analysis I reckon to be unnecessary, but the likes of Caitlin Moran – who suggested men rather than teenagers lusted after Jenny Agutter's nubility – wrote: 'For men of a certain age, *The Railway Children* exerts a very particular hold, not unrelated to Agutter being incredibly strong and sweet and beautiful throughout the film, and then waving her red flannel petticoats (Freudian translation – vagina) at a train coming out of a tunnel (Freudian translation – penis). Indeed, so potent is *The Railway Children*'s magic over the minds of bookish Freudians that it inspired one of the loveliest songs of the 1980s: the Lilac Time's *Girl Who Waves at Trains*, which rather wistfully compares Agutter to a "shotgun in a field of crows".' [40]

Lastly, the mother's dialogue at one point is pure Vicky Pollard out of the brilliant *Little Britain*. 'Poor dear head,' said Bobbie, 'does it ache?' 'No – yes – not much,' said Mother. To think Edith Nesbit created the prototype under-class single mother chav one hundred years in advance!

Live sex and ciggies

Those avid collectors and arbiters of contemporary legend Phil Healey and Rick Glanvill chose to treat as an urban myth the tale concerning an over-amorous couple whose lust led to having full sex before the eyes of fellow passengers, but who only fell foul of their companions when they lit cigarettes in the no-smoking carriage and were duly fined by a magistrate.[41] As is often the case, fact follows fiction, or as reviewer Neil Sears commented: 'Amusing it may be, mythical it ain't. That very incident was reported in *The Northern Echo* on 7 August 1992.' In fact, no doubt to the couple's embarrassment – nay, if they could have intercourse in public, amusement – it was plastered in almost every newspaper. So here's more publicity for John Henderson, then 29, and Zoe D'Arcy, 19, who worked together in Sainsbury's warehouse in West Ealing, London, who on a 25 May 1992, hot Bank Holiday train returning from Margate were seen performing fellatio in a first-class compartment by a woman who boarded at Whitstable with her children. The pair then moved to a packed second-class carriage. Pretty brunette D'Arcy went to the toilet, returned carrying her jeans and sat on Henderson's lap. They then performed full sexual intercourse. No one complained about the antics of the tiddly lovers until they celebrated with post-coital cigarettes. This serious breach of social etiquette led to a row, a complaint to the guard and eventually each being fined £50 with £20 costs. Magistrate Roger Davies told them: 'I'm surprised you can't restrain yourselves.' Henderson, of Pimlico, west London, explained: 'We had been on a works party to Margate and had a few drinks.' [42]

Also *The Sun* claimed testosterone-fuelled couples were taking over compartments on late-night trains to Brighton for sex sessions. Embarrassed guards purportedly turned a blind eye or risked being attacked by randy romeos. The tabloid reported that 'one guard found a half-naked couple embracing in a first-class compartment with third-class tickets.' So what did he do? 'He charged them the extra fare – and let them carry on cuddling!' How chivalrous.[43]

Left luggage gift

When it was her birthday, an adulterous Birmingham woman told her husband she was visiting her aunt in London. Actually, the subject of her trip to the capital was a rich boyfriend, who celebrated her birthday by buying her a mink coat. Travelling back to the West Midlands, she realised she must hide the coat. So she made it into a parcel, took it to the left luggage office and was given a ticket to collect the parcel later. Upon arriving home, she innocently mentioned to her cuckolded spouse that she had found the ticket and said she would go to make a claim with it. Unfortunately her husband insisted that he would collect whatever item it was. Upon discovering that the deposit was a parcel containing a mink coat, he presented it to his secretary, with whom he was having an affair. Returning home, he handed his wife the umbrella he had substituted. Suitably stunned, she could not say anything.[44] Fans of the work of Richard Curtis will recognise this tale as having been adapted as a thread in the film *Love Actually*.

Shame leads to suicide

A ubiquitous legend tells of an architect whose artisans misread his plans, build his design back to front and in a state of reflected shame, the architect commits suicide. A variant attaches to Holyhead breakwater, at 9,875 feet the longest in the UK. Avid shunter aficionados would make a pilgrimage to Anglesey to see the two '01' diesel mechanicals which, isolated from the national network, plied the breakwater carrying additional quarried stone to add to the harbour defences. I recall being on a society trip and as our bus negotiated the narrow lane to the port becoming stuck, being eventually freed, but at the cost of extensive bodywork damage. Welsh journalist Byron Rogers admired the 'crumbling towers of a Disneyland castle' built for the resident engineer who arrived 150 years previously to construct Anglesey breakwater. This was G.C. Dobson and the work took twenty-eight years to complete and ended in 1876. Inquiring of the engineer, a local man told Rogers: 'He killed himself here. He looked down one day, saw the channel he had designed had a kink in it and he couldn't bear the shame.'[45]

While researching a feature on London's St Pancras terminus, two writers stumbled upon a 'tantalising story' that while work was underway, architect Sir George Gilbert Scott discovered he had less land than he had anticipated and so curved the western end to fit the site. 'Without original plans we will never know... it sounds unlikely, but it is a good story!'[46]

Oldies... like this

As the unabashed filler of a column with urban myths on a slack day, no comparable diarist had more sluggish ones than Peter Tory. He shamelessly begins this opener with the warning: 'We have received the following unhappy little tale from a reader in Wales. It is faintly familiar to many of us. Did it happen? Somewhere, sometime, we feel, it most probably did.' For paucity of content, Tory spins it for a further eight paragraphs. To paraphrase would shamefully dilute Tory's shaggy doggedness.

> 'It concerns a small, dapper gentleman called Mr Brown, who had a most pressing engagement in Kettering. It was, so we are assured, an appointment of a lifetime. Mr Brown was travelling from London and fell asleep as the train approached Kettering station. In fact, the poor chap woke up as the express was pulling out. In a dreadful fluster he scrambled to the door of the coach and leapt out. Since the train was now accelerating fast, the

diminutive Mr Brown was required to run at an enormous speed
the moment his feet touched the platform in order not to be
pitched forward. He was still running as the last coach swept past.
As it did so the guard leaned out, grabbed Mr Brown by the scruff
of his overcoat and hauled him on board. "You are a lucky man,"
said the guard to the appalled and panting Mr Brown. "You very
nearly missed it." ' [47]

Poor wee Scottie

Two versions almost twenty years apart separate happy and unhappy endings. The
first claims to be true, in fact it names the witness as Stuart Oliver, of Fulton Street,
Anniesland, Stranraer, who had recently been driving to Glasgow. Approaching a
level crossing near Dunragit, he noticed the warning lights flashing and came to a
halt as the automatic barrier came down. The car behind did not stop in time and
slammed into the back of Mr Oliver's car. Both got out to inspect the damage.
Spotting a man walking his Scottie dog nearby, Mr Oliver called him over as a
witness. The passer-by tied his dog to the barrier and the three men set about
exchanging details as the train raced past. Suddenly the men heard the dog whining
behind them. They looked around and were horrified to see the wee Scottie swinging
by its lead ten feet off the ground. The owner had forgotten that once the train went
through, the barrier would lift – the dog with it – and being automatic, there was no
way of lowering it. The report ended unbelievably: 'The dog had to hang limply in
the air for 20 minutes until the barrier came down for the next train. Luckily, apart
from a bad scare, the Scottie was none the worse for its swinging experience!' [48]

A more recent version was submitted by Neal Hudson, of Sutton Coldfield, West
Midlands, who while walking witnessed an accident between a cyclist and a car.
The driver had hoped to make a getaway, but level crossing gates came down and
trapped him. The cyclist got back on his bike and rode up to confront him while the
storyteller jogged up, along with a woman out walking her dog, who had also
witnessed the incident, to give their accounts of what had happened. When they got
to the crossing, the cyclist was remonstrating with the driver and the situation looked
to be getting nasty. 'The woman and I intervened and managed to calm everybody
down. Eventually the level crossing went up, the cyclist rode off and the car sped
away, leaving the woman and I to shrug our shoulders at the state of the world,'
wrote the contributor. 'It was then we realised, with real horror, that the woman's
dog, which she had tied to the level crossing gate, was hanging from its lead a good
ten feet in the air, quite dead.' [49]

Where's Vernon?

We all know someone who believes the characters in TV soaps to be as real to them
as their family, friends and neighbours. A rail-based tale which relies for its
believability on this premise centres upon two old dears who got on a North
Yorkshire Moors Railway train at Goathland, intending to travel to Pickering.
However, they failed to read the notice which directed intending Pickering
passengers to cross the footbridge, resulting in them going in the opposite direction

to Grosmont. When inquiring at Grosmont how they might best get to Pickering (for the train they should have caught was the last train of the day), they were told that they would have to pay for a taxi to come from Whitby to Grosmont to take them to Pickering. At this point one of the old ladies asked: 'Can't we use Vernon Cripps?' (For the benefit of readers baffled by this inquiry, Vernon Cripps is the taxi-owner in the TV series *Heartbeat* based in Goathland, alias Aidensfield). Thet two old dears were told that he was around during the Sixties, but not in the twenty-first century.[50]

Out of the window...

First of three. A strait-laced office worker made a complete prat of himself at a New Year party in London's West End, ending up vomiting all over his pinstripes. Aware that he needed new clothes, but in a hurry to catch his train to Brighton, he dashed into Mr Byrite, in Oxford Street, spent less than two minutes hazily selecting fresh clobber, throwing into a pile by the till and hurriedly paying for it. He jumped aboard his train as it was pulling out and dashed to the toilet. Tearing off his stinking and soaking trousers, shirt and jacket, he recklessly threw them out of the carriage window. However, when he opened the bag to put on his new purchases, he discovered to his dismay that what he had hastily bought were some socks, a T-shirt and two cardigans.[51]

A second version purports to have actually happened to Spike Milligan's publisher, Jack Hobbs, who suffered embarrassment after eating something which did not agree with him. Hobbs rushed squelching into an Oxford Street store demanding a new pair of trousers, which to his impatience, the shop assistant spent ages parcelling up. Hobbs then raced to Waterloo station just in time to catch his train. Heading straight to the lavatory, he removed his trousers with relief and thankfully tossed them out of the window. Unwrapping the parcel, to his dismay he found a beautiful fluffy pink cardigan which had been so lovingly wrapped for him by the vengeful shopworker.[52]

Ricky Gervais, in a best British stand-up gags ever compilation, told it like this: 'My mate's brother was going for a job interview and he had to change trains. He was on the platform at Crewe and he shat himself, as you do. He looked around and saw Millets. So he squelched over and said, "Quick, Levis, size 36." So he got them, got the train and went into the toilet. He took his pants and trousers off, poked them out of the window, cleaned himself up and flushed it all away. Opens the bag – it was a jacket."' [53]

Dubious transmissions

Contemporary legend lore is replete with instances of communications transmissions variously picked up by the likes of church organs responding to local taxi firms' radios or teeth amalgam boosting some local radio broadcasting presenter. When the 6.45 a.m. express passenger train to London Euston ground to a halt shortly after leaving Birmingham New Street, after 'shuddering and juddering', a spokesman for InterCity West Coast explained: 'The computer on the rear loco threw a wobbler after picking up signals from Birmingham International Airport.' [54]

Previously, Tony Iommi, of Black Sabbath, decided too little attention was being paid to his guitar solo spot in the show. So he demanded fellow band members remain silent for the showcase performance, road crew stay quiet backstage on pain of fining and the audience be encouraged to keep schtum also. First night of the tour was a prestigious hometown date at the Birmingham Odeon. As the lights dimmed and the hall fell silent for Iommi's solo spot, an inaudible intake of breath across the hushed auditorium greeted Iommi's kaftanned arm raised above the strings... and from the speakers crackled the immortal words, 'Car 22, could you pick up at New Street station, travelling to Cradley Heath... ' [55]

Finally, a faulty sound system broadcast a reading of 'Thomas the Tank Engine' to churchgoers waiting for a sermon at Keighley, West Yorkshire. St John's vicar David Robinson said: 'The Fat Controller caused great hilarity.' [56]

When you're ready

The rural branch line and days when trains actually ran to cater for a social need are almost a memory. Just such was the tiny Bishop's Castle Railway which spent more than seventy years in the hands of the Official Receiver, and eked out a precarious existence in rural Shropshire. In the 1920s, not long before it gave up the uneven struggle, a hiker supposedly turned up at Bishop's Castle station to inquire about the next train to Craven Arms. Discovering the station deserted, and no timetable on display, he set off towards a loud clanging noise down the yard. Here he discovered an antediluvian locomotive, leaking steam from every joint, and a man in overalls striking something underneath with a spanner. 'Excuse me,' said the hiker, 'could you tell me the time of the next train to Craven Arms, please?' The station master, booking clerk, engine driver and fitter (for it was indeed he) looked anxiously at his watch and replied: 'Er... what time did you want to go?' [57]

Model behaviour

Same named culprit, six years between tellings and an ocean between. In 1994, a model train fanatic named as John Whelan, 37, of Christchurch, New Zealand, refused to put away the toy tracks and bride Joan, 33, refused to make love in the middle of the layout and stormed off home to mum.[58] In 2000, in Glendale, Utah, USA, John Whelan, by now only 33, and Joan, now 31, rowed when she refused to consummate the wedding in the middle of his toy railway and went back to mother.[59] The couple were last heard seeing a marriage counsellor. But where?

The gold train

A secret train and stolen gold, a three-month wartime journey at 3 mph, plus bombing, robbery, deceit and refuge in an Alpine tunnel hiding pending a deluded re-launch of Nazism from a mountain redoubt. All fact.[60] The same train in 1944 dynamited in a French tunnel, carrying gold worth 200 billion dollars on today's market, but which found its way to finance the Montauk Project. All unlikely. The project mentioned operated during the 1970s and 1980s at New York's Montauk Air Force Base and was supposedly an attempt to explore, chart and ultimately manipulate the flow of time. Kidnapped, tortured and brain-washed young men, the 'Montauk Boys' would be sent down a 'time tunnel' on missions to different times, places and alternate realities. Many never returned. Philip K. Dick's novel *Total Recall* is allegedly based on some of the Montauk Project reports. According to this worldview, time as we know it ends in AD 2012.[61]

Thai treasure hunt

Apparently even the country's Prime Minister, Thaksin Shinawatra, joined thousands of other Thais in a treasure hunt after a senator claimed he had found 2,500 tons of hidden Japanese booty. They headed for caves beside the notorious Burma-Siam 'Death Railway' in western Thailand, where Chaowarin Latthasaksiri, a veteran searcher for buried Japanese gold, claimed he had found treasure. Rumours had circulated locally in Kanchanburi province that at the end of the Second World War a hoard of gold had been abandoned by the Japanese. The senator had been lured by a story told him by a monk, who claimed to have found a way to the treasure several years previously after having been led there by a wartime guide for the Japanese. According to the monk, having passed through a labyrinthine series of underground caves, he came upon gold bars, samurai swords, bodies of prisoners of war and... a locomotive.[62]

Actually there's no need to go to Thailand for hidden locos; try Heapey or Rhyd-y-Mwyn or Hessay.

Chapter Eight

Rust never sleeps

There's this secret underground cavern crammed with mothballed steam locomotives under a hill in the Cotswolds. Or a disused tunnel in the Scottish Highlands filled with cocooned, greased engines. Or less romantically a huge warehouse at a military depot sardined with strategic six-coupled hardware. Ferroequinological fantasy? Of all the wish-fulfilment style rumours this one excites me – and many others – the most.

Those steam engines, once so common, chugged and clanked everywhere and then they disappeared with undignified haste. The British Railways Board, in its dubious wisdom, waved a magic wand and in a puff of smoke the once proud culture of glamorous steam locos was replaced by the relatively characterless and flick-a-switch-and-it-goes diesels.

Regular rail travellers during the Sixties will recall passing depots crowded with rusting hulks; an obvious embarrassment to officialdom. Also they may have reason to thank a begrimed freight engine commandeered to take over from an errant, new-fangled diesel. This sort of emotional interface created the beginnings of a smokescreen of myth, legend, apocrypha and blatant dreamy contemplation which has cast doubts on and within the Sixties' scrapping scenario supposed specifics.

Strategic steam reserve

In such a climate of disbelief at the authorities' foolhardy rush into dieselisation with untried types, plus a network devoid of the necessary infrastructure to support a viable transition to a revolutionary new transport mode, it is hardly surprising that steam's rapid eclipse brought the dawning of a fresh and pervasive myth. Perhaps these displaced dinosaurs did not all go for scrap. Occulted from prying eyes, their whereabouts known only to the chosen few, a cache was secreted away at a secret location or locales. This is the Strategic Steam Reserve (SSR) story.

It is certainly a rather offbeat myth. Like legendary King Arthur and his Knights of the Round Table awaiting the call to arms in time of England's need. For a thousand years he has been our sleeping hero and the tale of Arthur – *rex quondam rexque futurus*, the Once and Future King – appeals to the oppressed and disadvantaged. Others, too, have been held to lie in suspended animation such as Northern hero Harry Hotspur and his hounds holed up by a landslide at Hell Hole in the Cheviots awaiting release by a call on a hunter's horn; Earl Gerald, who lies below the Rath of Lullaghast, from which he will emerge to drive out the British and unite Ireland;

Welsh heroes Owen of the Red Hand and Owain Glendower; Roderick, last of the Goths; Don Sebastian of Spain; King Wenzel below Bohemia's Blanik Mountains; Frederic Barbarossa beneath a mountain in Thuringia; and many other national heroes.[1]

So offbeat a myth, in fact, I have been tracking it down for the past twenty-five years, noting the uniformities among my informants' stories and cursing the irritating irresoluteness of substantiating it.[2] There is a logic in the notion that some steam engines be retained mothballed, lubricated and kept in reserve in readiness for any circumstance such as war, civil unrest or even geophysical exhaustion. A reserve which could be easily resurrected as happened with the long-forgotten Green Goddesses during the fire brigades' strike.

Ironically, British private railways have been buying steam locos from other nations' disbanded strategic reserves. Swedish, Greek and Yugoslav stockpiled former reserve engines now work on preserved lines. One dump alone at Nizhmiy Tagil, in Russia, was reputed to hold no fewer than 1,500 steam locos, and nationally there were an estimated 9,000.[3]

When I began writing about the SSR in 1980 there were not the steam charters which ply our railway system every weekend or the network of volunteers and preserved railways where private locos could be maintained and prepared for main-line running. Back then there were doubts as to whether it could ever be feasible to resurrect steam for an infrastructure so changed by modern motive power requirements. The very ubiquity of steam operations today shows that the Doubting Thomases were so wrong and that human ingenuity and will has overcome all obstacles.

Just as surplus army Green Goddess fire-engines were retained, on the railway system there existed a number of emergency telegraph trains, placed strategically throughout the country. These coaching sets, with their radar and other sophisticated gear, were also taken out of mothballs in the late Seventies. Individual coaches were sold to preservation societies. Not until this commercial venture was undertaken did the coaching stock buffs feel safe to publish the minutiae of the operation in the railway press. Yet, doubtless, the revelations fuelled rather than dampened a similar notion of steam engines which could also come on to the open market.[4]

'Elephants' graveyard'

Commenting on an article I had written about the SSR, writer John Michell recalled that as an undergraduate he would wander around a dump beyond railway tracks in Cambridge. There were acres of old steam traction engines. He heard many of them went to East Africa for the abortive groundnuts scheme. He presumed the Africans must now have their own dump of them somewhere in the bush. He likened this to the 'Elephants' graveyard' myth and the SSR. This in turn triggered my memory of an Anthony Buckeridge novel about those schoolboys in his 'Jennings' series. The pupils found a scattering of bones in the English countryside. One imaginative boarder speculated they had found where elephants went to die. Another held his nose and suggested they used the place for a more functionary purpose. It seemed very radical humour in my pre-pubescent period.

Additional to the striking haste of withdrawals and disposal, foreign precedents, Green Goddesses and emergency trains, two other factors seemingly encouraged rumour mongering. There was a sudden cut-back in oil supplies to British Railways, which fuelled further the usefulness of coal-based energy. Then came a downturn in rail-borne freight traffic, resulting in a modest concentration of surplus diesels at Swindon.

While on a journalistic assignment to report on and road test a new, cheap (and nasty) lightweight diesel railbus, I fell into conversation with a British Railways commissioning engineer. We got around somehow to the subject of the SSR and coincidentally his previous brief had been to find a means of adequately storing those diesels at Swindon in such a fashion that they could be rapidly returned to traffic at a later date. With no precedent, he had approached the Royal Navy at Portsmouth, but found its warship mothballing techniques unsuited to a railway requirement. He presumed it would be even harder to have a fleet of steam locos available at short notice than would be any attempt to find a solution as to how to get valuable, technically-sophisticated diesels to run again. He then confided that as a steam buff and Cornishman, he would dearly love to believe that a squadron of ex-GWR 'Granges' lay in reserve in a tunnel below some Wiltshire hill. Just as I doubt the presence as ancient folklore maintains of golden calves, coffins and chariots buried in prehistoric barrows at locations such as Salisbury Plain, I would question that here could lie the Holy Grail of Ferroequinology.

But this is only a scene-setter for other familiar folklore motifs in new guises. The SSR deals with new versions of the interrupted journey, vehicle interference, abduction, special gift and altered time factor.

Interrupted journey

Here's the reserve lore version from *Steam Railway*: 'One old driver recalls an unusual incident on a Sunday when, only minutes after coming off shed with a convoy of scrappers, he was halted at signals and called up to the signalbox. The signalman explained that he had just received fresh "orders." The driver and his mate were to be relieved of this particular duty and they could book off with full pay. They never saw which crew it was that took over the train, and the engines were never seen again.'[5] Similarly, a friend of mine, Alan Shepherd, then a permanent way ganger, recalled how when working at West Hartlepool locomotive power depot, a crew was selected to haul a formation of former 'War Department' 2-8-0s for scrap around 1966. They were similarly halted after a short distance and replaced by a crew of strangers.

I have cautioned several times in this work, beware the interrupted journey. Here there's a reward factor; full pay a bonus for doing virtually nothing. Similarly the altered time factor; that unexpected benefit of extra leisure hours. Time also involved almost supernaturally in the recollection recalled only with the topic's rise into a more general consciousness. Not least strange is the mysterious arrival of strangers from who knows where and heading for... well, there are plenty of postulated destinations.

If circumstantial evidence proved a case in the face of commonsensical scepticism then the tale of a 'B17' makes for interesting reading. An émigré in Lima, Peru, John Botterill asked in all seriousness about the fate of 'Sandringham' class 4-6-0 No. 61633 *Kimbolton Castle*. He claimed that upon withdrawal this 'B17' spent several days in sidings at Peterborough East station, bereft of nameplates, before being hauled 'dead' to a siding near Kettering early in 1959. It was stabled overnight before a diesel shunter propelled it cautiously down a disused mineral line, perhaps to Cransley. It was then stored in a line-side farm building, covered with oil-soaked potato sacks and bales of hay. Its purchaser took great pains to make trespassers unwelcome. Botterill said he had reason to believe it was still there, hidden and forgotten, as recently as 1968. The mineral line had lost its connection with British Rail and he had left England. He kept expecting to hear of its rehabilitation and arrival at a preservation site, but to no avail. His letter appeared in *Railway World* (July 1983) and two months later the magazine published a categorical denunciation by Peter L. Robinson that after withdrawal from March depot in September 1959 it appeared at Peterborough that month, nameplates still in place, that he saw it personally at Doncaster Works the following month and that it was cut up there. Did John Botterill fabricate his story, was he mistaken about the engine's identity or was something truly weird going on here? The tracks certainly diverge.

What the sleepy head saw

A far more persuasive case, yet ultimately undoubtedly erroneous is a person who claims to have seen part of the SSR. This remarkable tale was unearthed by David Wilcock, who as editor of *Steam Railway* was the first to draw the public's attention to the SSR. Also as editor of the first issue of *Steam World*, it was he who unveiled his scoop find of Stephen Burgess.[6] The story reached Wilcock after a chance conversation between Burgess, then twenty-eight and a Bachelor of Science working as Service Manager for Renault UK in Birmingham, and colleague Terry Staines, a long-term steam buff. Staines decided to risk his credibility and that of Burgess. Through Staines, Wilcock got Burgess to write down all he could remember of the fateful day, 2 October 1975.

This is Burgess's account of the strange incident: 'Exactly what occurred, I cannot completely recall, and certain details I'm afraid escape me completely. However, the bulk of the story I can substantiate by diary entries made by myself during the autumn of 1975. I was returning to Aberystwyth to begin the winter term at my college.' He caught an early morning train from Birmingham New Street to Shrewsbury, where he needed to change trains. 'I'm not sure what time the train arrived, as I had fallen asleep during the journey. When I awoke, the train had stopped, but we had not, it seemed, arrived anywhere, as the train was not standing at a platform. Instead, it was in some sidings. The train (a DMU, I think) was segregated into compartments and I was alone. I ventured to look out of the window to see where I was, as I was feeling completely disorientated.' In addition to the general paraphernalia of sidings, there were two or three lines of steam locomotives. 'I am completely ignorant of steam locomotives, so I cannot describe their type, except that they were large and in good condition. They were painted a dull black, and bore large white painted numbers on their boilers. The cabins were boarded over, as were the tops of the tenders, as I could see the boards which overlapped the sides a little. The connecting rods were also removed, but I cannot remember if they were laying in the cabins – I think they were.' He did not know how many engines there were, but it was many. 'Further details than this escape me, as the more I think about the experience, the more the facts become blurred. I got out of the train, and began to walk along the sidings, where I was discovered by a railway worker, who led me back to the station which was nearby. It was Shrewsbury.' He continued his journey to Aberystwyth, arriving late in the afternoon. He apologetically concluded: 'I'm sorry I can't identify the types of engine, but my knowledge of steam locomotives is minimal.' [7]

Wilcock met Burgess and for three hours quizzed him on his story. Additional points which emerged were that at the time Burgess thought nothing surprising of the cache of locos, with no attempt to hide them, and the railwayman who aided him was neither alarmed nor secretive, but simply helpful. Burgess had never been a rail enthusiast and as a mechanic, noting the removal of the coupling rods was a technical observation.

The closest analogy to what he reported was the actual hoard of steam locos in Dai Woodham's scrapyard at Barry, South Wales. There, engines had highly-visible white paint daubing to denote preservation societies which had reserved individual locos, often with requests that no parts be removed. Burgess had never been to Barry, nor could he have confused the date. His engines were in reasonable condition; those at Barry were by then rusting hulks.

Burgess took Staines back to Shrewsbury and they located the sidings. The area was clearly visible to many people in Shrewsbury. Could he have seen ex-Barry engines en route to preservation? Fourteen locos left Barry that year, but only two by rail.

So what actually happened to Stephen Burgess that fateful day? Did he slip into some other dimension or separate reality? An out-of-the-body experience to God knows where, with his consciousness in some exotic situation while his unconscious body was in the unexotic location of a drab provincial train? Or did he slip back in time? A British Rail employee who worked in the department concerned at the time of the alleged 1975 sighting, Peter Trushell, assured *Steam World* readers no such movement took place at that time.[8] However, he pointed out that during the final years of steam, Shrewsbury acted as a staging point for withdrawn locos en route to south Wales scrap yards from the north-west. These were stabled at Coton Hill yard, north of the station on the Wrexham line, and in Coleham yard, south of Sutton Bridge junction.

Or did Burgess slip into the future? Prophecy – as revealed earlier in this work – is no stranger, and in fact often a major component, in modern legends, so did Burgess take a brief journey into the twenty-first century? Did he see steam power being mobilised for some forthcoming emergency?

He did not think he imagined the experience, but admitted feeling 'completely disorientated.' Temporal lobe dissociation has been a recent catchall to explain supernatural experiences and touted as a unified theory of the paranormal. Phenomena ranging from sightings of ghosts, UFOs and Virgin Marys to out-of-the-body experiences and near-death experiences have been forwarded as examples of dissociative states. Of interest here, sleep paralysis has also been associated with unusual activity in the brain's temporal lobe; I discuss a number of such personal experiences in the Appendix.

Two other exotic states which might apply to Burgess are quantum entanglement and depersonalisation disorder. My guess is that it was a hypnopompic experience. This is the period between sleep and final wakefulness which can produce images which are vivid and realistic, lasting in duration from a few seconds to minutes. There is an unusual clarity of detail. The events 'seen' are coloured, three-dimensional and indistinguishable from reality.

He recalled the train heating being full on and a sprinkling of people on the train. In his own words: 'The next thing I remember was waking with a sudden sensation of coldness – or at least that something was different. The train had emptied at Shrewsbury and I'd been left sound asleep.' He was subsequently happy to admit his story had no rational explanation. It would not, however, be irrational to compare Burgess with the average UFO abductee; a bemused, disorientated pawn suffering an interrupted journey on his way back to college. Even Burgess's testimony shares facets of signed affidavits familiar in ufology. Yet he obviously saw something which was very real to him at the time.

After all my proposed exotic explanations are exhausted, there is still the possibility of mythomania.

Supposed secret sites

Over the years several possible sites have been mooted as storage points for the SSR. This crock of ferrous metal at the end of the rail rumour rainbow is usually a rail-connected Ministry of Defence or Royal Ordnance location. Anyone with Internet access can at the click of a mouse find the list of operational MoD shunters and the varied sites at which they operate. In fact, stored private diesel and electric locos, plus surplus coaching stock, are scattered among may government locations. In the past, official spokesmen were often sniffy about revealing the extent of defence establishment locos, but they proudly displayed a MoD Kineton 0-6-0 at the last spotters' Old Oak Common open day.

Rhyd-y-mwyn

During the Second World War, operations at the Valley works at Rhyd-y-mwyn, in the Alyn valley of North Wales, were so secret that it was the only UK wartime installation that was never located by German intelligence. Four tunnels fitted with blast doors involved 2,200 miners and 'company security' officers. The Valley site and an overflow chemical weapons location code-named 'Woodside' did not officially exist until recently. In 1947 the surface site was redesigned and site guards re-housed to protect identification. There was a panic when television company HTV began prying in 1982, only to be fobbed off. By 1990 the visible portions of the original chemical plant air ventilation shafts were re-engineered to remove them from view. The document from which this information has been gleaned warns that 'it should be noted that photography and stationary vehicles are treated in the same manner as at Aldermaston and Hawthorn, and with the same calibre equipment.'[9]

Rail-connected to British Rail until the early-Seventies, the track had been lifted partially, but there remained a section continuing from Mold almost to its doorstep without apparent reason. Not that this proves the SSR lay a stone's throw away. Yet *Steam Railway* anecdotally reported: 'An unsubstantiated account is given by a policeman involved in a special exercise there some years ago, that steam locomotives were stored there, and he had seen them – but that the information was "classified".' The MoD told the reporter narrow-gauge diesels are used there to move stores.[10]

Also the Alyn valley is not far from Shrewsbury. But what seriously damages Valley works' role in the SSR saga is an account on the Internet, with many colour pictures, of a visit made by five members of Subterranea Britannica on 22 March 2001. Arranged and fully sanctioned by owners the Ministry of Agriculture (now Department of Environment, Food and Rural Affairs), no restrictions were placed on the party's visit and they videoed the whole site. As for any railway operation, they found a platform and siding, but no evidence of railway tracks in any of the tunnels. There were, however, sheds which housed shunting locos.

Hessay

Another favoured SSR location is Hessay, where a Royal Engineers' depot was linked to the York to Harrogate single railway line.[11] It had warehouses, workshops and offices with tracks running through them. Radio ham Roger Kendall told me that he heard from a fellow hobbyist that a pit had been dug there and surplus American radio receivers and transmitters, weighing around 70 lb each and valued at £100, had been dumped in it. Apparently this ex-Second World War equipment was all in its original wrappers and even in the technologically-sophisticated twenty-first century would be warmly welcomed by radio hams. However, a private developer paid £2m for the site in 1999 and it is now a business park.

Marchwood

The military port of Marchwood, Hampshire, is another choice. Speculation was fanned when it was learned that privately-owned '9F' steam loco No. 92203 had been moved into the complex. A correspondent in *Steam Railway* pondered: 'It is indeed intriguing to wonder what exists at Marchwood that can retube a '9F' in 1979.'[12] But less intriguing when you learn by reply that the MoD depot to service and supply the Fleet Auxiliary is adjacent to Husbands Shipyards Ltd, which actually

'Class 9F' No. 92203, which was believed to have been worked upon at Marchwood military port in 1979, but was in fact re-tubed at an adjacent factory. (Paul Screeton)

repaired the loco. Also the depot is – or was – open to the public once a year, and one of its tank engines was used for filming in the children's TV series *Enid Blyton's Famous Five*. Yet the informant for these facts pointed to another MoD depot with an extensive rail network near the A32 connected to the Fareham-Gosport branch. 'To date I have only seen diesel shunters in the area,' adding darkly, 'but what is hidden away in the many buildings is another story.'[13]

After writing in the *Hartlepool Mail*, I had a correspondent write about the possibility of the SSR being at the extensive MoD site at Shoeburyness, Essex; this, and depots at Kineton (Warwickshire), Bicester (Oxfordshire), Ashchurch (Gloucestershire) and Smalmstown (near Carlisle) have all been used to store private diesel locomotives and rolling stock.

Heapey

A Sunday lunchtime ritual was to join a retired signalman for a couple of pints. Alec 'Bollocky' Gray got his nickname from being a stickler for following the rulebook, but that did not stop one of his former expatriate signal-box 'boys' from joining him for a beer whenever he returned to the area. As I sat down in the Seaton Hotel, the émigré waved a copy of the local 'rag', open at the page on which was an article I had written on the SSR. 'The place where all those missing steamers are is Heapey.

It's in Lancashire. It's a big Ordnance depot and they've lifted the track, supposedly to camouflage the fact of what's in there.' This was a major breakthrough. So he had been in and seen the locos? 'No, but a friend who lives nearby has been in and definitely seen them.' It was sounding depressingly like foaflore. He took my address and promised to send further details. That was 1980 and I am still waiting. It seems closed doors, barbed wire, rusty rails and guards create James Bond fantasies and imaginative scenarios.

Peter lists the scrappers

Of course, if all the redundant locos which went for scrap or preservation could be accounted for, surely the SSR myth would fade into oblivion. One man, Peter Hands, set out to catalogue the disposals and eventually published the results in a series of booklets entitled *What Happened to Steam?*, running to around forty volumes. The booklets give allocations of each engine since 1957 up to withdrawal, places of storage pending disposal, locations for scrapping and – in lucky instances – preservation. Only a handful of engines escaped Hands' ten-year prodigious and meticulous research. He believes that had there been such a reserve, its location would have been definitively identified long ago. He admits it to be possible but almost nonsensical that 'British Rail publicised false sales to scrap merchants to satisfy enthusiasts.' Those few locos that he could not account for were of older classes and the least likely to be of future use. A long letter he sent me in 1980 was reproduced in an article I wrote on the topic.[14]

Another diligent rail fan with an interest in loco disposals, Nigel Trevena, has produced a series of books, *Steam for Scrap*. After discussing the SSR, Trevena recalls the rumoured existence of an ex-LMS 'Duchess' at the bottom of Troon harbour, tipped from the quayside by an act of over-enthusiastic shunting and a query as to the veracity of a pair of ex-LMS 'Princess Royals' saved from a Birmingham scrap yard and currently running on the Foxfield Railway in Staffordshire. 'The truth is more prosaic, but *Steam for Scrap* is intent on putting the record straight,' he wrote.[15]

Rory visits the sites

A former ufology investigator, Rory Lushman became seriously interested in the SSR, not least having been a keen trainspotter (and after reviving his rail enthusiasm was last heard of as an employee with Peter Waterman's new London and North Western Railway). I must take most of the blame or credit for encouraging his SSR enthusiasm. It was also helpful that he lives near the Heapey site, which is so closely identified with the SSR. Heapey is a small village just off the M61 and near the Botany Bay district of Chorley, and formerly served by a railway between Chorley and Blackburn. As at Rhyd-y-mwyn there are four main tunnels.

Rory made several visits to the Heapey site, taking photographs (even hiring a light aircraft), videoing the site and interviewing local people. Both a farmer and former resident recalled seeing steam locos parked outside the main complex. The former told Rory the locos were removed on low-loaders during the Sixties. The former resident's version of events was that during the mid-Fifties to early-Sixties, up to a

At Box tunnel, a flameproof loco hauls an ammunition train into Corsham depot.

dozen aged engines would be stored in the open, being replaced as the years went by with other locos. The local kids, he said, knew the place affectionately as the 'engines' graveyard.' Local people reported occasional nocturnal visits to the factory site by lorries and as Rory was to learn at close quarters, it is patrolled by the police.[16] He and a companion also travelled to Rhyd-y-mwyn, but found little to see due to the enclosed nature of the site.[17] Seeking publicity in his bid to find persons with information on Heapey's role in the SSR saga, Rory was interviewed by a local paper. This elicited a comment from a Ministry of Defence police spokesman, Mervin Dodd, who said: 'Our people look after the Royal Ordnance site at Euxton and the sub-depot at Heapey. Apparently trains used to go there but there is no basis for these stories of hidden locomotives at the site. A couple of people have been arrested there recently for stealing slates. Perhaps one or two "conspiracy theorists" have seen this and drawn their own conclusions.'[18]

Box tunnel

Members of the wilder fringes of ufology have pointed to the vast underground complex in Wiltshire, one of whose entrances was originally adjacent to the London-facing portal of Box tunnel, as the storage site for extraterrestrial craft. This exotic theory is briefly touched upon by Rory Lushman in an article on the SSR, published in the magazine of the Pendle, Hyndburn UFO Network.[19] Box tunnel extends 1¾ miles on the line from Paddington to Bristol. The tunnel presented great difficulties to the GWR and was said to have cost £100 for every yard advanced. In the earliest days, stagecoaches were run from Chippenham to Bath 'for persons fearful of Box tunnel.' Today, travellers on westbound trains speeding into the chasm can glimpse the fenced-off and overgrown entrance taking a parallel line into the heart of the hill where lies a once-secret underground town known as 'Turnstile.'[20] This entrance was created in 1844 by the quarrying firm Randall and Saunders and a vertical ladder down to the mouth of the tunnel was the workers' means of accessing the workings. The labyrinth later housed an aero-engine manufacturing facility and murals remain from those days, including one of an Anglican missionary being boiled in a pot by cannibals. It became Corsham Central Ammunition Depot, for which the sidings at Thingley Junction were constructed. Finally as the regional seat of government it was improvised from these eerie interlocking chambers, it being one of twelve post-nuclear 'kingdoms', echoing John Michell's twelve-tribe nations of antiquity and also mirroring those of the Anglo-Saxons.

Conspiracy buffs have made their mark on Box. With all the elan of the all-knowing, Anarchists Anonymous could proclaim: 'There are four sets of points inside the tunnel leading through steel gates into the interior of the hill.'[21] Untrue, of course. Another counter-revolutionary claim being: 'At Chinnor, in the Chilterns, the government is excavating a massive new tunnel – ostensibly as an experiment for the Channel tunnel.'[22] Back at Box, three men appeared in court in 2004 having been caught halfway into the tunnel, having believed there was a secret MoD munitions base inside the tunnel and gone equipped with tools to break into it. A train driver raised the alarm and in the ensuing search, fourteen services were delayed, resulting in delay attribution costs of £48,000.[23]

There were also sidings near Box at Farleigh Down with a narrow-gauge tracked platform and mile-long conveyor belt set at right angles to the main standard-gauge line. During the Second World War from the platform here troops maintained a 24-hour operation of moving in and out ammunition. In the 1970s these caverns were reopened as a tourist attraction for a few brief years.[24]

As a final comment on the Cold War, during 1956 a war game played by the Royal Air Force assumed that two hundred nuclear bombs had been dropped on Britain. There was good news for rail travellers in this post-apocalypse Britain, 'half the normal scheduled trains would be running four weeks after the world as they knew it had come to an end.'[25]

Modern traction reserve

Once the SSR rumour was up and running, it was not long before its diesel equivalent took to the rails. While the vulnerability of electrical systems in diesel-electric and AC and DC electric locomotives makes them probable non-starters for a reserve, just that factor makes steam such a more attractive alternative. This very issue was raised in the letters column of a ufologists' magazine by Nick Brown, of York. He sought information on the SSR after 'a local and highly-respected lecturer in engineering' told him that certain railway tunnels were being used for storing and maintenance of the SSR, because after a nuclear attack 'the resulting ionisation would render electronic and diesel rolling stock useless.'[26]

During the war in Serbia, electrical systems were allegedly knocked out by graphite bombs, which explode a cloud of ultra-fine carbon-fibre filaments to short-circuit electrical installations. A later version of the G-bomb was used by NATO in May, 1999, to successfully disable seventy percent of Serbia's power supply. When asked if the United States launched offensive cyber operations against the Serbs, Lieutenant-General William Donahue, director of communications and information for the US Air Force, said: 'I don't know, and if I did, it's too sensitive to talk about.' This is the hardware weaponry of mass disruption. Electromagnetic pulse bombs and high-energy radio frequency guns on board aircraft could put electronic targets out of action.[27] There is also the alternative of using software strikes; shutting down, deleting or modifying computer data. All this can be bloodless and not covered by the Geneva or Hague Conventions.[28]

To return to electrical shorting out, this takes us back again to ufology and the ubiquitous vehicle interference from flying saucers and the resulting classic interrupted journey. Of course, we now know that Guglielmo Marconi discovered that very low frequency waves can stall engines. Similarly a radioactive energy field will interfere with atomic structure in electronic apparatus. Ufolore crackles with stalled automobiles. Folklore reports instances from before the Industrial Revolution. John A. Keel boasted: 'This sounds like our first electromagnetic case – even though no motors or electrical circuits were involved.'[29] This involved no lesser person than a president of the USA, Andrew Jackson, when he reportedly paid a visit to the Bell Witch poltergeist manifestation homestead and his horses were unable to move the wagon and its baffled first citizen. Even earlier occurrences in the UK have been recorded, generally with a supernatural dimension and a witch's interfering spell.

So if there were diesel locos in a reserve, presumably the modifications touted would be ones to render them impervious to hardware designed to short out or burn up unshielded electronic systems. The hex would be deflected.

Rory Lushman has also suggested that not all the 'Blue Pullman' multiple units were scrapped and 'one unit was converted to a strategic mobile unit and painted black.'[30] Powercars W60090 and W60091 were listed as preserved by a Blue Pullman Group. He also came across vague references to 'Class 47s' being modified at a RAF base, plus NATO-liveried examples stored at Newton Abbot in 1981 and ones built new and immediately hidden away. This could be a garbled supposition from ten such extra '47s' (actually '48s' for the pedants) built by Clayton/Brush for Cuba, which due to the sensitivity of the export order were trialled on the Lickey incline in the middle of the night. Though a bona fide fact and pictures of them being built at the works of Combustion Limited, near Derby, in 1964,[31] and rusting away in Cuba have been published.[32] Also mechanically-dire Clayton 'Class 17s' were stored for future use near Carlisle. As with the SSR, disposal records had supposedly been fabricated.[33] As Rory put it in a letter to me: 'Much of the SSR information is from the brother of a friend whose auntie knows someone who used to work on the railway in 1956.'

Variations on a theme

Of course, the SSR is one of a great many variations on the motif of persons or objects secreted away from prying eyes. The regional seats of government so sought after by the oxymoronic Spies for Peace could be lumped together with identical 'decoy' farmhouses of Cold War fame and maps purportedly locating IRA weapons bunkers. The Bomber Airfield Society reckoned it had located twenty-three dismantled planes abandoned after the last war around the country and planned to assemble them at Binbrook airfield, but I have yet to hear of any restoration.[34]

There were those who believed the crew of the sunken trawler *Gaul*, an alleged spy ship, were prisoners-of-war in Russia, just as many Americans believe 2,266 servicemen listed as missing in action are still being held hostage in Vietnam. Before that, intelligence reports from the Korean War described trainloads of PoWs shunting through Manchuria to Siberia.[35] In the USA, Area 51 does not officially exist, but if it did it would house UFOs, back-engineering projects and a new generation of spy planes. Oh, and let's not forget the vast Tibetan cavern that contains a library of books saved from Atlantis. Yes, this is the same mega grotto where Jesus Christ stopped off on his way to China.[36]

In conclusion

It is truly sad that Britain did not follow other countries' example and stockpile redundant steam engines. The SSR depended for sustenance on how faithfully the group of spotters with its community of interests could express its need logically. The utopian myth was cultivated reasonably imaginatively, but sadly and reluctantly we must let it go. Rather than waiting as a once and future reserve to be reckoned with, the locos must be allowed to pound through ethereal junctions of a steam Valhalla beyond the clouds. So sad that there is no longer optimism to get steamed up over a supposed strategic reserve. Remember, as Loudon Wainwright III sang, memory lane is just a dead end track.

Chapter Nine

Platform souls

One of the lesser conspiracies of the last century was a rearguard action by a particular cadre within the Anglican Church to resist the ordination of female priests. These people were only too well aware that women make poor railway fanatics. I jest, of course, but a disproportionate number of Church of England vicars are bona fide railway enthusiasts. Politicians have no choice but to have an opinion of railway matters, if only to mollify their constituents. If princes with their luxury royal trains are the highest of the high, then media folk with their careless howlers and enforced proprietorial agendas are the paupers. Again, I jest. Engineers, clergymen, royals, politicians, journalists, the general public, and as seen with their partisanship, rail fans themselves, all come in every shade.

Engineers

The first chapter introduced several of the most prominent railway engineers who laid the pattern for today's transport system. I.K. Brunel alighted within several chapters through the pollinating apocrypha of the busy bee he was. A figure I draw from the shadows to which he has been unfairly cast is William Murdoch. The Stephensons and Joseph Locke find room, too.

Isambard Kingdom Brunel

Perhaps the greatest civil engineer in our history, he was born in Portsmouth in 1806, the son of an immigrant engineer who fled the French Revolution. Sir Marc Isambard Brunel named his son after both himself (Isambard is a Germanic name, appropriately for I.K.B. meaning 'bright iron') and Great Britain (Kingdom honouring his adopted country). He was appointed to build the GWR line from London to Bristol, and eventually down to the West Country, utilising deep tunnels and cuttings so as to maintain a level course. Many lives were lost through his methods and a comment on footplate men suggests a disdain for the lower classes: 'It is not only unnecessary but undesirable for engine drivers to be literate.' [1] He would not have appreciated today's political correctness which dealt a blow to Brunel's dandy image. The iconic 1857 photograph of him wearing black suit, top hat and smoking a large cigar, which hangs in the National Portrait Gallery, appeared on a brochure to publicise the restoration of his ocean-going iron ship *SS Great Britain*. However, the trademark cigar was stubbed out of existence. 'The cigar was airbrushed out because we felt it was not suitable for the target audience, which is quite young,' said Alex Timms, of Bath-based Timms Creative Communications. 'In these days of political correctness we thought it was inappropriate for a potential role model such

Brunel, pictured with the chains of the Great Eastern, and the offending cigar.

as Brunel to be seen smoking.' Timms admitted: 'A few people have queried it.' Marjorie Nicholson, director of Forest, the pro-smoking pressure group, described the cigar's removal as 'the worst kind of censorship, both pathetic and dangerous. This is distorting our history and our traditions.'[2]

Joseph Locke

No round-up of the top-flight engineers could be allowed to pass without mentioning Locke, though it is as the historian David Gilks perceived: 'In our grasp of events it seems that we cannot cope with more than a very few memorable names and characters. Often, it will be the early pioneer or the most flamboyant who is remembered and it seems inevitable that those who come after, whatever their merits, will be seen as merely followers. So, ultimately, the name of Joseph Locke passed from public view overshadowed by the Stephensons and Brunel.'[3] In fact, Locke's role in my tale is typically that of a bystander, but I felt he deserved some recognition. Robert Stephenson, Brunel and Locke were travelling in the same railway compartment. Being bitterly cold, Stephenson was well wrapped up in his Northumberland plaid. He jauntily turned to Brunel and proposed a wager: 'I bet you ten pounds you can't put it on properly first time.' Not one to turn down a challenge, Brunel even upped the stakes to the plaid itself. As the journey progressed, Brunel studiously sized up every fold of the woollen cloth over Stephenson's shoulder while his companions conversed. At their destination, the plaid was tossed to Brunel who, to Locke's great amusement and Stephenson's mortification, deftly put it on at one go and claimed his prize.[4]

William Murdoch

A brief letter in *The Times* caught my eye. It referred to a plaque which reads: 'William Murdoch lived in this house, 1782–1798; made the first locomotive here and tested it in 1784; invented gas-lighting and used it in this house in 1792.' My research found that Murdoch (1754–1839) did indeed give the world the high-pressure steam engine, without which there could have been no railway locomotives.

That first locomotive was a miniature and its testing suggests an element of the apocryphal about it. Employed as site engineer by James Watt in Cornwall, Murdoch privately experimented with high-pressure steam, previously regarded as too dangerous to develop. 'In one test, one of Murdoch's little "fire devils" cheerfully hauled a truck containing the coal tongs and shovel round and round the drawing-room of a friend's house in Truro. In another, he let his machine loose one dark night near his home in Redruth, and frightened the living daylights out of the vicar, who thought he had come face to face with Beelzebub himself as this spitting, hissing, sparking entity suddenly burst upon him out of the darkness on the church path.'[5]

Murdoch wanted to mount a steam 'car' on rails but his bosses persuaded him that moving engines could not possibly have any future. Had Watt not discovered what his employee had been creating, the construction of a full-sized machine might have been produced earlier and railway locos could have been running well before the end of the eighteenth century. Watt even surreptitiously added Murdoch's idea to his own patents, though having no intention of developing high-pressure steam himself. 'By this single action, Watt and his partner [Matthew] Boulton held up the progress of the Industrial Revolution by up to 15 years,' wrote one commentator.[6] Another writer put Murdoch twenty years ahead of Richard Trevithick and thirty ahead of George Stephenson. According to the Internet site of Illinois Saint Andrew Society, Trevithick saw a Murdoch prototype model loco and used the idea to gain his own patent in 1802. Boulton and Watt may not have done Murdoch's inventions any favours, but at least they looked after him financially. He continued to work for the firm until his retirement in 1830 at the age of 76.

Nevertheless, the miniature steam-driven self-propelling locomotive was possibly the first vehicle in Britain to run under its own power and places Murdoch as a giant automotive pioneer. Neglected by railway historians, he is also best known for the invention of gas lighting, which transformed society. He also earned the gratitude of beer lovers by inventing a means of making isinglass from fish which cleared ale. The folk of Redruth, where he lived, celebrate Murdoch Day every June with a street parade, local bands and old-time fair.

Born in Auchinleck, Ayrshire, he is also remembered in Scotland, but without any extravagance. While herding cows as a boy, Murdoch dug coal from a hillside and became fascinated by the inflammable vapours which were given off when heated. His obsession continued throughout his adult life and further experimentation led to him lighting his house in Redruth with gas. Back in Ayrshire there is 'Murdoch's Cave', situated immediately behind Bello mill, Lugar, near Cumnock, on the banks of the River Lugar. It is reputed to be where young William 'carried out experiments.' [7] It looks very haunting and redolent of magic and mystery; the site a junior shaman might choose for a vision quest. Perhaps the notions of locomotives and gas lighting incubated here? Had he gifts like his fellow countryman the Brahan Seer? Perhaps an attunement to wavelengths of the future; had been afforded glimpses he converted into inventions from a collective memory older than ourselves?

No lesser figure than the Shah of Persia declared Murdoch a deity, Nassred-din, believing he must have been a reincarnation of Marduk, God of Light. Perhaps the fact that Murdoch changed his name to the more Cornish spelling Murdock in later life helped – Murdock and Marduk certainly sound alike!

Robert Stephenson

Having pulped millions of pounds worth of new £5 notes after getting the date of George Stephenson's birth wrong by three years, there was still controversy as the fivers which went into circulation in 1990 depicted the engineer in front of the locomotive *Rocket*. Railway historian Victoria Haworth fulminated: 'George Stephenson most certainly did not design the *Rocket*. He was obstructive and negative about the whole thing and tried to prevent it from being built. The entire design has been credited to his son, Robert. The Bank's decision is morally wrong and I feel so strongly about this that I have decided never to handle the new notes. I simply won't touch the things. I even wanted to emigrate to get away from them, but my husband managed to persuade me not to.' She wrote to the Bank of England seeking pulping of the revised notes, but a spokesman dismissed this step: 'We chose George because of his general role as the father of railways.' [8] The ghost of the younger Stephenson appeared in her Newcastle home in 1978. 'There was an apparition,' she claims. 'A voice said "This is Robert Stephenson".' She subsequently discovered that Robert had worked on his locomotive *Rocket* at the house and that, overshadowed by his father George, he never gained the full recognition he deserved. Apparently the hauntings ended when she began research for her book.[9]

Just as he is claimed to have appeared from beyond the grave, a sample of Robert's hair has been resurrected for analysis. Scientists at Oxford University's Ancient Biomolecules Centre are examining the lock of hair from the National Railway Museum collection with DNA analysis expected to reveal details of his diet, health and environment. Robert, who died in 1859 aged 55, was known to suffer from what we today term 'executive stress' and one of the tests will be to establish whether he was taking medication – even opium – in his later years to ease his situation.[10]

Clergy

Long ago, before railways were pilloried by all and sundry, our train network was held in such high esteem that the initials GWR translated as both Great Western Railway and God's Wonderful Railway. One doubts that Aleister Crowley felt that way or deserves to be mentioned even in a chapter on men of the cloth. Obliquely, his father was a member of the Plymouth Brethren, a man from merchant stock, but who refused to buy shares in any railway companies on the grounds that there were no trains in the Bible. However, had the Great Beast's dad been more acutely versed in the Scriptures, he would have known the passage where a train is mentioned and suggests the Queen of Sheba was the first railway entrepreneur. According to 1 Kings 10:2, when she came to visit King Solomon, 'she came to Jerusalem with a very great train.'

The Reverend Wilbert Awdry

The 'Thomas the Tank Engine' series of books celebrated their diamond jubilee in 2005. The tales came easily to Wilbert Awdry for he was already a railway enthusiast who grew up near the GWR main line at Box, Wiltshire. To amuse his son Christopher, sick in bed with measles, Awdry made up a story about steam engines which spoke to one another. Later, when Awdry made a wooden model 0-6-0 tank engine for his son, Christopher decided to call it Thomas and insisted it feature in the next adventure. Some of the subsequent stories were based on railway folklore: the Furness Railway loco which plunged down an old mine shaft and the turntable at Garsdale spun by gale-force winds.[11]

The twenty-six books in total were a huge commercial success, but that did not stop the politically-correct brigade interfering. A reference to 'sooty black engines' brought a charge of racism, while his choice of 'male' engines as main characters and the 'female' carriages being either passive or argumentative, led to an accusation of sexual stereotyping.[12] He hated the first TV series in 1959 because the BBC wrote in a scene he believed inauthentic. He was better pleased with Central Television's animated production, narrated by Ringo Starr, but became exasperated when Central introduced its own story lines. Awdry received the OBE and died in March 1997, aged 85. His epitaph could well be his comment upon his two callings: 'Railways and the Church have their critics, but both are the best ways of getting man to his ultimate destination.'[13]

Chris Evans

Yes, an improbable entry! Multi-millionaire media mogul Evans, on one of his breakfast show broadcasts with sidekick Dan, the then Virgin Radio boss told listeners: 'A sure way to get Dan and I down to church would be to have some topless stained-glass beauties. Some lovely stained-glass "Sport" girls, that would get loads of people into church.' Evans was prompted to conjure up this novel vision after hearing of a Thomas the Tank Engine window at St Mary Magdalene church in Rodborough, Gloucestershire. Approached for a comment, Church of England spokesman Steve Jenkins said: 'You've certainly got guts. The Church is part of society and reflects the community, therefore all down the ages you would find various things represented in stained-glass windows. The reason Thomas the Tank Engine is in a window is his creator was a curate of that parish. But we don't think "Sport" topless beauties are part of the Church community. They may be part of national society but they don't qualify for being church windows.' [14] More's the pity. The paper reproduced a mock-up stained-glass window with three angels playing horns below a colourful topless image of model Belinda Charlton. The real inspirational window depicts Thomas with Wilbert Awdry and his wife Margaret. He had commissioned it before he died.[15]

Lewis Carroll

Born Charles Lutwidge Dodgson, when he was eleven his clergyman father was presented with a Crown living at Croft on Tees, a few miles south of Darlington. The vicarage had a large garden, sufficiently sized to accommodate several 'stations' constructed by the brood of which Charles was the eldest of eleven, seven of them girls. Their favourite game was pretending a wheelbarrow, truck and barrel was the train and it could stop at the stations for real or pretend refreshments. Charles was chief stationmaster and also ticket agent. Long before he wrote *Alice in Wonderland* and *Through the Looking Glass,* he was composing the rules for his railway system. These remain today in his own handwriting and Rule 3 is as follows: 'Station master must mind his station and supply refreshments: he can put anyone who behaves badly to prison, while a train goes round the garden: he must ring for the passengers to take their seats, then count 20 slowly, then ring again for the train to start. The L one shall be a surgeon, the wounded must be brought there gratis by the next train going that way and cured gratis. There shall be a place at the L station for lost luggage. If there is anyone to go, a flag is to be hoisted.' [16]

As an adult he became a lecturer in mathematics at Christ Church College, Oxford. In 1861 he was ordained a deacon but never proceeded to priest's orders, probably because of his stammer, though he preached occasionally. Toward the end of his life he began to have 'a very peculiar, yet not very uncommon, optical delusion, which takes the form of seeing moving fortifications.' [17] He died of pneumonia.

Bishop Eric Treacy

Known as the 'Railway Bishop', Eric Treacy was famed for his photography and died on Appleby station on 13 May 1978, waiting to get a shot of the final steam loco built for British Railways. His fame was such that two locos were named after him, 'Black Five' No. 45428 on the North Yorkshire Moors Railway and WCML electric No. 86240. He believed the three greatest manmade wonders were the S&C, York Minster and Hadrian's Wall. In his church career he rose to become Bishop of Wakefield and once preached a sermon from the tender of Stephenson's *Locomotion No. 1.* He began photography when still a junior clergyman in Liverpool and many thought tales that he could request prolific smoke effects to be mythical. However: 'In the old days, when the authorities were not so smoke-conscious as they became in latter days of steam, this co-operation took the form of massive smoke emission at prearranged locations.'[18] Indicative of the clergy's association with railways, he also wrote: 'There are many dignitaries of the Church who sneak away from formal occasions and have a crack with me about horizontal lines of communication instead of the vertical kind with which we are vocationally concerned.'[19] He found remote lines with infrequent services to photograph an aid 'for meditation and exercises in "transcendentalism".'

Politicians

When the Duke of York, later King George VI, visited Darlington on the occasion of the Royal Show staged there in 1920, mayor Tommy Crooks greeted his royal guest with a, 'Pleased to see you, lad, how's thi feyther?' Five years later the Duke of York again visited Darlington for the Stockton and Darlington Railway centenary celebrations, and it was his turn to inquire after the health of the 'bearded alderman who was mayor on my last visit.' [20] Radical Tommy thundered denunciations of both Tories and alcohol from the town's market steps and in this section are all shades of political opinion and spectrum of integrity.

On the subject of which, when the new 'Class 60' diesel-electrics emerged from the Brush factory they were unique in that part of the body on opposite sides had been cut away. The obvious nickname 'doughnuts' was quickly applied to the class members, but some preferred 'politicians' – because you can see right through them.

Dr Richard Beeching

I have placed him in this section because although not an elected politician (even one eminent TV quiz described him as Minister of Transport when he was actually chairman of the British Railways Board), what he is famous for was dramatically political. It was obvious folklore would have attached to him after the industrialist wrote his controversial report on the state of the railways. We always hear of Beeching's 'axe', but it was ministers such as cyclist Ernest Marples who cut away the dead wood Beeching identified. Remember, Beeching's brief was to make the railway system cost-effective rather than socially useful.

Actually finding the anecdotes and folklore was difficult and I am sure others will know of more examples. As a rail supporter myself, I bear Beeching no ill will and, in fact, see him as a necessary moderniser. Following his controversial plan to greatly reduce the network, he reluctantly accepted the British Railways Board chairmanship for four years and was rewarded with a well-deserved peerage. When in 1979 journalist David Wilcock asked if he would feel proud to have a locomotive named in his honour, he retorted: 'I'd rather have a pub named after me. Much greater distinction.' [21]

I looked all over the web for clues of apocrypha, found he was born in 1913, died in 1985 and, according to well-known retired railwayman Dick Hardy, 'had the gift of laughing at himself' and proceeded to claim that Beeching, upon walking into a station lavatory, was confronted by a statement written on the wall with great emphasis: 'Beeching is a prat!' The great man added underneath in a smaller but clear hand: 'No, I'm not!' [22] Scouring back numbers of *Fortean Times*, I found Beeching featured in one of three versions of a tale related by Nigel Pennick. Firstly, when the Lynton and Barnstaple Railway, a bankrupt narrow-gauge line in north Devon was slated for closure in 1935, it is claimed a delegation of local dignitaries visited the general manager of the Southern Railway in London to protest. It is said that he asked them how they had travelled and when they answered 'by car' he showed them the door and immediately closed their line. Another version tells of a visit to Dublin of petitioners from the west of Ireland who, when asked by Dr C.S. Andrews, the railway boss contemplating closures, answered similarly. Pennick adds that the story also attaches to the 'notorious' Dr Beeching, but tantalisingly gives no further details.[23]

Although the following tale is not directly connected to Beeching, in context the closure of one of two lines to Newquay, Cornwall, could obviously be seen as one of his examples of unnecessary duplication. The Chacewater referred to was on the former GWR main line to Penzance, and Newquay is still served from that major artery at Par. Known locally as the 'Rhododendron Line', Trevor A. Tremethick, after describing a steam-hauled journey over the tracks, concludes: 'As a postscript, I offer readers the alleged account of the attempt by a syndicate of local businessmen to buy the line upon closure. There is some doubt as to how serious and well thought-out this bid actually was, but it makes for a good yarn, which goes thus. British Railways set a price of £40,000 to which the syndicate agreed. BR then raised the price to £60,000. The businessmen's response was broadly that, although the price increase would make matters more difficult, they would make extra efforts and still meet BR's price. BR, taken aback by this show of determination, went in for the kill. "Ah, but we won't let you run private trains into either Chacewater or Newquay stations – it will be a railway from nowhere to nowhere," it said. The end of this sad tale goes that, having seen off the rescue attempt, BR sold the line for scrap to Ward's of Briton Ferry at a knock-down price – much less than the syndicate had been prepared to pay. That is the legend, anyway. So died this beautiful railway line.' [24] Of course, 'nowhere to nowhere' has not deterred many preserved railways, such as the Bluebell and Gloucestershire/Warwickshire, where I doubt strictures regarding entry to East Grinstead (where ironically Beeching lived) and Cheltenham applied.

Sir Philip Goodhart

This former Conservative minister favours converting railway tracks to tarmac, but I must applaud one of his gems of transport policy lateral thinking. Part of his Beckenham constituency was suffering blight caused by the proposed Channel tunnel rail route. Sir Philip argued that at least the affected houses in his fiefdom would remain no less attractive to deaf people, who would be in the envious position of being able to pick up property bargains.[25]

Adolf Hitler

Who would imagine Hitler could play trains with intense concentration to amuse a small boy? The future Führer was a close friend of Ernst Hanfstaengl during the 1920s and early 1930s. Hitler was godfather to Hanfstaengl's son Egon, who was 84 when he recounted this tale, but then four. Egon recalls:

'I loved him. He was the most imaginative playmate a child could wish for. My favourite game with him was trains. He would go on his hands and knees, and pretend to be a tunnel or a viaduct. I was the steam engine going on the track underneath him. He would then do all the noises of the steam train. As the train started up slowly, he would say "Help me! Help me! Help me!" in a rhythmic voice, then, with accelerating speed, "It's all right! It's all right! It's all right!", and finally "Wonderful! Wonderful! Wonderful!" He sounded just like a train rattling along the tracks. Then he would give me a description of the wagons I was pulling behind me. He was a wonderful mimic and could imitate people and animals extraordinarily well. When it came to the cattle truck bringing up the rear, he had the mooing of the cows perfectly.'

They say great events cast their shadows before them. The cattle trucks Hitler shared with his little chum would eerily be used in real life to transport millions of humans to their deaths.[26]

Karl Marx

I include this snippet only because I doubt its veracity. Those who enjoy surmising 'alternative history' scenarios could ponder how different the world would have been had two political strategists not changed their travel plans. Karl Marx and Fridrich Engels were spending Christmas 1879 with friends in Edinburgh, intending to go on to Dundee on the evening of 28 December. As fate would have it, the companions decided to stay another night and so missed being on the 7.15 p.m. departure from Waverley. While crossing the Tay bridge the central span collapsed, the train toppled and no one survived.

Benito Mussolini

The phrase 'At least Mussolini made the trains run on time' continues to be trotted out by persons wishing to damn their own governments as useless or by critics of privatisation in the UK. In fact, state railway general manager Cavaliere Carlo Crova's modernisation in the 1920s just happened to be completed coincidentally during Mussolini's heyday. Also some historians suggest this efficiency was itself mythical, but that the fascist spin-doctoring was effective.[27]

Royalty

Tales of royalty being inconvenienced on our railways teaches us that VIPs of such stature get the same treatment as we plebs. The Queen's ears assaulted by a 'ghetto-blaster', or 'grunts and groans' from a couple in the next compartment to the Duchess of Kent, are par for the course. Some incompetent buffoon locked a connecting door so the Queen's breakfast made an icy trip along the platform at Ely. In fact, royalty and railways have been together since the London and Birmingham Railway built the first royal coach for Queen Adelaide. The National Railway Museum, at York, has a handsome collection of royal carriages.

Queen Victoria

Her Highness made her first journey by train in 1842 and became an inveterate rail traveller and source of transport apocrypha. After she ceremonially opened the High Level bridge over the Tyne on 28 September 1849, a celebration banquet was held in Newcastle's Station Hotel. Before leaving, Queen Victoria was presented with a bill for the meal by the manager. So angry was she that Victoria vowed never to look upon the city again. For the following fifty years as she travelled back and forth to Balmoral for her summer holiday she drew the curtains of the royal train as she passed through Newcastle.[28]

The belief that she would also order the blinds of the royal train to be pulled down whenever she passed through Britain's industrial centres is widespread; either generally or particularly (Black Country, and so on). For a wholly different reason the blinds would be drawn when passing through Bridgwater, Somerset, so she would not have to look at the faces of 'those conspirators', a reference to the Duke of Monmouth, who recruited many of his followers from the district for the Battle of Sedgemoor in 1685. To this day, Bridgwater apparently still has a reputation for being anti-royalist.

I recall my late father telling me that because of her indignation at some report in the *Sunderland Echo*, she would have the blinds lowered so she need not look upon Wearside. Writer John Michell also reported that because of a certain Member of Parliament she refused to visit his constituency.[29]

Incidentally, she never said or wrote, 'We are not amused.' Doubtless directors of the GWR were not amused when she persuaded them to build an expensive and circuitous line between Windsor and Slough, so her view from Windsor Castle would not be inhibited. What would she have made of Heathrow airport (and the joke about why was the castle built so close to a major flight terminal?).

King George V

A tale which has become international involves King George V. When he went to Liverpool to open the Mersey tunnel, it was claimed false frontages were created to mask the slums. The story was told of similar efforts by Mussolini to fool Hitler on his railway journey into Rome, and Philippines dictator Ferdinand Marcos erecting miles of whitewashed walls alongside the road to Manila from the airport to block out the Pope's view of the shanty towns.[30] Also, the monarch, whose taste in entertainment ran more to Royal Variety performances than anything cultural, fell asleep in the Royal Box at Covent Garden during a Wagner opera. It was at a climactic moment in the music, with clashing chords, clanging cymbals, wailing woodwind, shrieking strings and blaring horns, that he awoke with a start and cried out: 'Good God! Willesden Junction! Euston in ten minutes... '[31]

Duke of Edinburgh

Best known for his gaffes and outspokenness, here is one of the latter. The Southern Region had the privilege of taking the Queen and members of her family every June from Victoria to Tattenham Corner to watch the Derby. For years a 'Schools' class 4-4-0 had been rostered, but this practice was changed abruptly when Prince Philip commented on how small the loco looked. Obviously unaware of the capabilities of the class, more than equal to their task on so short a journey, he requested a larger loco in future.[32] Also, on the occasion he caught a train to Bristol to pick up an honour from the Wildscreen Trust for his work saving endangered species, ironically the train preceding mowed down and killed twenty sheep which had wandered on to the line. The delayed Duke quipped to guests: 'This is a new excuse. There were sheep on the line.'[33]

Prince Charles

It has been customary to shunt the royal train overnight up some little-used branch line for obvious security reasons. Brian Redhead recalled the Prince of Wales spending a night on North Yorkshire's Wensleydale branch. He wrote: 'There is the story – probably apocryphal but even so a nice one – of the local girl who peered through a carriage window for a glimpse of her idol. However did she break the police cordon?' Just what is he suggesting? A lusty liaison? Maybe it's just me![34]

And did you know that as a child Charles attempted regicide by trying to squash his mother's head under the wheels of a train? Apparently the heir to the throne used to place pennies on track close to the royal station at Wolferton, near Sandringham, according to retired stationmaster Ted Skillings.

Journalists

People in glasshouses. Yes, I've had my fair share of embarrassment along the way during forty years in journalism, and if I've perpetrated some howlers in these pages, so be it. As a sub-editor I duly wrote clichéd headlines containing 'just the ticket', 'hit the buffers', 'going loco', 'Beeching axe' and so on. It would therefore be unfair to single out one particular member of my profession, but...

Amanda Mitchison

Take a bow for the sheer volume of nonsense in one article. The hackette descended upon the Severn Valley Railway and immediately latched on to its GWR pedigree. A design by G.J. Churchward became 'The Churchwarden' and an English Electric post-nationalisation 'The Deltic, another classic product from the GWR workshops' which she also mistakenly described as having hydraulic transmission; diesel-lovers are 'growlers' and steam-lovers are 'kettles' (neither are: 'Class 37s' are the former and any steam loco the latter). Also: 'They only tick off an engine once it has been seen in motion' – rubbish, it can be stationary or a kit of parts to be counted. Plus: 'Bashers only tick off a train once they have travelled in it' where 'train' should be 'loco' and 'in' should be 'behind.' Her writing often warrants inclusion in the Pseud's Corner of *Private Eye*, such as: 'For some the arrival of a diesel can be likened to the philosophy of Comte – a diminished bland abstraction usurping the mysterious, felt essences of an earlier age' or 'The famous onomatopoeic train poems... are based on phoney combinations of dactyls and spondees which bear no relation to the beats of a bogie'. Or else its sheer garbage: 'The lore of bogies is hard to master, and even great men have tripped up' and 'The passion of a true train buff is harder to explain, and cannot be discounted simply as nostalgia or sexual sublimation.' So we live in the past and/or are wankers. And to think this comedy of errors was ever printed and she got paid for it.[35]

The also rans haul of fame

Named locomotive: *The Dutch Hamilton (Duchess of Hamilton) Leicester Mercury.*

Loco types: Great Western 'haul' ('Hall' class) *Western Daily Press*; 'Drum and Tank' (Drummond tank) n.p.; mighty 'Bulleyed' Pacifics (Bulleid) *Bristol Evening Post.*

Builder: 'Bay of Peacock' (Beyer Peacock) *Ashton-under-Lyne Advertiser.*

Operations: 'And on the Tube they're trying to straighten out the Circle Line' BBC GLR Radio; 'soundditt' train (sandite) n.p.; 'Panda Graph' (pantograph) n.p.; the 'canapes' which overhang the platforms (canopies) *Loughborough Mail.*

Thanks to Nigel Harris and *Rail* for monitoring those abominations.

Fellow travellers

To conclude this section, a small motley crew of whom prominent is the neglected and downright weird Nikola Tesla and musician Graham Bond, perhaps a victim of the celebrated 'Maniac on the Platform.'

Nikola Tesla

It behoved well for the man who invented alternating current that Nikola Tesla was born during a severe electrical storm. Also that the polyphase A.C. system came to him in an overwhelming flash of illumination as he watched a beautiful sunset from a Budapest park. Without Tesla our technology would be decades behind the present. As the most important electrical genius of the nineteenth and twentieth centuries, Tesla remains a shadowy forgotten figure, and where mentioned is often depicted in bizarre terms, which I will come to. But firstly his achievements and their relevance to railways.

His favourite field was electricity and he advanced an alternative to the weak, inefficient and costly direct current system developed by Thomas Edison. Despite American industry's alliance with Edison, to build machinery to produce the limited range DC voltage, and Edison's attempts to block Tesla's patented polyphase system, Tesla installed his invention at Niagara Falls in 1895–6. Born on 10 July 1856, in the Balkan hamlet of Smiljan, he arrived in the United States in 1884. He quickly began developing inventions in the fields of radio broadcasting, radar, ultrasound, neon light, laser beam, beamed television transmission, microwave technology, electrical oscillators, alternating current, and wilder claims add death rays and guided missiles, plus an 'anti-war' machine designed to put up protective 'force fields' in the mode of the later 'Star Wars' programme.[36] A composite figure combining the nutty professor, Frankenstein and Dr Who; basically benevolent, otherworldly but not unworldly.

Tesla's influence on railway development in Britain is seen in the decision in the later Fifties to abandon the 1,500 volt DC system (e.g. Manchester to Sheffield and Wath) in preference to 50-cycle AC traction. The 1,796 miles of Southern Region track already electrified on the 660 volt DC third-rail system was retained and, in fact, extended to all Kentish main lines. Elsewhere AC became standard, despite being untried on a large scale under British conditions. Today the ECML and WCML, along with East Anglian caternary, are monuments to a neglected genius with their very high voltage, 25,000 volts, and relatively low current so as to minimise power losses in the cables.

Perhaps his only invention to be widely known, the tesla coil, owes its popularity to having made television and computer monitors possible. Many writers have paraded the most extraordinary claims on behalf of Tesla, such as that the thermonuclear-scale explosion which blasted Siberia's Tunguska region on 30 June 1908, was the result of Tesla's death ray.[37] A comet-meteor theory for the strange event struggles in the face of a lacking impact crater and no more was heard of Tesla's experiment. Another project based at a laboratory on Long Island was attempting to create a worldwide network of receivers transmitting unlimited power anywhere and in any quantity extracted from the air. Speculations as to how this scheme collapsed range from the pragmatic financial one that backers who had gained wealth from Tesla's electric inventions were not going to bankrupt themselves by financing unlimited free energy for all, to the conspiracy of the US government having the transmitter tower destroyed on the pretext that it was being used to signal German submarines.[38]

Claims as wild as Tesla's for his own technologies abound about the man himself. 'There are those people who believe Nikola Tesla was from another world.'[39] He certainly had visions and hallucinations; also enjoyed precognition. Futurist Robert Anton Wilson observed: 'Tesla went through something in his early adolescence; a very mysterious illness in which he almost died and hallucinated quite a bit. It sounds like the initiation of any shaman.'[40]

Tesla believed the Sun and Earth to be living creatures, thus predicating the Gaia hypothesis. He died on 7 January 1943, in his room on the 33rd floor of the New Yorker Hotel: 33 fittingly being the number of the solar hero.

Jeffrey Archer

I can recommend the self-effacing author's collection of short stories, *Twelve Red Herrings*, as several of these are bubonically-plagiarised urban legends. An equally scurrilous tale tells how during the launch tour for his previous novel, *Prodigal Daughter*, Archer was booked to travel from London to Edinburgh. Declining to fly or take an overnight sleeper, he chose a slow, stopping train from King's Cross. The piece of 'Archer folklore' as the writer admits, goes on: 'At every one of the stops en route – some 35 in total – young Jeffrey slipped out of his carriage, checked in the station bookstalls, and finding few copies of his cherished opus, returned to his seat and reached for his portable phone. His first call on each occasion was to the sales director at Hodder in London.'[41]

Adrian Bell

As a farmer, he wrote lovingly of pre-war rural life and his books are so cherished there is a thriving Adrian Bell Society. His greatest claim to fame, however, is as founding father of *The Times* crossword puzzle. It was an American fad which successfully crossed the Atlantic and after being adopted by *The Daily Telegraph*, Bell fell into the position of *Times'* compiler. His television reporter and politician son Martin relates a tale he 'cannot entirely swear by', but here it is: 'Once, on a rare train journey to London, he picked up a copy of *The Times* with one of his puzzles on the back page. Across the carriage he saw another passenger struggling with it. He whisked out a pen, completed his in 60 seconds, laid it on the seat beside him with the crossword uppermost, closed his eyes and smiled serenely.' [42]

Colonel John Blashford-Snell

After a return rail trip took 4½ hours longer than scheduled, 'Blashers' commented: 'Tracking through the Amazon avoiding crocodiles and snakes, pales into insignificance compared to going to Liverpool by train.' [43]

Graham Bond

Did he jump or was he pushed? There are many mysteries in the life and death of influential UK rhythm and blues musician Graham John Clifton Bond, born in Romford, Essex, on 28 October 1937. The general assumption is that as a Tube train entered Finsbury Park station, with arms outstretched Bond dived into its path. The driver applied the brakes but to no avail. It was to be two days before police could identify the body, and then only through fingerprints as the body had been crushed beyond recognition. At the ensuing inquest the coroner declared an open verdict. Suicide was not proved and many had reason to believe his death was due to other forces.

Bond played Hammond organ so the group he formed, the Graham Bond Organisation, had a punning title. His fellow members were future Cream superstars Jack Bruce and Ginger Baker, plus Dick Heckstall-Smith. However, at the time there was no star presence in the group and Bond's growling vocals did not have chart potential. There were internal band problems and Bond's substance abuse helped break up the band in 1967. His mental health deteriorated, exhibiting symptoms of what would today be diagnosed as bipolar disorder: manic episodes, mood swings and periods of intense depression. He was seriously obsessed with the 'black arts'; two of his later outfits were called Initiation and Holy Magick. Learning that one of Aleister Crowley's girlfriends had given birth to an illegitimate baby in 1937 (he was a Barnardo's boy), he declared that it was him.

Back at Finsbury Park station on 8 May 1974, the only factor which is certain is that Bond died beneath a train. All manner of theories and opinions have been paraded and I here offer a handful I feel significant.

In an extract from his unpublished manuscript 'The Loop', Paul Olsen, the last drummer to play with Bond, writes: 'Very depressed, one afternoon Graham donned his Lesley-jacket and said he was going to north London to try to get something sorted out. I never saw him again.' A month later a policeman arrived at his door, asked if Olsen could identify the jacket, and said Bond had 'fallen in front of a train.' Olsen recalled that Bond had scored some high-grade cocaine and shared it with friends. He continued: 'After talking with some of his friends and going to the inquest on Euston Road, I was convinced it was suicide because of his depression. Just as I am convinced that Graham took his own life (maybe because he couldn't pay the man) Ginger is just as convinced he was doing a runner and either slipped (because he was clumsy) or was pushed.' [44]

Jim Driver had a different theory: 'The common belief is that addled by drink and/or drugs, Graham Bond fell (or jumped) in front of a London Underground train. Those close to him insist he was pushed, because of a weird feud with a secretive black magic organisation. But even when pressed, no names are forthcoming. [He] probably took his secret – if there was a secret to take – with him to the grave.' [45]

While R. Gary Patterson, famous for his book on how Paul McCartney died and was replaced by a *doppleganger*, told radio host George Noory: 'A new story I'm developing is when Graham Bond performed an exorcism and then threw himself under a Tube train in London. Many of his friends claim he was possessed.' Yet another source revealed Bond received a telephone call from a music journalist and was upbeat about meeting him for an interview the following fateful day.

So was Bond in a positive frame of mind and his death a tragic accident or was he a mentally-unstable maniac on the platform? Was he pushed by a drug baron, an evil occultist or Mick Goss's 'Maniac on the Platform'? Or simply committed suicide?

Billy Bragg

The 'big-nosed bard from Barking' was passing through a London Underground station when he ran into a problem with the automatic ticket barrier. Collaring an unfortunate inspector, Bragg ranted: 'What are you playing at with these bloody machines? They never work, they cost a fortune, the public don't like them, your own unions don't like them and the fire brigade hate them because they're a fire hazard. Well?' Sharp as a razor, the Tube official offered: 'Write a fucking song about it then.' [46]

William John Cavendish Bentinck-Scott

The fifth Duke of Portland was a prolific tunneller at his Dukeries seat, Welbeck Abbey, but one should ignore the claim that he arrived at Worksop railway station by this secret means. The claim is made in a partly-biographical Booker-nominated novel and I spent a day ascertaining it to be fictional. [47] One of the co-owners of the pub at the station, the former buffet, told me I was wrong to suspect the cellar where a folk club met (freemasons met upstairs) was the end of the tunnel, nor had he heard of any other legendary subterranea appertaining to the station. The lady in the library/museum was certain the nearest tunnel culmination to the station was a mile away at Sparken Hill. More detective work unearthed an unfulfilled plan to tunnel to

Whitwell railway station and the possibility of creating a personal halt on the line. The Duke's story is fabulously bizarre.[48]

Hunter Davies

Author of many books, including ones on walking abandoned railways and George Stephenson, he deserves a mention if only for his splendid description of Carlisle Citadel station – built in 1847 and whose architect, Sir William Tite, gave it a curious mock-Tudor frontage – as 'a marshalling yard for Scottish drunks.' I attended the 1975 Stockton and Darlington Railway 150th celebrations, but unlike Davies was not tempted to buy a tin of Locomotion Steam. 'I still have it,' wrote Davies. 'Unopened. In very small type, it says on the side, "This is a collector's item – the can is empty".' [49]

Marilyn Monroe

What is contemporary culture's ultimate cult moment and defining image of its most iconographic figure? According to *The Times* it's the moment Monroe pauses above a New York subway grating in the film *The Seven Year Itch* as a train whooshes below; she luxuriating in the sensation as the air sends her white dress billowing around her shoulders, giving co-star Tom Ewell something to smile about.' [50]

Chapter Ten

Rail enthusiasm

Trainspotting is a healthy outdoor pursuit with an aim. Sharing camaraderie, the rail fan seeks to see every loco, and perhaps every multiple unit, carriage and wagon, and/or cover every stretch of track and/or be hauled by each engine of a particular class. It does involve collecting numbers, which for some reason attracts opprobrium from some quarters. Its detractors are probably blissfully unaware that it is simply the equivalent of their own addiction to football league tables or music charts. The wife who cannot understand the hours spent by her husband cataloguing train photos sees nothing peculiar in spending most of her leisure hours glued to QVC programmes on television ('I see you've got your porn channel on again,' I'll light-heartedly observe to my wife, which makes me sound as bad as the anoraknophobics I highlight later). I also outline a history of the hobby and the changing monikers for enthusiasts; an attempted demographic portrait of spotters; and a resumé of the many sub-species of train fandom.

'Railwayacs' to 'Gricers'

As with everything connected with railways, there are rival claims (or simply research deficit) as to when the rail enthusiasm movement was born. A starting point would be 1897, when *The Railway Magazine* was launched. Two years later, a letter was published in the second issue of *The North Western Locomotive Journal* from A.K. Bruce, who signed himself as 'Railwayite' – other railway afficianados of the time were known as 'railwayacs.' Bruce judged the time right to form an organisation for 'that great and growing hobby afforded by railways' and invited readers to help form a national club. Sufficient people responded for an inaugural meeting at the magazine's offices in Birmingham, where chairman S. Cotterell deprecated the restrictions then imposed by railway companies upon the supply to members of the public of train movements. Thus the formation of The Railway Club was proposed and carried unanimously. Birmingham and London groups co-existed and met at members' homes, having defined objects to engender camaraderie, study locomotives, share information on movements and infrastructure, exchange photographs and generally promote the hobby.

A sub-committee was formed in 1902 to prepare a complete list of all Britain's locomotives, but which was never completed. In fact, apathy was weakening the club and in 1904 it was first proposed to wind affairs up. A further blow came in 1909 when those members who believed too little attention was being given to loco matters resigned and formed the Stephenson Locomotive Society. Known as 'the great schism', there was much animosity between the two organisations for some time. A Cambridge University branch was formed in 1911, but that too is now run independently. Centenary celebrations were held in 1999 with several high-profile events.[1]

According to would-be humorist Andrew Martin 'trainspotting was invented in 1928 by two men with the somehow very trainspotterish names of A.E. Broad and L.B. Lapper' who in that year founded the Railway Correspondence and Travel Society. Its magazine, *The Railway Observer* 'whose price – 98p – reflects the numerological exactitude of the true spotter.' It is still going strong. Martin records the opinion of a rail enthusiasts' magazine editor who blames the dearth of young spotters on 'comedians and media types.' Martin's article was neither remotely funny, accurate nor informative; doubtless another reason why people are turned off the hobby.[2]

In 1944 a court case arose after up to two hundred trainspotters would gather at Tamworth and irresponsible individuals put pennies on the line. At Tamworth juvenile court it was reported that collecting engine numbers was 'sweeping the country' and the *ABC of LMS Locomotives* was produced as evidence. Police began touring schools to warn of the dangerous and anti-social activity. Publisher Ian Allan rose to the challenge, forming the ABC Series Locomotive Spotters Club (later renamed Ian Allan Locospotters Club – still without apostrophe), where members signed a declaration that they would not trespass. Thus began the era of official weekend enthusiast rail tours, works visits and 'shed bashes'. Ian Allan said: 'I was particularly keen that they be referred to as locospotters – not trainspotters – because of course at that time, locos were what they were spotting, not trains. I am often asked if I despair of the phrase "trainspotting," but in these modern times, that's just about all today's poor souls have got to spot, so I suppose it's fair enough!'[3]

In the 1950s came another name for spotters. 'Ferro-equinology', unnecessarily hyphenated, was allegedly coined by railway expert H.C. Casserley and appeared in his 1952 book *Locomotive Cavalcade 1920–1951*. It translates as study of the iron horse.

Another common term is 'gricer', whose derivation has been the subject of much heated debate. My favourite fatuous explanation – which I do not believe – was put forward in a letter by Harold D. Bowtell, denying its recent origin: 'It certainly dates back to August 1938, being coined by Mancunian enthusiasts on the grouse moors above Weardale in County Durham. The objects of their search were the relics of old lead-mining railways... and even a Black Hawthorn locomotive long disused in its remote shed. With the sight of shooting butts on the moor and the twelfth just past, the parallel between our pursuits and those of the guns on the moor was clear. As all know the plural of grouse is grice the true enthusiast is a gricer, entitled to record his bag of grice in brace – whether they be rare species of locomotives, relics of industrial archaeology, or whatever.' That's exactly as written.[4]

When *Steam Railway* initiated a correspondence on the subject in the wake of news that the compilers of the *Oxford English Dictionary* had a problem over the word's origin, Bowtell again put pen to paper, claiming he was the surviving member of that

Weardale sortie and repeated the packhorse trail tramp tale, all under the alias 'Colonel Soupspoon.'[5] Somehow the *OED* was not totally convinced. In fact, the *OED* had been led to believe the word dated from 1984 and derived from Richard Grice, an Essex enthusiast claiming to be the first 'world champion trainspotter.' Perhaps Flight Lieutenant Aidan Fuller originated the word by including a Grice Street in the fictitious map printed on the cover of his essential *British Locomotive Shed Directory*, or was the word already so well known by the mid-Fifties that he was actually lampooning it? The plethora of explanations submitted for 'gricers' origin would make any etymologist weep.[6]

Who are the spotters?

Before considering what trainspotters do, some of the facts about what constitutes such a species need to be examined. The demographic portrait is difficult to ascertain accurately, particularly as many spotters are of the armchair variety. Sympathetic journalist Stephen Moss estimated the number was down to 20,000, making us sound like some endangered bird species facing extinction.[7] Freelance writer Nicholas Whittaker puts the estimate at 200,000, but reckons the market for rail books, magazines and videos is larger than ever and worth upwards of £5.5M a year.[8] The total is probably more like three million if those who buy railway books, magazines and films, and those who visit heritage railways or travel on special trains, are included. Any tally would even include the unsighted. An account of The Sidings, a hotel complex with viewing conservatory overlooking the ECML outside York, reported that a group of blind trainspotters came to stay and spent several days spotting by ear.[9]

Publishers and editors of nostalgia magazines are well aware their readership is declining as buyers go to that great junction in the sky. As for new blood, any youngster close to a railway line is unlikely to take Edith Nesbit's fictional trio as role models. Rather than carrying a pen and notebook, he or she is more likely to be tagging a wall or coach with paint spray cans or throwing ballast at a passing carriage window. In a reversal of today, when I was a lad fifty years ago the nerds were 'Brainy Brampton' and other bookish swots; the likes of me admiring a 'Streak' on the 5.32 were 'normal' pupils. Today, modern technology has made youngsters more a stay-at-home breed and interest in trains has gone the way of stamps, toy soldiers and flower pressing. It was not like today when I started in 1956, with numbers into three figures at hot spots such as London terminii, Doncaster, Derby, Crewe, York and Carlisle. Here's a report from 1962: 'Five hundred determined trainspotters played hide and seek with harassed railway police at Crewe at the weekend. In train after train they poured into the Cheshire junction – to be met by a handful of police with orders to get rid of them.'[10] But where to?

As for women enthusiasts, these are not unknown but are still a small minority. There is no visible antipathy towards women at the lineside, but it has not always been an emancipated world. Even when The Railway Club organisation was struggling, it remained a bastion of male dominance and when it was proposed in 1930 to open membership to women, the move was rebuffed on the grounds that it was 'neither practical nor desirable.' The question of welcoming the fairer sex was again put to the ballot in 1936 and again the proposal was lost, although it was magnanimously agreed that they could attend the annual dinner and film show. It was not until 1988 that misogyny lost the day.

Most enthusiasts are perfectly normal middle-aged men with typical families and sensible jobs. There are, however, a minority of oddballs. These may be fanatical to the point of psychological pathology, the socially inadequate or downright perverted.

Paedophiles did not have the high profile they enjoy today when I was a lad and we just thought the 'Bamboo Kid' was a local eccentric. We thought this weirdo with bamboo canes in his bicycle basket simply believed he was a railway policeman, but now recognise him for the abusive pervert he was. More recently a well-known railway photographer committed a horrific sex attack on a boy at the lineside, escaped jail but later committed suicide in my home town.[11]

Recalling his spotting days, Stephen Moss commented that 'dodgy characters' were rare, but: 'The only really disconcerting moment was on Bristol Temple Meads station when an elderly man came up to a friend of mine and asked him whether he was his son. Oddly enough, he was.' [12]

Home for enthusiasts is the same selection of dwellings as the rest of us. That is except for the two-bedroom 'starter' house at 15 Buttercup Drive, Adswood, Stockport, known as 'The Crossbridge' and built on the site of a former spotters' mecca at a major junction.[13] Several train drivers past and present clubbed together to pay £56,000 for the property, and that was when their troubles began. Firstly Mel Thorley's wife Kate briefly walked out on him, feeling he put trains before her, then the neighbours complained about the amount of visitors[14] and builders Barratt threatened action over untidy memorabilia, the 15-foot set of signals and grass two feet high and in strips the width of standard gauge track, breaching agreements.[15]

They also live oop north. Or so thinks Amanda Mitchison, of last chapter infamy, who believes spotters 'tend to come from the big industrial towns of the North of England', escaping presumably the grimness for bucolic pastures of rural preserved lines.[16] But this can be proven to be nonsense as the Southern and LMS editions of Ian Allan ABCs of locomotives always outsold their GWR and LNER cousins, a situation which continued into BR days, suggesting that geographically not all the spotters lived in slums.[17] In Europe, rail enthusiasm is a very British pastime, but a national body, the National Railway History Society, has 170 chapters across the USA, Canada and the UK. In the USA, enthusiasts call themselves 'trainfans', with the verb 'trainfanning', or 'railfans', and attend 'railroadiana' shows.

On a serious note, what is rarely appreciated is that with their knowledge of railway infrastructure and architecture, enthusiasts are in a position to spot anything untoward. There is not the haste of the commuter or the harassed nature of rail company platform staff. They could hold vital evidence, such as photographs and video film, in cases of terrorism – going from national joke to national security. A good example of a rail fan's alertness distinguished an otherwise negative article: 'I spotted a broken rail in the rush hour at Clapham Junction once. They closed the line down for the rest of the day. It's just part of the job.' [18]

Finally are, as many people imagine, trainspotters several gronks short of a full set of shunters? Dr David Weeks, a clinical psychologist specialising in the study of eccentric behaviour, believes rail fans fall broadly into two main personality types. There is the obsessional type who wants everything to be tidy and perfect, for whom an incomplete set represents imperfection: such as collectors of stamps, personal genealogy or ornithological 'twitchers'. Dr Weeks' second set is the schizoid type, the person who feels ill at ease socially and prefers the company of inanimate objects, becoming unduly interested in say computer games or weight training. These personality traits, alone or combined, are present in a sizeable proportion of the population, and harmless unless taken to extremes. Dr Weeks, perhaps patronisingly, emphasised: 'The vast majority of trainspotters are perfectly normal and reasonable people.' [19]

Also, according to Dr Uta Frith, 'trainspotting is a fertile ground for people with Asperger's syndrome. Not all spotters have the syndrome, but I know one, for example, who is really interested in carriage light fittings. That is fairly specialist.' [20] It was first spotted, so to speak, in 1944 by Viennese paediatrician Hans Asperger. The syndrome is a mild form of autism characterised by having unusual and narrow interests, coupled with poor social skills, lack of humour and pedantry.

What spotters do

Primarily rail enthusiasm shares with most hobbies the urge to collect: be it numbers, haulage, track, photos or performance logs. Trainspotting's 'essence is an appreciation of numbers', wrote the hobby's chronicler Nicholas Whittaker. 'There is, as any mathematician, or accountant, or clerk, or engineer, or cricket fan will tell you if you give them enough to drink, a beauty and a cadence to numbers in themselves, as exciting to those in the know as poetry or Picasso.' [21]

Number crunching

I collect only the numbers of Network Rail registered locos, plus former British Rail ones. That's sufficient for one lifetime. When George Stephenson launched his railway career he not only named his first steam engine *Locomotion* but gave it a number, *No. 1*. Nowadays there are spotters who collect anything with a number, be it diesel multiple units, carriages or wagons, and books exist in which to underline all these. Some start afresh each year to see how many different locos they can spot annually. Many rail enthusiasts also spot buses and aeroplanes. Oh, and Eddie Stobart lorries.

Haulage bashing

Just as motorists have their favourite make of cars, horse-racing followers back a particular trainer or jockey, and soccer specialists may become ground-hoppers, so a sub-culture of rail enthusiasm is the desire to travel behind a particular class of loco – many having a favourite within that type. Over the years those classes with a

170

fanatical following have included 'Deltics', 'Whistlers', 'Westerns', 'Peaks', 'Growlers' on the Cambrian and 'Choppers' to Skegness. A cautionary tale regarding 'Duffs' unfolded at Oxford crown court after David Whitley, 19, a geography undergraduate at Oxford's Brookes University, caused £12,399 damage in a wrecking spree after hiding under a seat when passengers got off and stowing away for the return empty stock working. Whitley's hammer orgy involved shattering windows, ripping up seats and hurling a table which was hit by an oncoming express at 90 mph. He then ransacked the buffet and grabbed dustbin liners full of food and lager. When the train failed to stop at Oxford he applied the emergency brake in the guard's van.

Philip Shears, defending, said his client was 'shy, introvert, intelligent and artistic', had 'boiled over' and suffered from a rare obsessive compulsive disorder. He had been branded a homosexual at school, where he was badly bullied, and had been having girlfriend trouble. His advocate said Whitley was a member of the Class 47 Society and explained: 'The word "bashers" is not for those who intend to damage trains. Members of the "Class 47 bashers" produce magazines and photos and other material.' Whitley was ordered to do two hundred hours' community service after admitting damage, obstructing a train and stealing BR food. Sadly, the number of the 'Duff' involved was not revealed in court.[22]

Perhaps an even more outrageous case of haulage bashing came to light concerning Ben Hunt, from Stoke-on-Trent, who was jailed for making 150 separate rail journeys in just two months using a credit card he found and altered the signature to spend more than £7,500 bashing 'High-Speed Trains and purchasing food from buffet cars. He was found guilty at Derby crown court of 283 offences of theft, forgery and obtaining services by deception. He was attempting to tot up 10,000 miles of haulage behind power car No. 43127 and this included trying to sit in the same passenger seat for all his journeys. Psychiatrists' reports observed he had 'intellectual and emotional tunnel vision.'[23]

Neil Howard, recalling the era of 'Class 37' haulage on the Cambrian line patronised by 'sub-humans from the West Midlands', wrote that some of them would hurl full and well-shaken two-litre cola bottles onto cars and pedestrians. He went on: 'Others would dismantle the toilet plumbing – they called this "taking a shower." A few of them will have died by now (painfully in some ghastly accident, I hope) or moved on to Star Trek conventions. I doubt any of them have achieved anything worthwhile.' And 'The haulage men are so often all bellowing and arm waving – and that very unpleasant Nazi salute they think is funny.'[24]

Track bashing

Another group of enthusiasts collect lines they have travelled over and special trains are organised to cover rare freight-only routes, obscure curves and reaching the very last inch of a branch line. Part of the lore of organising rail tours to such tracks is to make painful punning names such as Rylstone Cowboy and Blyth Spirit. One man determined to travel every inch of the network was Avon county council accountant Tim Wallis, 37, who ended up being fined £500 with £525 costs at Bristol county court for forgery and deception. During ten years of bashing, bachelor Wallis covered 99 percent of the estimated 22,770 miles of track. He financed his obsession partly by forty bogus compensation claims for alleged bad service and pretending to be a student to get travel discounts. He was caught out by his own meticulous record of journeys he made.[25]

Shed bashing

After The Railway Club was formed on 27 June 1899, the first official club visit was made to London's Nine Elms engine shed on 11 November that year. Health and safety legislation and 24 hours a day seven days a week operation have all but curtailed official visits to depots and 'bunking' without permission is now the dangerous name of the game.

Subterfuge, however, is not necessary at open days, when a depot opens for the benefit of the family market and enthusiasts as a public relations exercise and charity fund-raising.

Modelling

Very expensive. Pete Waterman has one and he and his old mates play with it while sinking beers. Frankly if I had the dosh I'd have one, too. Also worth mentioning is the debt I pay to modellers' magazines, for they cater for the perfectionist and I've learned much about detail differences within classes of loco. Admirable and arcane.

Photographing

Old-style snappa Derek Cross literally tore pages he hated from an arty book of train shots by new-wave photographer Colin T. Gifford, saying he had binned better work. The very curious fact about rail photographers is that if they have a second Christian name they always use it as an initial at the end of the caption when publishing their work. Thus we have had Ian S. Carr, John M. Boyes, Norman E. Preedy, John E. Auguston, Colin J. Marsden, Michael J. Collins, Peter J. Robinson and Alan C. Hopkins.

Railwayana collecting

Railwayana auctions today are big business. In the Fifties a fellow West Hartlepudlian spotter, John Parsons, had us in awe when he announced he had just had delivered to his door a nameplate from a 'Hunt D49', for the all-inclusive price of 7s 6d. How I wish I had followed suit, for such a gem would fetch a five-figure sum today. As an indication of what a nameplate may make at auction, recently a buyer paid £37,000 for one from 'Merchant Navy' No. 35011 *General Steam Navigation*, and although a new record for the class, one wonders if that figure was enhanced by the fact that it is the only main-line steam loco to have contained the word 'steam' in its name.

Preserving

What the public sees at preservation sites is a jarring mixture of perfectly idealised period station buildings and pristine locomotives in combination with a depot yard which would do a scrap merchant proud and a trip in a carriage so filthy MRSA bugs would boycott it. A flick through any heritage railway magazine will dent the romantically twee image of everyone pulling together for the common good: motions of no confidence, boardroom coups, litigation, harsh evictions and even fist fights.

Reading

Literature on railways stretches from the 'Thomas the Tank Engine' series to the most arcane books on long-forgotten branches and obscure long-defunct wagon builders. There are probably more monthly periodicals than for any other hobby. Rail fans also have society magazines, videos and the Discovery channel had a regular programme on trainspotting. There are also a few books about spotting itself. A nostalgic memoir from a front-line publisher is *Platform Souls: The Trainspotter as 20th Century Hero*, written wittily by Nicholas Whittaker.[26] This rites-of-passage narrative begins in the dying days of steam and tells how the author learned to love diesels. The incredible amount of column inches and hours of radio interviews it garnered is either an indication of a well-oiled publicity machine or an indication of our perennial fascination with railways – even if in many instances it also constitutes revulsion.

Surfing

Almost daily I check my local Yahoo website – group/north-east-discussion – an electronic grapevine which tells me what's going on locally loco-wise, but there are hundreds of rail-devoted sites, particularly 'fotopic' ones. Many enthusiasts also now use the £90 software package Spotter's Mate for storing information. In 1997 the world's first solar-powered anorak, by fashion designer Ted Lapidu, was stolen from an exhibition in Paris. The nylon jacket had solar panels on the back and arms which could power a laptop computer. Was it designed with Spotter's Mate users in mind?[27]

Speaking

As with every sub-culture, a special language has been adopted by trainspotters. In addition to a panoply of nicknames, this enthusiast-speak jargon includes: 'bail out' (leave train), 'stopped all shacks' (train which called at every halt), 'wedged' (over-full train), 'flag' or 'flagged' (train to ignore), 'fester' (stand around waiting), 'insect' (rail fan who only comes out during the summer; they 'swarm' at open days), 'namer' (loco with a name), 'nonker' (loco without a name), 'beast' (special loco), 'hellfire' (loco putting in a splendid performance), 'bellowing' (hanging out of front carriage yelling, waving and generally willing a spectacular performance), 'thrash' (superb performance) and my all-time favourite, the more literary-sounding encouragement 'thrash horses, my lords!' to loco crew.[28]

Drinking

I enjoy a few beers in the buffet while spotting as much as the next man. In fact, a particularly enjoyable boozy afternoon was spent swapping yarns with a chap in the buffet on Preston station, where if we missed the number of a passing loco, my new-found drinking buddy would click his fingers and his obedient wife would sprint off up the platform for us. Apparently truly serious imbibers will count the number of pubs visited or keep a tally of all the beers tested. This latter practice is known as 'ticking', 'scratching' or 'scooping.' With 5,500 beers under his belt, Alan Douglas, producer of the boozers' bible *Guild of British Beer Samplers*, reckons 'well over 80% of tickers are or have been interested in railways.'[29]

Of course the mention of alcohol and trains requires at least one tale of over-indulgence. Step forward punk rocker Dan Hart, 31, who was arrested after a scuffle with staff on the posh Orient Express. Dan and fellow members of the Deltic Preservation Society were travelling to Berwick upon Tweed and during the four-hour journey Dan downed about eight pints of beer, a few glasses of champagne, some vodka and a whisky. The DPS banned him for a year for bringing the group into disrepute.[30]

Celebrity spotters

All manner of famous people are or have been keen rail enthusiasts. Former Chancellor of the Exchequer Kenneth Clarke ran his school's trainspotting club and took members on trips to stations and locomotive depots all over the country. 'I was addicted and had a fanatical interest in steam engines.' Nowadays he and his historian wife Gillian explore medieval ruins together. Ken calls it 'monument bashing.'

Hollywood heart-throb Robert Redford 'can sometimes be found watching locomotives in freight yards', which may explain why so much enthusiasm was put into the train scenes in the 1969 classic movie *Butch Cassidy and the Sundance Kid.*[31]

Chris Donald, founder editor of *Viz* comic, saw becoming a trainspotter as a major turning point in his life: 'I met lots of quiet, nice, well-behaved kids. I was a trendy trainspotter. I never wore an anorak.' But cautioned: 'I accept that taken to extremes, trainspotting can be a rather disturbing hobby.' However, when *Viz* published a two-page satire of tabloid coverage featuring murderer Michael Sams there was a predictable humour deficit in some quarters.[32] Sams, convicted killer of Julie Dart and kidnapper of Stephanie Slater, was last heard of writing his crime autobiography, cruelly and teasingly entitled 'Mr Kipper'. Second wife Jane left him after three years of marriage when Sams fitted model railway main lines and marshalling yards through the rooms of their home. He described himself as two personalities: 'The Hyde was my feelings when I was angry. But my trainspotting or modelling would soon return me to Dr Jekyll.' Detective Seargent Tim Grogan, who arrested Sams, said police had profiled a rugged, mobile, even SAS-type character, but 'I went to get Britain's public enemy No. 1 and found a shambling, one-legged trainspotter.' [33]

Multi-millionaire record producer and now boss of London and North Western Railway Pete Waterman commented: I've travelled more miles on the railways in the last 20 years than most drivers. That's one of the reasons I still trainspot – to help pass the time. I've cleared BR several times but I still log the numbers of the 37s and 47s because I love them so much and it's nice to see how many times you've seen a loco you now own.'

After I criticised ufologist/paranormalist author Jenny Randles for attacking rail enthusiasts in *Northern UFO News*,[34] I received an email via Rory Lushman to say that: 'Although I would not say I am a trainspotter, I am an enthusiast for this mode of transport as the most civilised on earth and know the ins and outs. I go over to Peak Forest whenever I can to see the "Class 60" stone trains (and occasional "66s"). One of my earliest memories was of travelling behind a "Crab" from Stacksteads to Blackpool and then seeing a real crab on the beach. I only found out the steam engine was called a "Crab" much later! I hope that Paul now sees that my comment in *NUN* about trainspotters was an affectionate one, not an attack.' So which part of 'anorak wearing, mentally challenged trainspotters' didn't I understand?

Also known to have a railway appreciation are musicians Phil Collins, Elton John, Justin Hayward, Captain Sensible, ex-railway fireman Joe Brown, Chris Rea, Jools Holland ('not many people can entertain themselves all day for the price of platform ticket'), and Mike Read (recorded as The Trainspotters); comedians Jim Bowen (lives in a converted station house) and Michael Palin.

Anoraknophobia

Anoraknophobia: noun. enduring irrational fear of or dislike of trainspotters [35]

Better start with a defence of 'anorak.' Back in the 1920s it was a word taken from the Eskimo for a hooded waterproof jacket. As we all know, by the 1980s it had taken on a second meaning to describe a supposed social misfit with an obsessive interest in something untrendy. Nobody, at least to my knowledge, despises me for my hobby. But there is ample evidence some lowlife find it irresistible to make fun of hobbyists and particularly trainspotters. I feel a hall of shame coming on. You may wish to blacklist these people's books, newspapers or programmes. Or would that be sinking to their level?

Firstly step forward Bill Bryson, American but former sub-editor on the *Bournemouth Evening Echo*, second book *Neither Here Nor There* about railway journeys in Europe, third book *Notes From a Small Island* which went stellar. An excellent profile included this putdown: '"He's screamingly funny and an absoutely first-class writer." Actually he isn't, his fans just think he is because he signals his unfunny jokes in flashing neon. But 'However plonkingly satirical he may be about our railways and landladies, he really adores Britain.' Here's an example of his mind-numbingly dire prose: 'I ended up feeling sorry for him. His wife had died two years before – suicide, I would guess – and he had devoted himself since then to travelling the rail lines of Britain, counting rivets, noting breastplate numbers, and doing whatever else it is these poor people do to pass the time until God takes them away to a merciful death. [...] He got off at Prestatyn – something to do with a Faggots and Gravy 12-ton blender tender that was rumoured to be coming through in the morning.'[36]

Then there is Ian Allan, the Gerald Ratner of publishing. He told Jane Kelly: 'What do I really think of trainspotters? I loathe them. I will do anything to keep away from them. They are utter bores. I like trains, but not these number crunchers... Spotters are reduced to taking coach numbers, and that is a really dreary thing to do. But some of them are human.'[37] Or did he tell her this? There was a furore over the article and Kelly subsequently told *Steam Railway* that some of Allan's quoted remarks had not been made directly to her but to another journalist who had passed them on. 'He was more cautious with me,' she admitted, 'but his remarks were genuine. I don't doubt that he said them.'[38] As for the 71-year-old Grand Master of Ashford Manor Lodge of the Freemasons and publishing magnate, in a letter to *Steam Railway* he compounded his original gaffe by claiming 'there was a five per cent fringe of sellotape-spectacled, multi-badge, dirty anorak, beret-wearing puffer nutters who did take their hobby a bit over the top.' Yet some people still never learn. In 1999 he had another go at the hand that feeds him. His intemperate outburst ended with: 'It's almost as though there's a trainspotters' army. The more pens they have, the higher the rank they hold.'[39] Pocket-size ABC lists of engine numbers benefited generations of spotters, people he so obviously has so little regard for.

Yet the worst and most surprising attack upon railway enthusiasts came from the man in overall charge of the National Railway Museum, Dr Neil Cossons (now knighted and well known to *Private Eye* readers as 'Dame' – and just why?). The Director of the Science Museum stunned his audience, at a four-day international railway symposium, by dismissing Britain's preserved steam railway network as a 'self-centred, self-serving movement that does little or nothing to further the knowledge of serious railway history.' He told *The Railway Magazine* afterwards: 'Gricing is a harmless hobby for consenting adults in private.'[40]

Professional humorists have naturally got in on the act. Discovering that membership of the Carnivorous Plants Society had reached an all-time high, Paul Merton suggested a few of these 'specifically designed to eat trainspotters' could be put at the end of railway platforms 'always supposing you could find a plant capable of swallowing an anorak.'[41]

Not known for a sense of humour (unless you count his Ali G impersonation), Richard Madeley was chatting cheerily to caller 'Elizabeth from Yorkshire' when she requested: 'Could you steal me a bottle of wine from Safeways please Richard?' This being a reference to the *This Morning* host being cleared of purloining booze from Tesco four years previously. His super-cool persona piqued, he blustered: 'These are sad people. These are anoraks ... It's like a train thing to do. Go and spot some trains or buy yourself an anorak, love.'[42] This book obviously has little chance of featuring on Richard and Judy's Book Club.

Politically-correct Camden and Islington Family-Health Services Authority, in north London, banned ridiculing colleagues' outside interests. Dubbed a 'trainspotters' charter', the offence was made a disciplinary matter.

Over the years I have catalogued the absurdities of reporting on railway matters in the Press and the supposed quality newspapers are as blameworthy as the downmarket ones. Also rail enthusiasm and sex has graced the pages of *The Guardian* and *Women Only* to *The Sun* and *Daily Sport*.[43]

So, to round matters off, some journalists' pearls of wisdom on trainspotters in customary reverse order:

> Sixth. 'Trainspotters are our worst nightmare.' – Jonathan Margolis [44]

> Fifth. 'We all know trainspotters are unhinged.' – Richard Tomkins [45]

> Fourth. 'It is a marriage of human and mechanical minds that we all feared: trainspotters have taken up the computer.' – Andrew Gilligan [46]

> Third. 'You can hardly hear the station announcements above the clack of anorak toggles.' – Christopher Middleton [47]

> Second. 'Gricers like to break into railway property late at night and photograph one another atop rare engines – in the nude.' – Jonathan Margolis [48]

> First. 'If I had my way I would round up all the weirdos from station platforms up and down the country and find them some charity work to do.' – Harry Blackwood [49]

Chapter Eleven

Journey's end

So now the pace is slowing. The terminus draws near. Time to pack away the notebook with its open page of arcane hieroglyphics; book of printed loco numbers, and copy of *Daily Sport* open at the most lurid page. A last swig to drain the contents of the eye-watering, gut-wrenching Tennents. To deter fellow passengers from sitting beside or opposite them, some trainspotters will go even further: wear clothes which would disgrace a tramp, scowl menacingly, cough consumptively and to really put the hex on would-be companions, don a home-made cardboard 'dog collar'.

In fact, many travellers dump luggage beside themselves in a bid to achieve more privacy for themselves. The aptly-named Candida Crewe claims to have been told that actor/comedian/author Barry Humphries, so as to ensure that no-one sat next to him on the train, would spoon out coleslaw on the seat beside him.[1] Sir Les Patterson, probably; Dame Edna, perhaps; Humphries, surely not.

On the subject of food and railways, passengers in the company of Francis Trevelyan Buckland received a gastronomic surprise. This nineteenth century pillar of the British Establishment, founder of the Buckland Museum of Economic Fish Culture and great improver of the nation's salmon fisheries, was carrying slugs on a train journey. Buckland feared he and his fellow Britons were facing a food shortage which would worsen, but he had produced a solution. Famine could be averted by the introduction of new, edible species of animal to farming and with messianic zeal he was driven to eat at least one of every kind of creature. To speed this gourmet revolution he set up the Acclimatisation Society, whose inaugural dinner was held on 12 July 1862. This being an age before home refrigeration, Buckland had no option but to keep many of his future meals about his person or home. Thus a number of slugs that he had concealed in his overcoat for a mid-journey snack escaped and unsympathetic fellow passengers found the slimy gastropods attaching themselves to their clothing.[2]

Other rail travellers had more convivial companions. On the Southern Region arose several 'W' clubs. These were formed of affluent commuters who bought only second-class tickets as they congregated at the then-large buffet counters each evening. Standing chatting, every time a station beginning with 'W' was passed they would down a whisky. The journey began with first snifter at Waterloo, speeding firstly to a second short at Wimbledon, followed in succession by Walton-on-Thames, Weybridge, West Byfleet, Woking, Worplesdon and Witley. A journey of thirty-eight miles and a consumption of eight shots. Apparently there were three clubs, one servicing each main line. Commuters for Salisbury having Winchfield and Whitchurch in place of Worplesdon and Witley, while Southampton travellers had Winchfield and Winchester. There is no record of this behaviour extending to Weymouth, whose patrons would have had to stand and see Wareham and Wool to make eleven whisky purchases.[3]

The mention of Salisbury recalled for me a letter printed several years ago which proves some railway enthusiasts have a finely-honed sense of humour. Responding to Vaughan Gallois' reminiscences of spotting trains fifteen miles in the distance, F. Parsons, of Fordingbridge, Hampshire, painted a picture of creative hyperbole:

> He will be most tickled to learn that during school holidays, a bevy of some five friends and myself went trainspotting from Salisbury Cathedral spire. In fact, we frequented the cathedral so often the works mason rigged up a special chain and pulley system so that in fine weather we could haul ourselves up the outside without having to go into the building during services etc. Strange to learn after all this time that the schoolboy we spotted up Coventry spire was also trainspotting. Was Vaughan Gallois the lad with the top button missing from his jacket and the crisps jammed in his left hand pocket? Those were certainly the days: steam drifting upward from the Western lines to the north from Swindon as 'Castles' hammered through, the 'West Country' Pacifics which we picked up at Reading and could follow until Axminster, and a stone's throw to the south, the little Isle of Wight railways.

These were Parsons' friends' favourite and he recalled observing from his eyrie the stationmaster at Brading eating sandwiches and whose small Jack Russell terrier ate the crumbs. At a crossing junction near Bembridge an elderly ganger would pause to take a drag of his fag, a pile of butt ends on the ground by the LSWR sign, with a clearly missing bolt.

The eagle-eyed correspondent continued: 'Summer weekends were so busy we could follow the trains out of Waterloo by the smoke drifting over the North Downs. Visually we could pick them up as they broke through the South Downs and coasted down to Portsmouth, where the paddle steamers ferried the trippers across to Ryde. I well remember one regular visitor; we could always pick him out by his green plastic mac, the ABC stuffed in his left-hand pocket and his map of the island's railways in the other. Unfortunately we always lost sight of the trains at Ventnor Tunnel, and missed the activity in the station.'

Finally: 'Alas, these days have gone. Who would bother to climb Salisbury Cathedral spire these days to see a diesel chug out of Waterloo?'[4]

Exactly. Today's spotter shuns so physical an activity as ascending a cathedral and sharing long-distance sightings, being happier indoors and in cyberspace. Here is a brief Internet exchange which has all the incestuous drama of shared-interest hobbyists. Unfolding over an hour or so on 20 February 2006, it shows how elation can rapidly morph into deflation. It is recorded as seen by group members:

> 'I've now had this from two different sources so it's beginning to look more than just a rumor. It's been alleged that Immingham TMD is currently working on EWS class 56 locos with a view to them being reinstated to traffic in the UK to replace a significant number of class 66s which are to move to EWS's French operation. Some class 58s are also likely to receive attention. The suggestion is that as many as 40 class 56s and 58s may see reuse in the UK. – Phil (Hayden Glynn)

> 'This was mentioned on "End of the Line" last week. It is rumoured that the 56s and 58s currently in Europe may form part of this plan as and when the hire contracts expire.' – Mark Harrington

> 'I can CONFIRM that EWS Immingham are NOT working on any locos e.g. 56/58 or 37's.' – Oliver Optuk

> 'Gentlemen, calm, calm. Neither Immingham or Toton are to work on any 56s or 58s, nor are they to start resurrecting 37s.' – tractormad37264 [5]

There you have it: The Rumour Millers' Tale.

Perhaps this is a symptom of a modern world of chatrooms and Googling, but it shows that common-interest sharing is alive and well; also that a rumour can be scotched far quicker than in the past. As long as there are railways there will be commentators. It remains to be seen whether the Internet will have much effect upon the folkloric dimension of railways. My suspicion, based upon the above correspondence, is that dissemination will quicken, but also that there will be greater perception of what are and what not travellers' tales.

So, our journey has taken us through the calendar year and period from genesis of the 'iron road' to its pinnacle; we have met railwaymen, commuters and gricers; been into supernatural realms and the dreamland of the strategic steam reserve; judged criminals and blunders, praised pioneers and wonders; finally reaching our destination.

Appendix

It takes a lot to laugh, it takes a train to cry

Around 6.30 p.m. on 2 October 1995, I was travelling second class on a 'High-Speed Train' between London Paddington and Newton Abbot. At some point during the journey an image of a familiar book cover, *Margaret Clitherow* by Mary Claridge (Fordham University Press, USA, 1966) appeared to my right side peripheral vision. St Margaret Clitherow was martyred in York for harbouring recusant Roman Catholic priests. Her shrine is in The Shambles and I have held a fascination for her over many years. I had the feeling that she was here to give me a message and it was 'Be yourself.' A dread feeling overtook me and in a state of utter panic I dashed down the carriage and locked myself in the toilet. I curled into the foetal position on the floor and cried uncontrollably for around fifteen minutes before normality returned and I could resume my seat.

Conclusion: At the time I put this down to being a quasi-mystical experience, though I am not a Roman Catholic or sympathiser, being Protestant Gnostic.

Upon reading about an aberrant working of the brain known medically as temporal lobe epilepsy or, more appropriately, dissociation, I attributed the episode to the strobe lights above the train aisle flashing on and off and causing dissociation. I should add that I was not aware of any lighting malfunction at the time, though have observed this subsequently with 'HSTs.' Novelist Will Self (self-confessedly no stranger to Class 'A' substances) wrote jokingly in a column: 'Now as any fool knows, the way industrial designers proceed with two-class transit systems is to design the first class and then make the second class worse. This was evident on the old British Rail, where the lighting in first class was just about tolerable and the lighting in the second class modulated so as to provoke an epileptic seizure in every third passenger. ('Self critical' column, *The Times Magazine*, 21 March 1998)

Also the 'Be yourself' message may have been illusory – the vision was obviously hallucinatory, so perhaps too the auditory adjunct – but quitting my job on its say-so to seek greater fulfilment is solid enough. Others undergoing alien abduction, near death experience and so on, often report dramatic changes in personality and lifestyle. I know I am a damn sight poorer financially, but more extrovert, easy-going and enjoying greater quality of life. Some false epiphany, perhaps, though neurologists at the University of California in San Diego have located an area in the temporal lobe regarded as a spiritual 'hot-spot.'

This could also have been a hypnopompic hallucination if I had dozed off and awoken. Also to reach God, so the Gnostic credo goes, is to make a 'call to self.'

I have, over the years, had other strange experiences. With regard to railways, when young, I could see a steam loco approaching in the distance, concentrate and know its number: this scrying would entail a feeling at the lower back of the head and this would confirm I was predicting correctly. More singular and significant transient personal episodes include the following.

Starry-eyed and laughing

During the mid-Sixties, I was employed as a junior reporter on the Billingham and Stockton *Expresses*. One day prior to a regular pub lunch, I accompanied colleague Geoff Daniel to the Billingham Synthonia theatre, where Geoff was to report on a performance by one of the foreign dance groups appearing at the annual Billingham Folklore Festival. Seated in the auditorium, I not only found the sight of men in *lederhosen* amusing, but when they began a rhythmic dance and banging pieces of wood together I began laughing uncontrollably. Embarrassed, I pushed my way through the audience, who obviously thought my behaviour even more bizarre. I walked around Mill Lane still laughing helplessly, tears streaming, for fifteen minutes until it subsided.

Conclusion: music combined with wood-banging ritual activated the temporal lobes and caused the hysterical behaviour. It may also link with the 'Toronto Blessing' charismatic phenomenon which led to Christian worshippers falling down laughing. Or as Groucho Marx observed: 'He who laughs, lasts.'

Chimes of freedom (flashing)

One Bank Holiday weekend in the late Seventies I was passing a night-club in Seaton Carew to find for the first time ever its ground-floor bar doors wide open. It was lunchtime and out of curiosity I went in and ordered a pint of bitter. I had only drunk a little when the flashing lights and tempo of the disco music took a hold on me. I realised that if I did not leave quickly I would pass out, so drank up swiftly and once back on the street normality returned.

Conclusion: Bright flashing lights and musical beat pattern caused temporal lobe dissociation.

Rainy day women Nos. 12 and 35

Against what in soberer times I would have avoided, I decided to sample a largish mushroom growing on a willow tree stump in our Seaton Carew back garden. Trusting my ability to match it to an illustration and description (edible and safe) in Richard Mabey's book *Food for Free*, and having previously been told by gypsy friend Tom Cole that if the setting looks pleasant then the fungi should match that, I ate some. The next day, cycling to work along Coronation Drive, Hartlepool, I saw a jogger approaching who suddenly vanished into thin air. Later, mentioning this to my son Ian, he pinpointed the exact location and said others he knew had been the subject of similar weird experiences there; on one occasion two youths tripping on the drug LSD were passed by a jogger at this spot soaked to the skin and with rain falling only on and just around him, but not on them or elsewhere. That lunchtime I had a couple of pints in the Jackson Arms and as I climbed the steps to the *Hartlepool Mail* offices, someone came out with a hand covered with and dripping blood – or so it seemed to me. During that afternoon I was in the toilet urinating when the door opened and I turned to see reporter Paul Wenham, who began to shrink and took on the partial form of a zebra before unexplainably retreating out.

Conclusion: these seem to describe involuntary drug-induced 'flashbacks' rather than any form of temporal lobe dissociation.

Do my experiences appertain to a 'unified theory' for all paranormal events, as attributed by some to temporal lobe dissociation and neurological trauma theory (or for that matter electromagnetic pollution or tectonic stress in the Earth's crust). Forteana mates with neuro-theology.

Or has what has been described been a sequence of brief psychotic events as initially diagnosed in me by psychologist friend Dr Neil Robson, but who is not absolutely certain, though adamant I do not have temporal lobe epilepsy.

This appendix is based on what I have called my exegesis, or neurological status report, on trying to make some sense out of strange personal experiences. During its evolution I have shown it to, and sought comments from, a few trusted friends.

Earth mysteries, ufology and consciousness author Paul Devereux reckoned my experiences were 'just altered states triggered at different times by different things. You may be particularly prone – you probably would have been a shaman in another culture/epoch.'

John Michell, the radical-traditionalist whose book *The View Over Atlantis* influenced the Sixties' counter-cultural generation, wrote to me: 'You are, as I've recognized all along, a man of deep perception, with insights and experiences that cannot well be expressed – a shaman, if you like. But there's nothing unusual in being "gifted." It's how you use it that counts. I liked reading your accounts of your mental adventures and thoughts on them. You have made use of them rather than becoming their victim – which is the hallmark of a real shaman. I hope you'll continue writing and make your knowledge and enthusiasms of use to other people. There is no one else like you.'

Much of my experiences are echoed in two works of fiction by Philip K. Dick, *Radio Free Albemuth* and *VALIS*. Dick deserves the last word as he sums up my current state of play trying to make sense of my place in the world: 'Every day he developed a new one [theory], more cunning, more exciting, more fucked.'

End notes

In the references, changes in certain newspaper titles may seem inconsistent. Max Hastings introduced the definitive article to the *Telegraph* titles during his editorship; *Daily Sport* spent a brief period as *The Sport*, *Daily Mirror* similarly spent some time as *The Mirror* and *Daily Express* as *The Express*. *Northern Earth Mysteries* shortened itself to *Northern Earth*.

Chapter 1 (pages 5 to 23)

1. R.A.S. Hennessey, *Railways*, B.T. Batsford, 1973
2. Harold Pollins, *Britain's Railways: An Industrial History*, David and Charles, 1971
3. Charles Fort, *Lo!*, first published New York, 1931; reprinted John Brown Publishing, 1996
4. *The Best of Mayfair*, Vol. 5
5. Jan Harold Brunvand, *The Baby Train and Other Lusty Urban Legends*, W.W. Norton, 1993
6. *Sunday Sport*, 23 May 1993
7. Reuters, 26 January 1996; *Fortean Times*, No. 87, 1996
8. *Daily Star*, 28 February 1992
9. *Daily Telegraph*, 27 February 1984
10. *Daily Telegraph*, 16 March 1984
11. *The Railway Magazine*, May, 2003
12. *Heritage Railway*, October, 2004
13. *Steam Railway*, October, 1998
14. Ibid.
15. *The Sun*, 1 June 1996
16. *Daily Sport*, 10 March 2004
17. *Sunday Mirror*, 16 February 2003
18. *Steam Railway*, January, 1999
19. *Daily Sport*, 28 February 2000
20. *The Railway Magazine*, August, 2003
21. Paul Screeton, 'Rod the Mod(el railway fanatic)', *Folklore Frontiers*, No. 49, 2005
22. For a detailed and moving account of just such a railway funeral see *The Daily Telegraph*, 27 February 1999
23. *Steam Railway*, January, 1996
24. *Daily Telegraph*, 17 February 1996
25. *Daily Telegraph*, 6 November 1999
26. *Steam Railway*, June, 1996; *Daily Mail*, 11 June 1996
27. *New Scientist*, 13 March 1998
28. *The Express*, 23 January 1999
29. *Daily Sport*, 6 August 1993

30. *Steam Railway*, January, 1996
31. *Heritage Railway*, October, 2004
32. *Daily Mail*, 13 November 1999
33. *Daily Sport*, 1 November 1995
34. *The Sport*, 29 October 1996
35. *Rail*, No. 409, 2001
36. *Daily Sport*, 14 October 1998
37. *Daily Sport*, 17 December 1998
38. *The Sun*, 20 June 1992
39. Diana Lainson, 'Chinese Steam', *Railway World*, April, 1976
40. *The Sunday Times*, 1 January 1978
41. *Daily Mail, Daily Express, Daily Sport*, 6 June 1996
42. *The Railway Magazine*, June, 1999
43. *The Railway Magazine*, May, 2002
44. *The Guardian*, 3 January 1992
45. *Rail*, No. 282, 1996; *The Sun, The Sport*, 27 February 1997
46. *Steam Railway*, No. 225, 1998
47. *Eastern World*, February, 1991
48. *The Mirror,* 24 November 2000; *Daily Sport,* 24 November 2000
49. *Daily Star*, 21 November 1996
50. *Leyton Guardian*, 5 November 1998; *Fortean Times*, No. 119, 1999
51. *Daily Sport*, 10 March 2000
52. *Sunday Sport*, 23 May 1993
53. *Sunday Sport*, 3 November 1996
54. *The Sport*, 15 June 1998
55. *The Railway Magazine*, September, 1996; *Fortean Times*, No. 89, 1996
56. *Daily Sport*, 7 June 1996, and 11 August 2000
57. *Rail Express*, November, 1996, via *Gridiron* newsletter
58. *The Sunday Telegraph*, 2 May 2004
59. *The Sunday Telegraph*, 13 June 2004
60. *The Railway Magazine*, April and June, 2003
61. *The Railway Magazine*, December, 1998
62. Paul Slade, 'Riding the Death Line', *Fortean Times*, No. 179, 2004
63. *The Railway Magazine*, February, 1986
64. *Railnews*, January, 2005
65. *The Times*, 1 January 2000
66. *Heritage Railway*, November, 1999
67. *Rail Enthusiast*, April and May, 1986
68. *Sunday People*, 16 May 1986
69. *Rail Express*, May and June 1999
70. *Steam Railway*, July, 1996
71. *The Railway Magazine*, January, 1999
72. *The Sunday Telegraph*, 28 March 1999
73. *Daily Sport*, 19 February 2002
74. *Steam Railway*, October, 1991
75. Paul Screeton, 'More than one face to railway graffiti', *The Mail* (Hartlepool), 17 November 1987

76. Henry Chalfant and James Prigoff, *Spraycan Art,* Thames and Hudson, 1987

77. *Rail,* No. 509, 2005; *The Railway Magazine,* May, 2005

78. For display advertising on the sides of trains see 'Platform Announcer', 'Is it all done in the best possible taste?', *Rail Express,* November, 2000; for anti-tagging see Laura Richardson, 'The writing's on the wall', *e-motion* (South West Trains), No. 10, 2005

Chapter 2 (pages 24 to 52)

1. Noel Turnbull, 'A rail ghost', *The Northern Echo,* 3 January 1977

2. Brian Redhead, 'Railside tale of terror', *Darlington and Stockton Times,* 5 April 1986

3. Paul White, 'Identity of the railway ghost is ... ', *The Northern Echo,* 8 May 2001

4. Hugh Watson, 'Old 69 – Thornaby T.M.D. – "The Ghost"', *Folklore Frontiers,* No. 15, 1992

5. Ibid.

6. *Folklore Frontiers,* No. 2, 1986

7. W.B. Herbert, *Railway Ghosts,* David and Charles, 1985

8. *Folklore Frontiers,* No. 3, 1986

9. Paul Screeton, 'Ghost Trains – the myth of the Strategic Reserve', *Common Ground,* No. 3, 1981

10. W.B. Herbert, *Phantoms of the Railways,* David and Charles, 1989

11. Paul Screeton, 'A hoax repeated', *The Mail* (Hartlepool), 28 April 1989; *Folklore Frontiers,* No. 9, 1989

12. W.B. Herbert, *Railway Ghosts and Phantoms,* David and Charles, 1989

13. *Rail Express,* March, 1999

14. *Rail Enthusiast,* February, 1984

15. 'Collision at Wrawby Junction, ER', HMSO; precis in *Modern Railways,* April, 1987

16. *Rail Enthusiast,* March, 1984

17. Graham Bell, 'Fate rides on the 5.32', *Sunday Express,* 1 April 1984

18. Paul Screeton, 'Railway Rites – The Renumbering of 47216', *The Symbol,* No. 4, 1984

19. Paul Screeton, 'From George Stephenson to Carole-Anne Stephenson (Changing Locomotive Numbers and Names)', *The Shaman,* No. 9, 1985

20. *Rail Enthusiast,* February, 1985

21. Jenny Randles, *Beyond Explanation?,* Robert Hale, 1985; Jenny Randles, *Strange But True?,* Judy Piatkus, 1995; Jenny Randles, *Truly Weird,* Collins and Brown, 1998

22. *Rail Enthusiast,* No. 109, 1989

23. *Rail Enthusiast,* No. 131, 1990

24. *Rail,* No. 162, 1991

25. Paul Screeton, 'Ariadne Lives!', *Folklore Frontiers,* No. 16, 1992; *The Labyrinth,* Issue 3, 2000; Paul Screeton, '47299 – Predicting the future', *Traction,* September, 1999

26. W.B. Herbert, *Railway Ghosts,* David and Charles, 1985; W.B. Herbert, *Railway Ghosts and Phantoms,* David and Charles, 1989

27. Anna Gizowska, 'The Haunted Locomotive', *Sunday (News of the World)*, 1 November 1998
28. Nigel Antolic, '47299', *Forty Seven Forum,* No. 18, 2000
29. www.geocities.com/Athens/Forum/8287/brahan.html
30. Nicholas A. Macleod, *Scottish Witchcraft,* James Pike, 1975
31. *The Brahan Seer,* Clan Mackenzie Society of Scotland and the UK web site
32. Justine Glass, *The Story of Fulfilled Prophecy*, Cassell, 1969
33. Jamie Stokes, *Strange People*, Parragon, 2000
34. *The Brahan Seer,* Clan Mackenzie Society of Scotland and the UK web site
35. Nigel Pennick and Sheila Cann, *Mother Shipton*, Fenris-Wolf, 1980
36. John Michell, editor, *Mother Shipton*, West Country Editions, 1976
37. Paul Screeton, 'Hare-brained behaviour', *The Mail* (Hartlepool), 8 November 1976
38. David Joy, *Main Line Over Shap*, Dalesman Books, 1979
39. John and Anne Spencer, *The Ghost Handbook*, Boxtree, 1988; www.unexplained-mysteries.com/forum/index.php?showtopic=11131andst=o
40. *The Sunday Telegraph*, 23 January 2005
41. Lynn Picknett, editor, *The Encyclopaedia of the Paranormal,* Macmillan, 1990
42. Justine Glass, *The Story of Fulfilled Prophecy*, Cassell, 1969
43. Peter Bishop, 'Dream that ended a marriage', *Sunday People*, 5 February 1978
44. *Fortean Times,* Nos. 77 and 78, 1994
45. Chris Milner, 'Riding on the Redland', *The Railway Magazine*, January, 1993
46. Paul Screeton, 'Two Middridge fairy tales', *The Mail* (Hartlepool), no date, March, 1977
47. Noel Turnbull, 'Strange ladies', *The Northern Echo*, 6 December 1976
48. John Billingsley, *Stony Gaze*, Capall Bann, 1998
49. Paul Screeton, 'Shap Avenue and Memory Lane', *Northern Earth Mysteries*, No. 11, 1981
50. *Traction*, October, 1999
51. John Palmer, 'Return to the stones', *The Ley Hunter*, No. 126, 1997
52. *The Crop Watcher*, Issue 2, 1990 (monitored from *Steam World*, September, 1990)
53. Patrick Harpur, 'Mercurius in the cornfields', *The Cereologist*, No. 1, 1990
54. Ronald Hill, 'Hums, stones and circles', *The Cereologist*, No.17, 1996
55. *The Times,* 20 March 2002; *The Mirror,* 20 March 2002
56. *Steam Railway*, February, 1990
57. Geff Vinter, *Railway Walks: LNER*, Alan Sutton, 1990
58. William Howitt, *Visits to Remarkable Places, Vol. 1*, Longman, Green, Longmans and Roberts, 1841
59. Chris Cubitt, 'Peggy Engines', *Moorsline*, No. 16, 1997
60. *Steam Railway*, December, 1996
61. Bryan McAllister, *The Guardian*, 11 August 1990
62. Paul Screeton, *The Lambton Worm and Other Northumbrian Dragon Legends*, Zodiac House, 1978; Paul Screeton, *Whisht Lads and Haad Yor Gobs*, Northeast Press, 1998
63. Philip Young, 'Going Underground', *The Northern Echo*, 24 October 1989

64. Paul Screeton, 'Long Man of Wilmington column', *The Ley Hunter*, No. 113, 1990.
65. Peter A. White, *Portrait of County Durham*, Robert Hale, 1967
66. Paul Screeton, 'The flying dragons of steam', *The Dragon Chronicle*, No. 17, 2000
67. Paul Screeton, *Seekers of the Linear Vision*, Stonehenge Viewpoint, 1994
68. John Michell, 'Lung Mei and The Dragon Paths of England', *Image*, No. 1, 1967
69. Deryck Lewis, 'The Flying Saucer now standing on launchpad one ... ', *The Railway Magazine*, May, 1996
70. Paul Screeton, 'Sky Westbury and Crooked', *Touchstone*, No. 64, 2004; *Amskaya*, No. 57, 2004
71. Arthur Shuttlewood, *The Flying Saucerers*, Sphere, 1976
72. Peter Gray, 'The Glorious Years', *Steam Railway*, September, 1998
73. John Rimmer, 'Hold the back page', *Magonia*, No. 63, 1998
74. Paul Sussman, 'In the news', *The Big Issue*, No. 200, 1996
75. Alan Falconer, *The Cleveland Way*, HMSO, 1972
76. Ginny Dougary, 'The New Romantic', *The Times Magazine*, 27 March 1999
77. Paul Screeton, 'Jodrell Bank (Simon Says)', *Folklore Frontiers*, No. 26, 1995
78. *The Times Magazine*, 7 October 2000
79. *The Mirror*, 18 March 2000
80. *The Daily Telegraph*, 6 February 1999
81. Bill Pertwee, *The Station Now Standing*, Hodder and Stoughton, 1991
82. Cristina Odone's Diary, *The Observer*, 26 September 2004
83. *The Sunday Telegraph*, 30 January 2000
84. Iain Mayhew, 'The Original Cook's tour', *Daily Mirror*, 28 May 2005
85. John Stephenson, 'The Romance of a Railway Ticket', *Canny Crack,* privately published, 1982
86. *You*, 9 November 1997
87. *Traction*, September, 1999
88. *The Sunday Telegraph*, 28 May 2000
89. *The Daily Telegraph*, 12 December 1998
90. *The Daily Telegraph*, 11 October 1997
91. Colin Wilson, *The Directory of Possibilities*, Corgi, 1982
92. Colin Wilson, *Mysteries*, Hodder and Stoughton, 1978
93. Philip Atkins, 'Sudden death', *The Railway Magazine*, September, 2003
94. *Daily Telegraph*, 3 January 1984; *Railnews*, May, 1984; *Fortean Times*, No. 50, 1988
95. Robert Rickard and Richard Kelly, *Photographs of the Unknown*, New English Library, 1980
96. *Rail*, No. 502, 2004
97. *Fortean Times*, No. 52, 1989
98. John Chesterman, 'The Middlesbrough Meteorite', *Curious Facts Monthly*, No. 4, 1981
99. Paul Sieveking, 'Mysteries column', *The Sunday Telegraph*, 14 May 2000
100. Charles Fort, *Lo!*, first published New York, 1931; reprinted John Brown Publishing, 1996

Chapter 3 (pages 53 to 74)

1. L.T.C. Rolt, *Red for Danger*, Pan Books, 1967
2. Nigel Pennick, 'Urban folklore of the London Underground', *Folklore Frontiers*, No. 6, 1987
3. *Daily Mirror*, 1 May 1975
4. . Nigel Pennick, 'Urban folklore of the London Underground', *Folklore Frontiers*, No. 6, 1987
5. *Daily Sport*, 27 October 1999
6. *Financial Times*, 6 September 1991
7. *Daily Telegraph*, 11 February 1991
8. *Fortean Times*, No. 59, 1991
9. *Mid-Wales Evening Leader*, 9 May 1991
10. P.W.B. Semmens, *Railway Disasters of the World*, Patrick Stephens, 1994
11. Philip Atkins, 'Sudden Death II', *The Railway Magazine*, July, 2004
12. *Daily Mirror*, 17 April 2002
13. John F. Clay, 'Foolish legend but honourable history – 1', *Railway World*, August, 1976
14. *Steam Railway*, Spring 1998
15. Paul Screeton, 'Hush-hust rail record', *The Mail* (Hartlepool), 1 July 1988
16. *Steam Railway*, November, 1994
17. Michael Harris, 'No. 4468 'Mallard': Fastest of them all', *Railway World*, November, 1986
18. *The Railway Magazine*, December, 2002
19. *The Times*, 29 May 2004
20. Francis O.J. Otway, letter, *The Sunday Telegraph*, 4 April 2004
21. O.S. Nock, 'Stockton and Darlington', *The Railway Magazine*, September, 1975
22. Chris Lloyd, 'New contender for the title of rail birthplace', *The Northern Echo*, 11 April 1990
23. *The Railway Magazine*, June, 1999
24. *The Northern Echo*, 3 February 1990
25. L.T.C. Rolt, *George and Robert Stephenson*, Longmans, 1960
26. Thomas Insull, *Transport by Land*, John Murray, 1948
27. Hunter Davies, *A Walk Along the Track*, Hamlyn, 1982
28. *The Times Magazine*, 13 October 2001
29. Robert Hawkins, *Steam Railway*, June, 1995
30. John Williams, 'Station demolished for want of a comma', *Daily Telegraph*, 3 November 1984
31. Sean O'Neill, 'Train supersaver offers 10-minute visit to London', *The Daily Telegraph*, 21 September 1996
32. *Daily Sport*, 15 February 1998
33. *The Railway Magazine*, April, 1997
34. *Steam Railway*, June, 1995
35. Crispin Gill, *Things to see and do in South Devon*, The Raleigh Press, 1967
36. Dr David Norman Smith, 'Railway's early opponents', *The Railway Magazine*, January, 1989
37. *The Sunday Telegraph*, 20 September 1998

38. John Stephenson, *Canny Crack*, privately published, 1982
39. Norman Harper, 'On the other hand ... ', *Press and Journal* (Aberdeen), 24 September 1994
40. *Daily Sport*, 20 September 1993
41. *Daily Sport*, 14 December 1999
42. *Daily Sport*, 11 February 2000
43. *Rail*, No. 415, 2001
44. *Daily Mirror*, 14 August 2004
45. *The Times*, 18 January 2003
46. Roy Stevens, 'Refreshing changes', *Steam Railway*, October, 1991
47. *The Times*, 18 September 2004
48. Anthony Trollope, *He Knew He Was Right*, n.p., 1896–7
49. *Steam Railway*, No. 313, 2005
50. *The Railway Magazine*, November, 1980
51. *Daily Mail*, August 24, 1996
52. Howard Johnston, 'Doncaster works "secret engines": will they finally be revealed?', *Steam Railway*, No. 313, 2005
53. *The Railway Magazine*, October, 1995
54. Ben Webster, 'Rail enthusiasts let off steam over mock Nazis', *The Times*, 19 February 2005
55. *The Railway Magazine*, December, 1992
56. *The Railway Magazine*, April, 1979
57. Nigel Pennick, 'The Great Central Railway Cup Final Prophecy, 1904', *The Symbol*, No. 3, 1984, via *The Railway Magazine*, vol XXII
58. *Daily Mirror*, 18 May 2004
59. *The Daily Telegraph*, 17 February 1996
60. *Daily Mirror*, 25 October 1990
61. *Rail*, No. 304, 1997
62. Paul Sieveking, 'Bigfoot turns down dates with Chinese', *The Sunday Telegraph*, 17 October 1999
63. *Fortean Times*, No. 40, 1983
64. Lynn Picknet, *The Encyclopaedia of the Paranormal*, Macmillan, 1990
65. Ron Toft, 'On the trail of Big Cats', *Canal Boat and Inland Waterways*, July, 2004
66. *Daily Sport*, 17 July 1996
67. John Michell and Robert J.M. Rickard, *Phenomena: A Book of Wonders*, Thames and Hudson, 1977
68. Paul Screeton, 'A Personal Black Panther Sighting in Northumberland, 1983', *The Shaman*, No. 10, 1985

Chapter 4 (pages 75 to 86)

1. *The Railway Magazine*, May, 2002
2. *The Daily Telegraph*, 13 December 1997
3. *The Sport*, 8 September 1998; *The Railway Magazine*, November 1998
4. *The Sun*, 12 July 2000
5. *The Times of India*, 2 January 2003; *Rail*, No. 454, 2003

6. *The Times*, 8 January 2000
7. Michael Persinger and Gyslaine F. Lafreniere, *Space-Time Transients and Unusual Events*, Nelson-Bell, Chicago, 1977
8. *The Railway Magazine*, July, 2002
9. *The Sunday Telegraph*, 6 August 2000
10. *The Railway Magazine,* January, 2004
11. *The Daily Telegraph*, 20 February 1999
12. Associated Press 16 May 1996; *Fortean Times*, No. 90, 1996
13. *The Railway Magazine*, April, 1997
14. *The Sunday Telegraph*, 6 February 2000
15. *The Mirror*, 18 August 2001
16. *The Sunday Telegraph*, 22 December 2002
17. *Rail*, No. 296, 1997
18. *The Railway Magazine*, February, 2003
19. *Daily Mirror*, 17 May 2004
20. *The Times*, 9 April 2003
21. *The Railway Magazine*, May, 2003
22. *Steam Railway*, October, 2002
23. Graham and Lynne Jones, *I Love Sex I Hate Sex*, New English Library, 1989
24. *The Times*, 12 June 2004
25. *The Sun*, 3 January 1995
26. *The Sport*, 11 November 1996
27. *Daily Star*, 27 June 1996
28. Dr Robin Smith, *The Encyclopaedia of Sexual Trivia*, Robson Books, 1990
29. *Sunday Sport*, 23 February 1997
30. *Daily Star*, 30 October 1996
31. *The Independent*, 26 January 1994
32. Dr Peter Kinnell, *The Complete Illustrated Encyclopaedia of Erotic Failure*, Futura, 1989
33. *The Times*, 26 January 1987
34. *Rail*, No. 249, 1995
35. J.B. Hollingsworth, *The Atlas of Train Travel*, Sidgwick and Jackson, 1980
36. *Rail Express*, December, 1999
37. *Rail*, No. 336, 1998; *The Railway Magazine*, November, 1998
38. Paul Sussman, *Death by Spaghetti*, Fourth Estate, 1996
39. *Daily Star*, 4 October 1996
40. *The Sun*, 15 July 1992
41. *Daily Star*, 22 June 1993
42. *Daily Telegraph*, 28 April 1987
43. *Daily Sport*, 1 August 1996
44. *Daily Sport*, 27 October 1998
45. *The Sun* 15 December 1980; *The Northern Echo* 15 December 1980; *The Mail* (Hartlepool) 15 December 1990
46. Tom Fort and Tom Gatt, 'Lost for words', *The Times*, November 8, 2003; Aubrey Malone, *Literary Trivia*, Prion, 1999
47. Mark Sanderson, 'The Literary Life', *The Sunday Telegraph*, 26 January 2003
48. *The Railway Magazine*, August, 1998

49. *The Mail on Sunday*, 21 October 2001
50. *Daily Mirror*, 22 January 2001
51. *The Railway Magazine*, May, 2003
52. *The Daily Telegraph*, 12 June 1999
53. *The Times*, 18 September 2004
54. *The Sunday Telegraph*, 22 August 2004
55. *The Daily Telegraph*, 27 October 2001
56. *The Railway Magazine*, June, 2004
57. *City of London: Volume IV – A Club No More 1945–2000*, Chatto, 2001
58. *The Sunday Telegraph Magazine*, 23 April 2000
59. *The Railway Magazine*, March, 2002
60. *The Railway Magazine*, February, 1999
61. *The Daily Telegraph*, 30 October 1999

Chapter 5 (pages 87 to 102)

1. *Night and Day*, 22 October 1995
2. *The Journal* (Newcastle), 22 April 1994
3. *Daily Star*, 24 June 1997
4. *The Times*, 30 October 1997
5. *Daily Star*, 26 July 1995
6. *Heritage Railway*, November, 1999
7. *The Sun*, 6 July 1996
8. Anthony Roberts and Geoff Gilbertson, *The Dark Gods*, Rider/Hutchinson, 1980
9. John A. Keel, *Operation Trojan Horse*, Souvenir Press, 1971
10. *The Independent*, 30 March 1991
11. *The Sun*, 1 April 1991
12. *Daily Telegraph*, 22 March 1997
13. Michael Goss, *The Halifax Slasher*, Fortean Times Occasional Papers, 1987
14. Willy Smith, 'Mattoon Revisited', *Magonia*, No. 48, 1994
15. *News of The World*, 7 November 1999
16. Jonathan Margolis and Gabrielle Morris, *The Commuter's Tale*, Chapmans, 1992
17. *Night and Day*, 14 April 1996
18. Michael Goss, 'The Maniac on the Platform', *Magonia*, No. 19, 1985
19. *The Mirror*, 7 November 2001
20. *The Times*, 31 January 2004
21. *The Times*, 25 February 2004
22. *The Sun*, 2 December 1987; *News of The World*, 6 December 1987
23. Michael Goss, 'The Maniac on the Platform', *Magonia*, No. 19, 1985
24. Tobias Hill, *Underground*, Faber, 1999
25. *The Times Magazine*, 3 October 1998
26. *The Sunday Telegraph*, 3 October 1999
27. Jonathan Margolis and Gabrielle Morris, *The Commuter's Tale,* Chapmans, 1992
28. *The Sun*, 5 March 1992
29. Jonathan Margolis and Gabrielle Morris, *The Commuter's Tale*, Chapmans, 1992

30. Nigel Blundell, *The World's Greatest Crooks and Conmen*, Hamlyn, 1991
31. *Daily Sport*, 4 May 2001
32. *Daily Sport*, 13 August 2001
33. *The Sunday Telegraph*, 31 December 2000
34. *Evening Chronicle* (Newcastle), 3 September 1998
35. *Fortean Times*, No. 114, 1998
36. *Daily Sport*, 22 October 1999
37. *Daily Sport*, 25 October 1999
38. *The Daily Telegraph*, 22 August 1997
39. *The Sport*, 20 May 1997
40. *Daily Sport*, 26 January 1999
41. *The Sunday Telegraph*, 28 November 1999
42. *The Guardian Weekend*, 8 June 1996
43. *Daily Star*, 19 March 1996
44. Jonathan Margolis and Gabrielle Morris, *The Commuter's Tale*, Chapmans, 1992
45. *The Sport*, 10 September 1997
46. *Eastern World*, 1989
47. *The Guardian*, 1 March 1991
48. *Fortean Times*, No. 86, 1996
49. *New York Daily News*, 6 May 1996
50. *The Sunday Telegraph*, May 23, 2004
51. Paul Screeton, 'Obsolete railway trackbed offers an important challenge', *The Mail* (Hartlepool), November 18, 1980; Paul Screeton, *The Man Who Ate A Domino*, privately published, 2002

Chapter 6 (pages 103 to 119)

1. *RailStaff*, February, 2005
2. *Steam Railway*, December, 1991
3. Philip Atkins, 'Death by unnatural causes', *Steam Railway*, November, 1991; Philip Atkins, 'Sudden death', *The Railway Magazine*, September, 2003
4. Philip Atkins, 'Death by unnatural causes, Part II', *Steam Railway*, August, 1992
5. Letter in *Steam Railway*, April, 1988
6. Letter in *Steam Railway*, May, 1988
7. Terry Sykes and Helen Smith, 'The mystery of the loco chimney', *Darlington and Stockton Times*, 13 April 1990; as 'Searching for Lost Treasure', *Steam Railway*, June, 1990; as 'Loco chimney mystery solved', *Folklore Frontiers*, No. 11, 1990
8. *The Railway Magazine*, May, 1996
9. Letter by Colin Cowell, *The Times*, 5 March 2005
10. *Daily Star*, 13 May 1997
11. *Modern Railways*, December, 1985
12. Nigel Pennick, personal communication dated 23 November 1990
13. *Hartlepool Star*, 25 September 1997
14. *The Railway Magazine*, November, 2004
15. *Steam Railway*, January, 1991

16. Paul Screeton, 'Exploding Egbert the Tank Myths', *The Mail* (Hartlepool), 21 July 1987
17. Letter by James Burton, *The Mail* (Hartlepool), 24 July 1987
18. *Eastern World*, April, 1989
19. Keith Miles, 'The Highland Clearance of '46', *British Railways Illustrated*, October, 1995
20. Nick Piggot, compiler, 'A to Z of Railways', *The Railway Magazine*, April, 2005
21. Colin J. Marsden, compiler, 'Slugs, Skodas and Skinheads', *The Railway Magazine*, November, 1997
22. *Rail Express*, January, 1999
23. *The Railway Magazine*, June, 2004
24. *The Guardian*, 11 December 1996
25. *Rail*, No. 355, 1998
26. Marcus Stent, 'Tinsley Class 45 Unofficial Names', *InterCity*, Vol. 22, No. 12, 1994
27. 'Rumours of Names', *Folklore Frontiers*, Nos. 40, 41, 42, 2002; No. 44, 2003; No. 50, 2005
28. *The Independent Saturday Magazine*, October 25, 1997
29. *Metro*, 11 April 2005
30. *Steam Railway*, July, 1993
31. Peter N. Walker, *Folk Tales from the North York Moors,* Robert Hale, 1990
32. Nigel Pennick, *Skulls, Cats and Witch Bottles*, Nigel Pennick Editions, 1986
33. Michael Behrend, *The Symbol*, No. 5, 1984
34. David Wilcock, 'Impostor!', *Steam Railway*, March, 1998
35. Letter to Reg Appleton, *The Railway Magazine*, July, 1998.
36. Philip Atkins, 'Sudden death', *The Railway Magazine*, September, 2003
37. *The Railway Magazine*, November, 2004
38. *Steam Railway*, March, 1995
39. K.S. Farr, 'Fifty Years a "King"', *The Railway Magazine*, June, 1977
40. John H. Bird, 'Winston Churchill's funeral train', *The Railway Magazine*, March, 2005
41. *Steam Railway*, November, 1993
42. *Steam World*, June, 2005
43. John Carter, 'A right old shindig at the Cotswold Olimpicks', *The Mail on Sunday*, 29 May 2005
44. Robin Coulthard, 'It Was Their Express Wish ... ', *Mission Impossible*, January, 1991
45. 'Captain Oates', 'Football transfers', *The Railway Magazine*, December, 2002
46. David Jackson and Owen Russell, 'The "Footballer" Interlude', *Railway World*, January, 1981
47. Mike Amos, *Backtrack* columns, *The Northern Echo*, 8 January, 18 January, 25 January, 15 February, 19 February 1991
48. Mike Amos, 'The Darlington Now Leaving ... ', *The Northern Echo*, 7 May 1984
49. Anon, *Darlington and South-West Durham*, Bellcode Books, 1990
50. *The Railway Magazine*, August, 1999
51. *The Railway Magazine*, April, 1999

52. Letter by Keith Farr, *The Railway Magazine*, October, 2001 (The 'A3' boiler has a 220 lb pressure and the class normally had 19 by 26 inch cylinders. Farr's tractive effort is challenged by the Ian Allan ABC book, which gives it as 32,910 lb. Also 39,745 lb seems unusually high.)
53. *Modern Railways Pictorial*, May, 1981
54. *Steam Railway*, April, 1998

Chapter 7 (pages 120 to 136)

1. *The Northern Echo*, 29 June 1979
2. Malcolm Parsons, 'Truth behind viaduct legend', *Railnews*, June, 2001
3. *Rail*, No. 396, 2000
4. Nigel Pennick, *Skulls, Cats and Witch Bottles: The Ancient Practice of House Protection*, Nigel Pennick Editions, 1986
5. Rodney Dale, *The Tumour in the Whale*, Universal, 1978
6. *The Guardian*, 14 September 1990
7. Paul Screeton, 'Folklore of the Settle-Carlisle Railway', *The Labyrinth*, No. 3, 2000; *Folklore Frontiers*, No. 39, 2001, *Northern Earth*, No. 102, 2005
8. W.R. Mitchell, 'Iron Road to Carlisle', *Cumbria*, May, 1973
9. Paul Screeton, 'Thorpe Thewles story without foundation?', *The Mail* (Hartlepool), 23 July 1980
10. V.P. Mitchell, 'High Arches', *The Dalesman*, January, 1933
11. Anon, *Welcome to Cameron Country*, Sheila P. Fowler Associates, *circa* 1988
12. *Daily Telegraph*, 8 November 1983
13. *New Scientist*, 29 April 1995
14. *PC Dealer*, December, 1995; *The Railway Magazine*, September 1996
15. *Front*, April, 2004
16. Peter Welbourn, 'Thawed class travel on BR!', *Daily Star*, 31 May 1993
17. *Mail on Sunday*, 14 May 2000
18. Frank Earp, *At the Edge*, No. 1, 1996
19. *The Times* bodyandsoul section, 18 June 2005
20. *Modern Railways*, September, 1984
21. Paul Screeton, *Who Hung the Monkey?*, Printability Publishing, 1991
22. Peter E. Baughan, 'Centenary of "Long Drag"', *The Railway Magazine*, no date
23. Brian Page, 'Steam, speed and our Sid', *The Northern Echo*, 24 November 1988
24. Peter Semmens, '1945: The year sanity returned to the nation's railway', *The Railway Magazine*, May, 1995
25. Anthony Lambert, *Settle to Carlisle*, Siena, 1997
26. Stanley C. Jenkins, *The Wensleydale Branch*, The Oakwood Press, 1993
27. Peter Brock, 'Steam Finale over Ais Gill', *Railway World*, no date
28. E.S. Youldon, 'Garsdale turntable: an alternative theory', *Steam Railway*, November, 1987
29. W.R. Mitchell, 'Ribblehead Remembers the Great Days', *The Dalesman*, March, 1972
30. Anthony Lambert, *Settle to Carlisle*, Siena, 1997
31. W.R. Mitchell, *Summat and Nowt*, Castelberg, 1998
32. *Rail*, No. 517, 2005

33. Screened on Channel 4, 6 September 1993
34. Nigel Pennick, 'The Fare-Dodger: a German legend', *Folklore Frontiers*, No. 23, 1994
35. 'Light Rail and Modern Tramway', July, 1994; *Magonia*, No. 50, 1994; *Magonia*, No. 51, 1995
36. *The Sun, Daily Sport*, 3 December 2004
37. E. Nesbit, *The Railway Children*, reprinted Wordsworth Classics, 1993
38. *Folklore Myths and Legends of Great Britain*, Reader's Digest Association, 1973
39. Paul Screeton, 'Waving at trains: A life of the swinger Edith Nesbit', *Folklore Frontiers*, No. 49, 2005
40. Caitlin Moran, 'Why I'm mad about *The Railway Children*', *The Times*, 13 December 2003
41. Phil Healey and Rick Glanvill, *Now! That's What I Call Urban Myths*, Virgin, 1996
42. *Daily Telegraph*, 7 August 1992; *Daily Mirror* 7 August 1992; *Fortean Times*, No. 65, 1992; *The Sun*, 29 December 1992; *Magonia*, No.51, 1995; *The Northern Echo*, 9 March 1996
43. *The Sun*, 11 May 1987
44. Letter from Brian McConnell, *Dear Mr Thoms*, No. 23, 1991
45. *The Daily Telegraph*, 22 November 1997
46. Adam Page and Nigel Harris, 'The secrets of St Pancras', *Rail*, No. 382, 2000
47. Peter Tory Diary, *The Star*, 1 August 1986
48. *Sunday Post*, 24 August 1980
49. Neal Hudson, *The Best of Bar Room Jokes and True Stories*, free with *FHM*, June, 1999
50. *Rail Express*, December, 2004
51. Healey and Glanvill's Urban Myths, *The Guardian Weekend*, 2 January 1993
52. Jonathan Margolis and Gabrielle Morris, *The Commuter's Tale*, Chapmans, 1992
53. *Zoo*, 4–10 March 2005
54. *Daily Star*, 27 September 1995; *Daily Sport*, 27 September 1995
55. Danny Kelly, editor, 'Apocryphal Now, Part I', *New Musical Express*, no date, 1991
56. *The Sun*, 21 May 1994
57. *Eastern World*, April, 1989
58. *The Sun*, 4 November 1994
59. *Daily Sport*, 13 December 2000
60. Ronald W. Zweig, *The Gold Train: the Destruction of the Jews and the Second World War's Most Terrible Robbery*, Allen Lane, 2002
61. Michael Craft, *Alien Contact*, St Martin's Press, 1997
62. Andrew Drummond, '"Mad Senator" sparks Thai treasure hunt', *The Times*, 14 April 2001

Chapter 8 (pages 137 to 149)

1. Paul Screeton, 'Resurrection Shuffle (From King Arthur to Rock 'n' Roll Olympus)', *Pendragon*, Vol. 19 No. 2, 1989

2. Paul Screeton, 'Steamed Up – About 'Strategic Reserve'', *The Mail* (Hartlepool), 29 August 1980; *The Labyrinth*, Issue 3, 2000; Paul Screeton, 'Tracking down steam engines of yesteryear', *The Mail* (Hartlepool), 11 November 1980

3. *Steam Railway*, February, 1991

4. Murray Brown, 'Gresley's "Hush-Hush" Coaches', *Railway World*, June, 1981; Paul Johnston, 'The Other Control Trains', *Railway World*, March, 1982

5. David Wilcock as '45050', 'Strategic Reserve', *Steam Railway*, Nov./Dec., 1979

6. David Wilcock, 'Strategic Coincidence?', *Steam World*, April, 1981

7. Rory Lushman, 'The Strategic Reserve Refuses To Die', *The Labyrinth*, No. 3, 2000

8. *Steam World*, May, 1981

9. Ian Davies, *Rhydymwyn: The Valley Works, North Wales*, Subterranea Britannica, 1997

10. David Wilcock as '45050', 'Strategic Reserve', *Steam Railway*, Nov./Dec., 1979

11. Ibid.

12. *Steam Railway*, No. 6, 1980

13. *Steam Railway*, No. 8, 1980

14. Paul Screeton, 'Steamed Up – About 'Strategic Reserve'', *The Mail* (Hartlepool), 29 August 1980; *The Labyrinth*, No. 3, 2000

15. Nigel Trevena, *Steam for Scrap, Vol. 2*, Atlantic Transport Publishers, 1985

16. Rory Lushman, 'Heapey – There's Trains in Them Thar Hills', *Down to Earth*, Vol. 1, No. 5, 1998

17. Rory Lushman, 'Rhydymwyn, the First Outing', *The Labyrinth*, No. 2, 1989

18. Mike Whalley, 'Ghost trains', *Chorley Citizen*, 18 June 1999

19. Rory Lushman, 'The Box Hill Tunnel – An Anoraks' Paradise or a Passage to Narnia', *Down to Earth*, Vol. 1, No. 4, 1998; *Folklore Frontiers*, No. 33, 1998

20. Alan Franks, 'The End of the World', *The Times Magazine*, 27 March 2004

21. Anarchists Anonymous, 'The Other Underground', *Undercurrents*, No. 8, 1974

22. Ibid.

23. *The Railway Magazine*, March, 2004

24. John Baxter, 'Secrets and Lines', *Steam World*, September 1998

25. Ben Fenton, '12 kingdoms of the nuclear Apocalypse', *The Daily Telegraph*, 7 August 1998

26. *UFO Brigantia*, No. 50, 1991

27. Robert Moore, 'The "Strategic Reserve" – A Practical Consideration', *The Labyrinth*, No. 3, 2000

28. Michael Evans, 'War planners warn of digital Armageddon', *The Times*, 20 November 1999

29. John A. Keel, *Operation Trojan Horse*, Abacus, 1973

30. Rory Lushman, 'The Box Hill Tunnel – An Anoraks' Paradise or a Passage to Narnia', 'Down to Earth', Vol. 1, Issue 4, 1998; *Folklore Frontiers*, No. 33, 1998

31. *Rail*, No. 521, 2005

32. Mark Saunders, 'The Cuban 47s', *Forty Seven Forum*, 1995
33. Rory Lushman, 'On the trail of the Strategic Reserve', *The Labyrinth*, Vol. 1, No. 1, 1999
34. *The Guardian*, 1 January 1997
35. *The Sun*, 19 June 1992
36. David Hatcher Childress, *Lost Cities of China, Central Asia and India*, Adventures Unlimited Press, 1991

Chapter 9 (pages 150 to 165)

1. Nick Pigott, 'Taking the Mic', *The Railway Magazine*, April, 1999
2. Tim Woodward, 'Spot the difference', *Daily Mail*, 9 October 1998
3. David Gilks, 'Joseph Locke and the Stephensons', *Backtrack*, June, 2005
4. Ibid.
5. www.cottontimes.co.uk/murdocho.html
6. www.cumnock.net/murdoch.php
7. *Steam Railway*, July, 1990
8. Victoria Haworth, *The Making of a Prodigy*, The Robert Stephenson Trust, 2005
9. Ibid.; *Metro*, 4 May 2005
10. *The Railway Magazine*, December, 2003
11. 'Thomas at 60', *The Railway Magazine*, July, 2005
12. David Wilcock, obituary, *Steam Railway*, June, 1997
13. *The Daily Telegraph*, 22 March 1997
14. John Warburton, 'Evanly body', *The Sport*, 19 March 1998
15. *Steam Railway*, Spring, 1998
16. Frank Morley, *The Great North Read*, Hutchinson/Readers Union, 1962
17. www.victorianstation.com/authorcarroll.htm
18. Bishop Eric Treacy, 'Reflections of a railway photographer', *The Railway Magazine*, December, 1967
19. Ibid.
20. Bob Page, 'Home Town: Darlington', *The Dalesman*, December, 1976
21. *Steam Railway*, November/December, 1979
22. R.H.N. Hardy, *Beeching: Champion of the railway?*, Ian Allan, 1989
23. *Fortean Times*, No. 37, 1982
24. Richard A. Tremethick, 'The Rhododendron Line', *Steam Days*, June, 2005
25. *The Sunday Telegraph*, 24 December 2000
26. Ulrich Chaussy, 'My kind, funny Uncle Dolf', *The Sunday Telegraph*, 27 February 2005
27. Matt Howard, Mythconceptions, *Fortean Times*, No. 160, 2002
28. Terry Deary, *The Vile Victorians*, Scholastic Publications, 1994
29. John Michell, *Eccentric Lives and Peculiar Notions*, Thames and Hudson, 1984
30. Nigel Pennick, letter, *Fortean Times*, No. 37, 1982
31. *Eastern World*, April, 1989
32. *The Railway Magazine*, March, 2002
33. *The Sun*, 26 October 1996
34. Brian Redhead, 'An old diesel returns to glory on the sleepy Wensleydale branch', *Darlington and Stockton Times*, 14 November 1981

35. Amanda Mitchison, 'Going loco', *The Independent Magazine*, 2 September 1989
36. John Freeman, *Suppressed and incredible inventions*, A.H. Fry (California), 1976
37. Jamie Stokes, *Strange People*, Parragon, 2000
38. Joseph Goodavage, *Storm on the Sun*, New American Library, 1979
39. Ibid.
40. Robert Anton Wilson, 'Illuminatus! The Robert Wilson Interview, part 2', *Quicksilver Messenger*, No. 9, 1984
41. *The Digger*, Vol. 1, No. 3, 1987
42. *The Sunday Telegraph*, 24 January 1999
43. *The Mail on Sunday*, 2 December 2001
44. www.grahambond.net/loop.html
45. Jim Driver, *The Mammoth Book of Sex, Drugs and Rock 'n' Roll*, Robinson, 2001
46. Danny Kelly, editor, 'Apocrypha Now, Part I', *New Musical Express*, 1991
47. Mick Jackson, *The Underground Man*, Picador, 1997
48. Paul Screeton, '"Invisible Prince" of Worksop', *Folklore Frontiers*, No. 32, 1998; *Northern Earth*, No. 75, 1998 (abridged as 'Worksop's "invisible prince"')
49. Hunter Davies, *A Walk Along the Track*, Hamlyn, 1982
50. *The Times*, 21 February 1998

Chapter 10 (pages 166 to 177)

1. Dr John Millbank, 'The Railway Club, 1899–1999', *The Railway Magazine*, June, 1999
2. Andrew Martin, 'Going loco', *Evening Standard*, 17 October 1997
3. Nick Pigott, 'Ian Allan... the man who launched a million locospotters', *The Railway Magazine*, February, 1999
4. *The Railway Magazine*, March, 1974
5. *Railway World*, June, 1970
6. *Steam Railway*, June 1982; *Steam Railway*, March, 1991; *Steam Railway*, April, 1991
7. Stephen Moss, 'The engine of love', *The Guardian*, 22 September 1995
8. *The Sunday Times*, 16 May 1993
9. Neil Sears, 'With notebook and platform souls', *The Northern Echo*, 14 October 1995
10. *Manchester Guardian*, 27 August 1962
11. Paul Screeton, 'Sex on the tracks', *Folklore Frontiers*, No. 50, 2005
12. Stephen Moss, 'The engine of love', *The Guardian*, 22 September 1995
13. *Rail*, No. 181, 1992; *The Sun, Daily Star*, 25 June 1992
14. *The Sun*, 27 June 1992
15. *The Sun*, 5 July 1993; *Daily Express*, 5 July 1993; *Daily Mirror*, 5 July 1993
16. Amanda Mitchison, 'Going loco', *The Independent Magazine*, 2 September 1989
17. *The Railway Magazine*, February, 1999
18. Jonathan Margolis, 'Platform Souls', *The Sunday Times*, 16 May 1993

19. Richard Tomkins, 'Spot the anorak on Platform 5', *Weekend Financial Times*, 8–9 May 1993
20. Jack O'Sullivan, 'Train spotters "may suffer from autism"', *The Independent*, 14 September 1991
21. *The Sunday Times*, 16 May 1993
22. *Daily Star* 17 August 1993; *Daily Mirror* 17 August 1993; *Daily Sport* 17 August 1993; *The Sun* 17 August 1993
23. *The Railway Magazine*, October, 1999
24. Neil Howard, 'Inside the head of a trainspotter', *RailStaff*, May, 2002
25. *The Sun* 16 February 1995; *Today* 16 February 1995; *Daily Star* 16 February 1995
26. Nicholas Whittaker, *Platform Souls*, Victor Gollancz, 1995
27. *Daily Express*, 16 October 1997; *Fortean Times*, No. 108, 1998
28. My thanks to Alan Hopkins, of Seaton Carew, for translating these terms overheard or noted in railway publications.
29. Ticking them off, 'A Thirst for Steam!', *Steam Railway* supplement 1997
30. Martyn Sharpe, 'Orient Excess', *The Sun*, 28 September 2000
31. *The Railway Magazine*, October, 2003
32. Gregg Bakery, 'Inside the brain of a killer', *Viz*, No. 61, 1993
33. *The Sun*, 9 July 1993
34. *Folklore Frontiers*, No. 35, 1999; *Northern UFO News*, No. 181, 1999
35. The title of a 2001 Marillion album is *Anoraknophobia* and is used as a title of a Wallace and Gromit book and another by David Pickering, subtitled 'The A to Z of Frightening Football Facts'. It is also the title of a two-page centre-spread by me in *The Mail* (Hartlepool) on 30 March 1995, adapted and extended over seven pages in *Folklore Frontiers*, No. 25, 1995.
36. Bill Bryson, *Notes From a Small Island*, Doubleday UK, 1995
37. Jane Kelly, 'It's the rail thing', *Daily Mail*, 14 December 1993
38. *Steam Railway*, March, 1994
39. Nick Pigott, 'Ian Allan... the man who launched a million locospotters', *The Railway Magazine*, February, 1999
40. Nick Pigott, 'Preservationists attacked by Science Museum head', *The Railway Magazine*, December, 1993
41. Paul Merton, *The People*, 30 May 1993
42. *Daily Star, The Sun*, 11 February 1995
43. Paul Screeton, 'Sex on the tracks', *Folklore Frontiers*, No. 50, 2005
44. Jonathan Margolis, 'Overnight sleeper', *The Mail on Sunday*, 24 May 1998
45. Richard Tomkins, 'Spot the anorak on Platform 5', *Weekend Financial Times*, 8–9 May 1993
46. Andrew Gilligan, 'Trainspotters can go on line', *The Sunday Telegraph*, 27 August 1995
47. Christopher Middleton, 'He's got the rail world in his hands', *The Daily Telegraph*, 29 January 2000
48. Jonathan Margolis, 'Overnight sleeper', *The Mail on Sunday*, 24 May 1998
49. Harry Blackwood, 'Spotting a way to beat the anoraks', *The Mail* (Hartlepool), 27 August 1994

Chapter 11 (pages 178 to 180)

1. Candida Crewe, 'Someone's got to do it… the stage vomit mixer,' *The Times Magazine*, 4 February 2006
2. Jamie Stokes, *Strange People*, Parragon, 2000
3. Barry Doe, 'Toasting the "W" clubs with a wee dram!', *Rail*, No. 527, 2005
4. Letter by F. Parsons, 'Trainspotting "up the spire"', *Steam World*, n.d
5. http://finance.groups.yahoo.com/group/north-east-discussion/messages

Index

Pre-nationalisation, British Rail/ways and post-privatisation locomotive numbers:

Mystery Big Cats

Merrily Harpur

In the past twenty years every county in Britain, from Caithness to Cornwall, has had recurrent sightings of 'big cats' – described as being like pumas or panthers. These anomalous big cats sightings are now running at an estimated 1,200 a year.

Farmers, gamekeepers, ornithologists, policemen and even parents on the school run have all been thrilled – or terrified – to see what they assume is a big cat escaped from a zoo. Yet these big cats are neither escapees from zoos nor, as this book conclusively argues, the descendants of pets released into the countryside by their owners in 1976 when the Dangerous Wild Animals Act made it too expensive to keep big cats.

The questions therefore remain, what are they and where have they come from? With the orthodox explanations overturned, Merrily Harpur searches for clues in the cultures of other times and places. She discovers our mystery felines have been with us for longer than we imagine, and throws unexpected light on the way Western civilisation looks at the world.

Mystery Big Cats is the first serious and comprehensive book on the subject. From the drama of eyewitnesses' verbatim accounts to the excitement of new perspectives and insights into a strange and often terrifying experience – it gets to grips with what is now the commonest encounter with the unknown in Britain.

Merrily Harpur is a cartoonist and writer. She has published three books: *The Nightmares of Dream Topping, Unheard of Ambridge* and *Pig Overboard*. She divides her time between Dorset and Ireland, where she founded the Strokestown International Poetry Festival.

EAN 978 1872 883 922. ISBN 1 872883 92 3. March 2006.
245 x 175 mm, 242 + viii pages, 55 b&w photographs, paperback
£16.95

Explore Phantom

Black Dogs

edited by Bob Trubshaw

Contributors: Jeremy Harte, Simon Sherwood, Alby
Stone, Bob Trubshaw and Jennifer Westwood.

The folklore of phantom black dogs is known
throughout the British Isles. From the Black Shuck of
East Anglia to the Moody Dhoo of the Isle of Man there
are tales of huge spectral hounds 'darker than the night
sky' with eyes 'glowing red as burning coals'.

The phantom black dog of British and Irish folklore, which often forewarns of death,
is part of a world-wide belief that dogs are sensitive to spirits and the approach of
death, and keep watch over the dead and dying. North European and Scandinavian
myths dating back to the Iron Age depict dogs as corpse eaters and the guardians of
the roads to Hell. Medieval folklore includes a variety of 'Devil dogs' and spectral
hounds. Above all, the way people have thought about such ghostly creatures has
steadily evolved.

This book will appeal to all those interested in folklore, the paranormal and fortean
phenomena.

> 'I think this must be the best entry in the Explore series I have seen
> so far... ' **Aeronwy Dafies** *Monomyth Supplement*

> 'This is an excellent work and is very highly recommended.' **Michael
> Howard** *The Cauldron*

ISBN 1 872883 78 8. Published 2005. Demy 8vo (215 x 138 mm), 152 + viii pages,
10 b&w half-tones, paperback. **£12.95**

'Highly recommended'
Folklore Society Katherine Briggs
Award 2003

Explore Folklore

Bob Trubshaw

**'A howling success, which plugs
a big and obvious gap'**

Professor Ronald Hutton

There have been fascinating developments in the study of folklore in the last twenty-or-so years, but few books about British folklore and folk customs reflect these exciting new approaches. As a result there is a huge gap between scholarly approaches to folklore studies and 'popular beliefs' about the character and history of British folklore. *Explore Folklore* is the first book to bridge that gap, and to show how much 'folklore' there is in modern day Britain.

Explore Folklore shows there is much more to folklore than morris dancing and fifty-something folksingers! The rituals of 'what we do on our holidays', funerals, stag nights and 'lingerie parties' are all full of 'unselfconscious' folk customs. Indeed, folklore is something that is integral to all our lives – it is so intrinsic we do not think of it as being 'folklore'.

The implicit ideas underlying folk lore and customs are also explored. There might appear to be little in common between people who touch wood for luck (a 'tradition' invented in the last 200 years) and legends about people who believe they have been abducted and subjected to intimate body examinations by aliens. Yet, in their varying ways, these and other 'folk beliefs' reflect the wide spectrum of belief and disbelief in what is easily dismissed as 'superstition'.

Explore Folklore provides a lively introduction to the study of most genres of British folklore, presenting the more contentious and profound ideas in a readily accessible manner.

ISBN 1 872883 60 5. Published 2002. Demy 8vo (215x138 mm), 200 pages, illustrated, paperback **£9.95**

The Autobiography
of a Rail Fan

James Alan Bousfield Hamilton
and John Brooke Hamilton

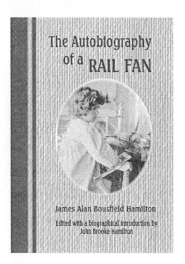

The Autobiography of a RAIL FAN

James Alan Bousfield Hamilton

Edited with a biographical introduction by
John Brooke Hamilton

As a boy at the start of the twentieth century, Jim Hamilton grew up in the heyday of railways. By the age of three he was in love with steam locomotives. He enthusiastically compared the different competing rail companies that flourished around his home in Nottingham: the Great Central, Great Northern, North Western and his favourite because its engines were painted red – the Midland. His interest was greatly aided and abetted by *The Railway Magazine*, which rapidly became his preferred reading.

Holidays in his father's native Scotland soon added the Caledonian line to his store of knowledge. Then boarding school in Yorkshire meant travelling on the trains of the 'cold, unfriendly' North Western line. In a sometimes turbulent working life Jim ensured that either holidays or the job gave him occasion for extensive travel by train throughout Britain. But not only Britain: as a soldier in both World Wars he made the most of the opportunity to study trains in France, Belgium, the Netherlands and Germany. He also made several trips to Denmark and became enchanted with the country – but not its trains!

The author of several railway books, Jim Hamilton brings a wide-ranging knowledge of railways and an exceptional memory to his story. He recounts his varied life in a lively style that intrigues and entertains. His autobiography is augmented by his son John Hamilton, in an introduction which covers Jim's life when not on a train, and by 57 photographs of relevant locomotives, key places and family members. The author's detailed recollections of locomotives and their specifications when steam ruled the rails brings life to a subject often dismissed as 'train spotting'.

EAN 978 1872 883 839. ISBN 1 872883 83 4. **October 2005.**
245 x 175 mm, 232 + xviii pages, 56 b&w photographs plus colour frontispiece, paperback. **£16.95**

Heart of Albion

The UK's leading publisher of
folklore, mythology and cultural studies.

Further details of all Heart of Albion titles online at
www.hoap.co.uk

All titles available direct from Heart of Albion Press.

Please add 80p p&p (UK only; email
albion@indigogroup.co.uk for overseas postage).

To order books or request our current catalogue
please contact

Heart of Albion Press

2 Cross Hill Close, Wymeswold
Loughborough, LE12 6UJ

Phone: 01509 880725
Fax: 01509 881715
email: albion@indigogroup.co.uk
Web site: www.hoap.co.uk